Theorizing European Integration

Sage Politics Texts

Series Editor
IAN HOLLIDAY
City University of Hong Kong

SAGE Politics Texts offer authoritative and accessible analyses of core issues in contemporary political science and international relations. Each text combines a comprehensive overview of key debates and concepts with fresh and original insights. By extending across all main areas of the discipline, SAGE Politics Texts constitute a comprehensive body of contemporary analysis. They are ideal for use on advanced courses and in research.

Published titles:

The Politics of Central Europe
Attila Ágh

The New Politics of Welfare
Bill Jordan

Rethinking Green Politics
John Barry

Democracy and Democratization
John Nagle and Alison Mahr

International Political Theory
Kimberly Hutchings

Politics and Society in South Africa
Daryl Glaser

Transforming the European Nation-State
Kjell Goldmann

Local Governance in Western Europe
Peter John

Theorizing European Integration

Dimitris N. Chryssochoou

SAGE Publications
London • Thousand Oaks • New Delhi

SAGE Publications Ltd
6 Bonhill Street
London EC2A 4PU

SAGE Publications Inc.
2455 Teller Road
Thousand Oaks, California 91320

SAGE Publications India Pvt Ltd
32, M-Block Market
Greater Kailash – I
New Delhi 110 048

British Library Cataloguing in Publication data

A catalogue record for this book is available from the British Library

ISBN 0 7619 6285 9
ISBN 0 7619 6286 7 (pbk)

Library of Congress Control Number 2001 131843

Typeset by Keystroke, Jacaranda Lodge, Wolverhampton.
Printed in Great Britain by Biddles Ltd, Guildford, Surrey

To the memory of Alexandra Moschonidou
Her love will always be a blessing to an innocence preserved

Summary of Contents

Contents

Abbreviations

AMT	Treaty of Amsterdam (1999)
CFSP	Common Foreign and Security Policy
EC	European Community
ECJ	European Court of Justice
EMU	Economic and Monetary Union
EP	European Parliament
EPC	European Political Cooperation
EU	European Union
IGC	Intergovernmental Conference
JHA	Justice and Home Affairs
QMV	Qualified Majority Voting
SEA	Single European Act (1987)
TEU	Treaty on European Union (1993)

Acknowledgements

This book owes a great deal to the continuous encouragement of friends and colleagues. For providing unsparingly of time and constructive comments on my work throughout the years, I am particularly indebted to Paul Taylor, Michael J. Tsinisizelis, Stelios Stavridis, Geoffrey Edwards and Richard Gillespie. I have also benefited immensely from exchanging ideas with such exemplary colleagues as Fulvio Attinnà, Richard Bellamy, Wayne te Brake, Simon Bulmer, Dario Castiglione, Iain Hampsher-Monk, Simon Hix, Kostas Ifantis, Emil Kirshner, Thomas Lancaster, Arend Lijphart, Anand Menon, Christos Paraskevopoulos, Ben Rosamond, Martin Schain, Jo Shaw, Amy Verdum and Antje Wiener. I am grateful to Ian Holliday for inviting me to undertake this task and to Lucy Robinson for her generous editorial support. I would also like to thank Michael J. Tsinisizelis and Latis Kanatidis for their unreserved friendship and support, and Dimitris K. Xenakis who, in the process of becoming a doctor in politics, also became such a good friend. I am equally grateful to my students for putting up with my continued insistence on theory!

Two institutions in particular have had a great impact on the development of this book by providing a most congenial environment for research and debate: the Centre of International Studies at Cambridge University, where I spent the first academic term of 1999 as a visiting fellow, and the Institute on Western Europe at Columbia University, where I was a visiting scholar during the spring semester of 2000. I am greatly indebted to Geoffrey Edwards and Glenda Rosenthal for welcoming me so warmly into their respective academic families. I also extend my gratitude to Mary Demeri and Seena Srinath at the Institute on Western Europe, and to the Master and Fellows of Pembroke College, Cambridge, for honouring me with an associate scholarship. Life at Pembroke has been a unique experience, much enriched by long discussions with Dimitris Livanios at the Senior Parlor – usually over a glass of port! I am equally grateful to the Italian Academy for Advanced Studies in America at Columbia University or, simply, Casa Italiana, and particularly to Richard Brilliant, Maria Francesca Nespoli, Kathleen Madden, Allison Jeffrey and Jaime Perez for their unparalleled hospitality, as well as to the Fellows of the Academy, especially considering their forbearance when I insisted upon practising my – all too often self-invented – Italian! I have found a second home in the Casa, which I will always remember with the greatest affection.

My work has also greatly benefited from comments, suggestions and constructive criticisms of the various parts of this book that have been presented to audiences at Reading, London, Cambridge, Oxford, Athens, Rethymno, Nicosia, Braga, Brussels, Turku, Pittsburgh and New York. Likewise, participation at the 26th ECPR Joint Sessions at Warwick in March 1998 on comparative federalism proved extremely beneficial, as did my involvement in the 17th Annual Graduate Student Conference at Columbia University in March–April 2000. Finally, I owe a special debt to my great friend and colleague Dario Castiglione, coordinator of the ESRC project on 'Strategies of Civic Inclusion in Pan-European Civil Society', financed by the ESRC Programme 'One Europe or Several? The Dynamics of Change across Europe', under the directorship of Helen Wallace. This book is a product of that project. Of great intellectual benefit to my research has also been my participation to the TSER Network on 'European Citizenship and the Social and Political Integration of the European Union', financed by the European Commission, under the coordination of Richard Bellamy.

In these opening pages, I would like to pay tribute to the memory of two individuals: Vincent Wright, whose constant encouragement and advice were instrumental in finding my way into British academia, and Peter F. Butler, former Head of the Department of Politics at Exeter, who within such a short period of time did so much to make me feel at home in an educational environment that meant so much to him. His thoughts, taken from his paper on the purpose of a university education *Do Not Go Gentle into that Good Night* can be read as a blueprint of hope for the shape of things to come:

> To provide students with an understanding of the reflections that have taken place on such matters as the nature of the best state and on the relationship between and among citizens and subjects and rulers and governments seems to me to offer them both a sense of, and a capacity for membership of, a human community, one of the primary characteristics of which is its members' ability – too often latent – to reflect on the conditions of their common existence.

I also proudly acknowledge the support of my father Nikitas who has always been so immeasurably confident about the destination of my intellectual departures, no matter how long or arduous these journeys may have been. Above all, my greatest debt is to my mother Karolina and my stepfather Dimitris. Their love means the world to me. As always, I am wholeheartedly grateful to Panagia Gorgoepikoos for answering my prayers. Finally, a word about the person to whom this book is dedicated, Alexandra Moschonidou. She has been by my side from the day I literally took my first steps, dedicating her life to me ever after. I have never stopped missing her, although I know, as profoundly as she does, that she will always live in my heart.

Introduction

No one who has heard a whispered intimation of the power and greatness of theory will ever surrender to despair, nor will he doubt that this sound of thought will one day awaken the stones themselves.

R. M. Unger, *Knowledge and Politics* (1975)

Theorizing in the social sciences is a path to making sense of complex social reality. This intellectual route to explaining and understanding real-life events is central to the study of European integration, for it reveals the underlying structure of relations among a plethora of public, semi-public and private actors involved in the process of steering the political system of the European Union (EU). They include: institutions of collective governance; national and subnational authorities; interest associations; civic organizations; policy communities; ordinary citizens. Theorizing also helps to break down the complexity of the regional system, whilst systematizing its study with a view to deepening our understanding of large-scale polity-formation, novel patterns of institutionalized shared rule and instances of formal and informal interaction among different domains of policy action. In a word, theorizing becomes an indispensable tool for knowledge acquisition.

Having welcomed the new millennium, and after nearly five decades of uninterrupted theorizing about European integration, international scholarship is still puzzled as to what exactly the EU is or may come to resemble in the future. Today, both 'process theories' of international integration, such as functionalism, neofunctionalism and transactionalism, and others that focus on alternative integration outcomes, such as federalism and confederalism, find it difficult to grasp the distinctive nature of the European polity and its complex and increasingly overlapping governance structures. The same can be said of those theoretical perspectives that were advanced during the 1970s, such as international regimes, interdependence and concordance systems, or even of recent theoretical insights drawn from the likes of consociationalism, liberal intergovernmentalism, new institutionalism and multi-level governance, to mention but a few. Whether a good part of these theoretical approaches are trapped in a process of inventing a series of neologisms to conceptualize the evolving polity of the EU, no conceptual consensus has thus far emerged over this uniquely observed regional formation. Rather, integration scholarship is still in search of a reliable theory as the basis for the future of the political system that is currently coming into being at the regional level. But such is the complexity of the Union's ontological conundrum that many promising theoretical departures confine themselves to the microcosm of sector-specific analyses, often professing an almost explicit antipathy to the construction of a 'grand theory' of regional integration, or to the development of a foundational discourse and epistemological awareness within the discipline on what constitute legitimate questions and answers for integration scholarship.

For its part, this book aims to do justice to those who have contributed to the theoretical study of European integration, as well as to advance a particular conception of the European polity, best captured by the term 'confederal consociation'. The proposed model, which in large measure aspires to transcend the 'international-comparativist' divide in EU studies, has considerable implications for the way in which sovereignty relations are to be reconceptualized within a highly interactive system of mutual governance such as the EU. But the changing conditions of European statehood, in turn, entail serious implications for the democratic organization and social legitimation of the European polity and, given the increased levels of political interconnectedness, its component political systems. Hence, one may legitimately raise the question whether the segments, in the form of distinct politically organized entities, form a constitutive part of a larger, purposive whole – i.e. a polity in its own right – or whether they represent an instance of (mainly) horizontally cooperating states, whose respective governments retain ultimate political control over the pace and range of the regional arrangements.

The view taken in this book is that the present-day EU contains elements of both, and that the theory of consociationalism exemplifies its essential character as a composite political structure composed of both states and demoi. The message is clear: the EU is not a state as conventionally understood by political scientists, nor have the member publics developed (as yet) a sense of belonging to a transnational polity. Consistent with this view, the overall conclusion to be drawn is that the building of a democratically organized European polity composed of multiple civic spaces and public spheres depends ultimately on the development of effective European 'civic competence': the institutional capacity of European citizens to engage themselves in the governance of the larger polity.

A few words about the organization of the book are in order here. It is divided into four parts, each reflecting a particular concern with the theoretical study of European integration. Part I, comprising Chapter 1, links the uses of regional integration theory with the broader exercise of theorizing in the social sciences. In doing so, it justifies the centrality of theory in the process of developing a more profound understanding of complex social and political phenomena. Moreover, it identifies the new challenges confronting EU scholarship and attempts, in a theoretically informed manner, to unfold Europe's social scientific puzzle so as to get to grips with the uniquely observed process of European polity-formation.

Part II, including Chapters 2 and 3, deals more specifically with those integration theories that aim to explain the nature, conditions and dynamics of regional international integration in general, and its application to the postwar West European order in particular. While Chapter 2 focuses on the formative theories of European integration and the relationship between structure and process (functionalism, federalism, transactionalism and neofunctionalism), Chapter 3 suggests a number of questions about the dynamic interplay between autonomy and control through the conceptual lenses of a group of theories that form part of what might best be termed as the 'second wave' of theorizing European integration (confederalism, international regimes, interdependence and concordance systems). Part III, including Chapters 4 and 5, offers an account of recent trends in theorizing the political system of the EU. In this context, Chapter 4 draws its insights from an examination of formal treaty reform in the mid-1980s and early 1990s and the emergence of new, multi-level governance arrangements which, taken together, lead towards the formation of a pluralist regional polity. In terms of theorizing the EU during the past decade or so, the result is a shift in paradigm 'from policy to polity' with serious implications about the changing nature of sovereign statehood in contemporary Europe. Chapter 5 explores the pattern of relations between state and regional organization, by portraying a particular image of the EU as a confederal consociation: a consensual form of union, whose distinct culturally defined and constitutionally organized polities have established among themselves a symbiotic *modus operandi* based on the practice of political co-determination. Finally, Part IV, comprising Chapter 6, investigates the recent normative turn in EU studies and shifts the emphasis from theory to metatheory and from questions of 'who governs and how?' to questions of 'who is governed?' in the evolving structures of the European polity.

PART ONE

THEORY

1

Integration Theory and its Uses

CONTENTS

In defence of theory

Theory and good social science are mutual reinforcements. This is the underlying premise of this book, based on the following intellectual proposition: theory generates pluralism, pluralism produces choice, choice creates alternatives, alternatives formulate debate, debate encourages communication, communication increases awareness, awareness minimizes dogmatism and, in this way, there is a propensity to develop a greater and better understanding of social phenomena. This is a book about the theoretical study of European integration, rather than the praxis and assorted praxeology of the regional process *per se*. To reflect on a recent paradigm shift in integration studies, namely 'from policy to polity' (see Chapter 4), this is also a book about the ontology of the emerging European polity, rather than the day-to-day running of its constitutive policy processes and technical forms and mechanisms of collective regulation. In it, engagement in concept-building, normative theorizing and the advancement of ideational formulations of human governance are taken as positive developments in the search for the kind of polity we want to build in Europe. The wider methodological claim put forward in this chapter is that good (or better) social science is theoretically informed. Accordingly, scholarly attempts at new theory creation, theory development and metatheory or 'second-order theorizing' (see Chapter 6) should be much welcomed.

But perhaps the strongest case to be made for theory in general, and against the raw positivism of self-styled 'social scientists' confining the art of theorizing to a narrow set of verifiable or falsifiable hypotheses, is that its role is to reveal ways of improving the conditions of human governance itself. The latter may be defined as the art of organizing the production of knowledge about the constitution of social activity. By theorizing is meant the systematic study of the conditions, structure and evolution of that constitution, by means of explicating, interpreting, understanding and, where possible, predicting individual, small- or large-scale social action. Although some theories tend to direct their conceptual and analytical *foci* on one, more or even all of the above categories (of which, each may form in itself the basis of a given research programme), what they all have in common is an explicit and unequivocal commitment to the search for reliable answers. But theories entail different notions of knowledge as well as cognitive resources for developing working conceptions and, accordingly, employ different approaches to knowledge acquisition, application, evaluation and critique. In short, theories as distinct knowledge domains allow room for a variety of methodologies and lines of social inquiry to be pursued, the biases and particularistic concerns of the researcher notwithstanding.

According to Mjøset, there exist four different notions or understandings of theory in the social sciences: law-oriented, idealizing, constructivist and critical. The first, by avoiding the search for truly universal laws as in experimental natural science, where 'theory is compact knowledge', but without rejecting social scientific claims to generalization, focuses on 'regularities that apply only within specific contexts': theory thus becomes 'a collection of "lawlike regularities" or "quasilaws"'; the second, in accepting that social science 'laws' are 'ideal types', focuses 'on the conditions which establish the *ideal* situation': theory, in this sense, is capable of yielding predictions in an idealized (or model) world and, to that end, 'perfect knowledge must be assumed'; the third notion questions 'any foundation for the social sciences', implying that no alternative ethical foundations can be found': as '[s]ocial science theory is not in principle different from everyday knowledge', it follows that 'social processes define (construct) certain realms of knowledge as science' – with theory itself taking the form not of axiomatic models, 'but of contextual understanding of interacting motives'; the fourth notion is based on an 'internal linkage between theoretical and ethical reflection', with social science being defined 'by its commitment to universal ethical principles': this notion of theory focuses 'more on ethical foundations and less on concrete paradigms involved in the explanatory efforts of applied social sciences'.[1] Hence, the first notion focuses on 'theory testing, the second on modelling, the third on theory formation and the fourth on ethical reflection'.[2]

In the context of this discussion of the epistemological underpinnings of social science research, one has to take into account Laski's assertion that its variables are human beings whose uniqueness prevents their reduction to law in the scientific sense of the word.[3] To borrow Lieber's metaphor, 'we are all forced to acknowledge that water freezes at 32° Fahrenheit';[4] yet, how can we accept axiomatically that a given social phenomenon or for that matter the substance of a given political process or institution can only be subjected to a single pattern of systematic inquiry resulting in an impersonal form of knowledge driven by the explanatory power of formal rationality? As problems of recognition, classification and definition have not been solved in the social sciences, its theory is not defined by its ability to 'prove', but rather by its ability to 'illustrate'. But 'crass positivism' in the social sciences is also untenable, for the meanings and understanding of the concepts themselves are affected by the cultural context of both the researcher and the social phenomenon being studied.[5] And given the difficulties in using a tightly controlled experimental design to study social phenomena and to establish relations among variables that are consistent and generalized across time and space (through the generation and testing of hypotheses), explanation through the employment of vigorous causal mechanisms – i.e. the mechanistic approach – is but one element of the feasible end of social inquiry. More important, perhaps, it is highly doubtful whether too much 'social sciency' can help the analyst to uncover the alleged coherence that underlies the apparent chaos of contemporary social and political life through the operations of deductive logic (as the apparatus of social scientific theory) and modelling (as an expression of empirical observation), in turn inspired by rationalist explanations.

As Tilly suggests, three styles of explanation generally compete in those portions of social science that seek explanations of social phenomena:

> The first expects social life to exhibit empirical regularities that at their highest level take the form of laws . . . The second accounts for particular features of social life by specifying their connections with putative larger entities: societies, cultures, mentalities, capitalist systems, and the like . . . The third regards social units as self-directing, whether driven by emotions, motives, interests, rational choices, genes, or something else.[6]

Each style corresponds to a different account of explanation. In the first style, for instance, 'explanation consists of subsuming particular cases under broadly validated empirical generalizations or even universal roles'; in the second, it 'consists of locating elements within systems'; and in the third, it 'consists of reconstructing the state of the social unit . . . and plausibly relating its actions to that state'.[7] To these, Tilly adds a fourth style/account that deserves attention, according to which 'explanation consists of identifying in particular social phenomena reliable causal mechanisms [events that alter relations among some sets of elements] and processes of general scope [combinations and sequences of causal mechanisms]'.[8] The emphasis in this fourth category is on the nature and range of social mechanisms, with explanation being assigned the task of 'locating robust cognitive, relational, and environmental mechanisms within observed episodes'.[9]

But a useful and perhaps more ambitious theoretical enterprise has to incorporate a sense of understanding as a valued claim to the pursuit of unfolding the puzzling features of complex social processes, organizations, episodes or system-steering events, and even to allow for 'an intuitive organization of perception'.[10] At the same time, such an intellectual strategy should also be able to identify parallels or suggestive analogies among comparable case studies (even if the latter have come under the close scrutiny of adjacent disciplines); draw attention to schemes of understanding the evolutionary nature of political processes as constitutive of wider social phenomena; trace the broader intellectual environment within which concepts and assumptions are used to facilitate the production of explanatory patterns, i.e. the genealogical method; and attempt to make advances in the realm of social inquiry itself, by being prepared to take risks – as well as accept, or at least constructively respond to, possible criticisms from methodologically competing research programmes – in the generation and framing of hypotheses that aim to state the general conditions of the social phenomenon under investigation.

The above methodological reflections suggest that integration theorists, instead of exhausting their analytical talent in applying the logic of 'strict' science in the ever-changing social and political environment of the European Union (EU), should strive for a more profound understanding of the existing and emerging constitutive public spheres and political spaces of the larger entity. This is by no means a negation of disciplined social inquiry or a more or less implicit attack on empirically grounded social research. It is merely to make the point that 'the value of theory is not determined by any rigid criteria',[11] and that narrow training, rationalist rule application and the employment of an overly 'scientific' procedure that rests on the illusion of ethical neutrality in social inquiry are not the most appropriate methodological blueprints for enriching our understanding of European integration as an essentially political phenomenon. All the more so, if one takes into account the patterns of human behaviour, institutional interaction and societal mobilization that integration has produced in such diverse fields as collective norm-setting, authoritative value allocation, large-scale constitutional engineering, economic governance, transnational civil society formation, joint problem-solving, multiple identity-holding, loyalty-sharing and so on.

In summary, theorizing about the past, present and future of European integration is as much about explaining the causality of multiple interactions as it is about developing feelings for the play of collective European governance and polity-building, as well as the inevitable normative and ethical questions to which these processes give rise. Normative as the above claims may be, it seems that the highest educational purpose the theoretical study of social phenomena can serve is to venture for a deeper and more penetrating understanding of the conditions of human association, the forces that shape the range and depth of societal interactions and the possibilities of improving the quality of debate about such self-inquiring questions as 'where we are now, from where we have come and to where we might go'.[12]

Why theorize?

Half a century of uninterrupted theorizing about the structure and dynamics, substance and procedures, forms and functions of European integration has produced a situation where, *prima facie* at least, little remains to be said. This critical and rather pessimistic syllogism is not intended to offer an apology for theoretical inaction, or for that matter a justificatory basis for a methodological blueprint inspired by atheoretical observations. Likewise, it should not be seen as an attempt to escape the intellectual responsibility of developing a more insightful understanding of the multiplicity of forces (and causes) that constantly form and reform the regional system. It is only to state that the theory of such a polysemous and still largely elusive concept as 'integration' appears to have reached a high *plateau* in its West European context. Similarly, this is not to imply that integration theorists should start looking for new regional experiments of comparable conceptual and analytic potential. Rather, the idea is that the new challenges confronting the study of European integration, concerning both its theoretical boundaries and operational reality, do not take place in a theoretical vacuum: they are an extension, if not a refinement, of older theoretical endeavours, necessitating the striking of a balance between explanation and understanding, or between 'first-' and 'second-order theorizing' (see Chapter 6). At the same time, however, the task for contemporary integration scholarship still remains to discover a reliable theory of integration as the basis for the future of the Union and, in doing so, to offer a convincing response to the challenges of large-scale polity-formation.

Legitimately though, one may wonder whether Puchala's cynical prophesy that integration theory will amount to 'a rather long but not very prominent footnote in the intellectual history of twentieth century social science' will prove as accurate as the author would have us believe.[13] A first response is that *theory matters*, whether its conceptual findings and qualifications are to be evenly appreciated by scholars and practitioners alike (the latter being in principle much less interested in theoretical purity than operational reality). For familiarity with theory helps to test our analytical tools and appreciate their relevance in real-life situations. As Taylor puts it, 'Each theory . . . leads to unique insights which are valid starting points for the purpose of comparison and evaluation.'[14] Or, in the words of Keohane and Hoffmann, 'Attempts to avoid theory . . . not only miss interesting questions but rely on a framework for analysis that remains unexamined precisely because it is implicit.'[15] 'Therefore', Church asserts, 'awareness of theory is a necessary ground-clearing measure.'[16] True, a great deal still remains to be accomplished in the theoretical study of European integration. But as long as theory-building activities remain at the top of the academic agenda, there are good grounds for thinking that important possibilities are deemed to be explored. To borrow from Rosamond: 'Theorizing intellectualizes perceptions. It is not that theory just helps us to identify that which is significant.'[17] Thus, as Groom rightly points out, '[t]heory is an intellectual mapping exercise which tells us where we are now, from where we have come and to where we might go.'[18] Even more than that, however, theory is a means of linking 'the order of ideas' (as conceptual entities) to 'the order of events' (as actual occurrences),[19] without being created merely in response to the latter. Church explains:

> Theories have a life of their own related not just to what happens outside but to general intellectual changes, and, especially, to who supports them and why. Political commitment and self interest like academic investment all play a part in keeping theories going in altered circumstances. Hence theories keep re-appearing and debate between them is continuous.[20]

But what might constitute such 'possibilities'? How are they to be explored? What is the appropriate methodological line to that end? To start with, substantive progress in the field requires the transcendence of purely narrative and/or descriptive approaches about, on the one hand, the form and functions (or structure and dynamics) of the integrative system and, on the other, the resolution of fundamental ontological issues confronting a discipline that has become subject to diverse interpretation. This, in turn, requires 'structured ways of understanding changing patterns of interaction',[21] free from the inherently fragmented boundaries of micro-analysis. Put differently, the aim is to project a macroscopic view of European governance based on systematic conceptual explanation. As Church rightly observes: 'We need to be aware of the conceptions we use since they determine our perception of things.'[22] The *locus classicus* for this contention is found in Allison's influential *Essence of Decision*, stating that 'different conceptual lenses lead analysts to different judgements about what is relevant and important'.[23] After all, as Hamlyn reminds us, albeit in a different, philosophical context, 'one cannot get at reality except from within some system of concepts'.[24] Groom makes the point well:

> Our conceptualization does . . . give a context to the activities of practitioners and provides them with an opportunity of learning from the experience of

others . . . And different projections show us different worlds so that we may find what we are looking for in the sense that we impose meaning on 'facts' rather than their speaking for themselves. There is a sense in which one can be pragmatic, but behind every 'pragmatic' approach lies a theory of conceptualization – no matter how inchoate. All social activity requires choice and that choice cannot be exercised without some criteria for judgement – in short, a theory, a conception, a framework.[25]

This methodological pathway to the study of European integration allows the researcher a higher access to reality or, alternatively, offers the necessary conceptual infrastructure from which 'a hierarchy of realities' might emerge.[26] The hypothesis in the latter case is that a continuum of accessible knowledge domains might bridge the distance from the study of specialized issue areas to the understanding of collective conduct on institutional design and the exercise of specific political choices. As a result, important connections will be established between knowledge acquisition and knowledge evaluation in the process of theorizing the transnational political system: integration theory may thus be see as a system of interdependent principles and ideas, relationships between concepts and practices, as well as links between wholes and parts or, to put it somewhat differently, between universals (totalities) and particulars (substructures).

But there exists considerable variation in the way in which scholars ascribe different meanings and interpretations to concepts whose examination is nevertheless crucial for furthering our understanding of the social phenomenon under investigation – in our case, the theory of European integration and, at a more specific level, the changing relationships between the Union's multiple arenas of governance. Moreover, there are those who are interested only or primarily in the larger picture (the hierarchy, to borrow from the above metaphor); others who aim to capture only part of the overall image (a particular reality); others who focus on the relationship (or interdependence) among different realities themselves; and others again who concentrate more on the process of theorizing, its underlying antinomies and dialectics, as well as the various methods employed for studying the phenomenon in question. As Rosamond tellingly reminds us in his excellent contribution to the literature: 'Theories are necessary if we are to produce ordered observations of social phenomena.'[27] This view is in full harmony with Stoker's understanding of the uses of theory in the contemporary social sciences: '[t]heories are of value precisely because they structure all observations'.[28]

The analytical validity of these suppositions is justified further when trying to establish a link between continuity and change within a system of multinational shared-rule; when attempting to identify the common values of distinct polities and the prospects for the emergence of new ones; when aiming to throw light on the dialectical (i.e. harmonious and contentious at the same time) union between a highly interactive society of states and new sources of legitimate authority; and when engaging in a process of investigating the allegedly 'part-formed' or *sui generis* physiognomy of a union composed of distinct culturally defined and politically organized units, where the dynamics of domestic policy-making are intimately linked to those of large-scale polity-building within a system of interlocking and overlapping authority structures: a transnational polity, that is, which lacks a single locus of decision-making. In addition to this, theory helps to conceptualize the emerging European polity by assessing the changing nature of sovereignty (defined not only as ultimate responsibility or final power but also as an inclusive unit of participation) and its implications for the governance of the constituent polities.[29] The argument advanced here (see Chapter 5) is that national sovereignty has not been superseded by a new European political centre as part of a new constitutional order, but that the delegation of policy competences to regional institutions of governance passes through, rather than goes beyond, the capacity of states to exercise considerable control over the development, depth and range of the integration process. In accordance with this argument comes the view that the question of sovereignty has to be placed within a context that takes account of the consensus-seeking norms embodied in joint decision-making practices that affect the behaviour of states in the general system. These norms do not promote the retreat of the West European state nor do they enhance its capabilities at the expense of the central authorities in a conventional realist zero-sum fashion. Rather, a symbiotic relationship has emerged between state and international organization, according to which the growth of central competences does not represent a direct challenge to sovereign statehood: 'Any assertion of the former was likely, in the pattern of the historical evolution of the latter, to be accompanied by its countervailing force.'[30] Put differently, the conditions for sovereignty and, hence, the effective exercise of political authority have adapted to the practical need for developing collective modes of governance and problem-solving within a larger management system.

At the scholarly level, even more challenging is to evaluate critically an ever-expanding corpus of literature dealing with such a rich kaleidoscope of relations, whose thorough examination often defies our traditional methods of analysis. And all this whilst trying to make sense of a hidden political agenda concerning the future of the European state system; the viability of democratic arrangements within and across pre-established borders; novel forms of transnational community-building, multiple citizenship and identity-holding; formal and informal processes of constitutional engineering; the locus of sovereignty in relation to an ever-growing array of European competences; the relationship between the functional scope, territorial scale and integrative level of the regional arrangements; the institutionalization of new avenues of communication across a plurality of national citizen bodies (or demoi) and their identification with emerging governance structures, and so on. In fact, this list may well be extended to cover most areas of regional life, cutting across conventional disciplines in the study of European integration. 'And yet', Pentland notes with some apparent optimism, 'we need not be routed by the apparent diversity and chaos of the field.'[31] In this light, whatever lessons are to be drawn from the process of bringing together a cluster of democratic polities under the organizational logic of a common management system, this study will have made a contribution if it offers the opportunity to communicate the major concerns underlying the evolutionary nature of European polity-formation in relation to the no less challenging and dynamic process of theorizing its defining properties and functions.

Such a task is, above all, a pragmatic one, confronting, on the one hand, the transformation of international rule-based behaviour and, on the other, the assertion of a new set of principles, norms and values in the organization of EU politics. In the context of integration theory, the ordering of relations among the component polities amounts to what might best be described as the practice of political co-determination: the forging of new cooperative arrangements for jointly managing their internal and external affairs. The perennial question to ask here is whether the political system of the Union will prove capable of striking a positive balance between its becoming the main locus of collective decision-making for the participating entities, including both national and subnational structures of governance, and, at the same time, the dominant focus of popular political identification. Chapter 6 puts forward an analysis of these increasingly topical themes, linking the question of EU polity-building and its democratic implications for the constituent publics to the search for legitimate shared rule, and particularly the need for a vibrant transnational 'civic space' and with it a more demos-oriented process of union.

The challenge to EU theorizing

It does not take a specialist in international and comparative politics to reach the conclusion that, more than any other organization, the Union has contributed to the systematization of regional politics in such diverse fields of activity as solving problems of collective action, satisfying conditions of stability, managing complex interdependence and striking a balance between collective governance and self-rule. Most important in this context is the sharing of experience among the participants in developing a transnational cooperative culture as a learning process of peaceful social and political change. 'Cooperative culture' should not be confused with a certain type of diplomatic accommodation based solely on *quid pro quo* practices of interstate bargaining, but rather should be understood as stemming from participation in a purposive forum that is capable of impinging upon the behaviour of the participating units. Elements of this multifaceted experience, a clear manifestation of which is the Union's institutional sophistication, provide the intellectual (and cognitive) capital needed for integration theorists to capture the transformation of a 'community of states' into a regional pluralist polity, or the dynamics of system-wide structural change from a 'diplomatic' to a 'domestic' arena.

Although no shortage of available theory exists in contemporary EU studies that might be used to inform and guide integration scholarship, the entire field is embroiled in theoretical controversy compounded by conceptual complexity and a propensity to adopt the logic (and tactics) of methodological individualism. In some interpretations, the EU system is called complex, not because it is seen as a dynamic polity composed of a multiplicity of interactive actors and institutions, but because it defies any easy notions of how it is organized or functions in relation to other systems of domestic or international governance. This gives rise to a wider issue concerning the validity of core integration theories as to why, even when taken in a complementary manner, they generally fail to capture the dominant character of the relationship between the collectivity and the segments. Indeed, Mitrany's functionalism, Haas's revised version of it – what was rather conveniently labelled 'neofunctionalism' – and the many different federalist approaches to European integration, ranging from the American model of 'dual federalism' to the 'cooperative federalism' of the German political system, find it equally difficult to reconcile two apparently contradictory principles: the preservation of high levels of segmental autonomy within a nascent, yet constitutionally uncrystallized, system of mutual governance. From this angle, the challenge to scholarly inquiry is to capture the dynamics of two complementary objectives: strengthening the political viability of separate but not entirely autonomous (as opposed to idealized notions of the Westphalian nation-state system) domestic orders through the institutionalization of the principle of joint sovereignty and the practice of political co-determination.

The intellectual problem associated with such an ambitious task is rooted in the different treatments and perceptions of such 'general concepts' as sovereignty and integration, government and governance, policy and polity, order and fragmentation, unity and diversity, autonomy and interdependence, management and control. But which of the many interpretations these concepts entail ought we to utilize to improve the reliability of our understanding of such a macro-level political phenomenon as European integration? Particularly given its inherently dynamic nature and even its capacity for institutional self-renewal, both of which are of importance when employing different lines of (theoretical) inquiry to 'rise above [mere] observation of specific events'.[32] As Kuhn pointed out some forty years ago, without a theoretical model, 'all facts are likely to remain equally relevant'.[33] Whatever the mixture of evidence and method embedded in existing models of European integration, whether their emphasis is on conflict or equilibrium, and irrespective of their preference for the familiar (concrete) or the unique (unidentified) in describing or prescribing a possible end-point towards which the Union may be developing, their systematic examination becomes a prime theoretical requisite for the crossing of a qualitative research threshold in the field, while serving the purpose of suggesting potentially fertile questions for further research.

Both normative and narrative interpretations of European integration, purporting to identify the logic of a distinct form of regionalism and its implications for the subunits, often tend either to underestimate the importance of the central institutions and, more generally, the common functional arrangements or to overemphasize the role of national governments in setting the integrative agenda and then acting authoritatively upon it. Arguably, much theoretical writing on European integration has been trapped in the 'supranational–intergovernmental dichotomy', leading 'to an unhelpful focus on the formal characteristics of the actors at the expense of the processes which characterize, and flow from, their interactions, making the latter entirely dependent on the former'.[34] From a different perspective, competing theoretical approaches tend to disagree on background conditions and process variables, where power lies in the general system, the need for more or less integration, the impact of formal or informal structures, the feasibility or desirability of ascribing a political *telos* to the process and so on. This 'battle of theories' has often in the past led to zero-sum notions of interstate bargaining, coupled with unjustified confidence in how the EU system actually works and in which direction it might develop. The 'elephant', however, to recall Puchala's colourful metaphor, is not easy to manipulate in theoretical terms: it often turns into a 'chameleon' adjusting itself to the actual requirements of the day. In other words, it may not only be the case that the various integration theorists are aware of a rather limited picture of a barely describable and, hence, conceptually evasive political animal, but also that the creature itself may indeed change so rapidly as to render the whole process of its study (including both sector-specific analyses and system-wide theorizing) an exercise that is ultimately misleading.

Be that as it may, the fact is that, almost axiologically, the Union remains an unresolved social scientific puzzle with an 'open *finalité politique*'.[35] It represents a form of regionalism that more than any other 'form of deep regionalism . . . has displaced the potential to alter the relative congruence between territory, identity and function which characterised the nation state'.[36] All of the above defining properties of statehood are subjected to change: national territories are embedded in a wider socio-political space; identity displays the potential of multiple loyalties and affiliations; while state-controlled functions have been influenced by the emergence of new strains generated by a dramatic increase in the levels of interdependence and internationalized governance.[37] As Laffan *et al.* assert, 'the EU is more than an expression of modified interstate politics: it is the focus for processes that bring together new varieties of identity and need.'[38] But let us now turn to the question (or problem) of defining this elusive political formation.

Europe's social scientific puzzle

The above theoretical concerns are compounded further by the fact that, on the basis of existing typologies, the Union remains a 'half-way house' between the worlds of 'federal state' (federation) and 'federal union of states' (confederation).[39] Although it is often taken to imply something more than the mere aggregate of its component parts, perhaps even in the form of a higher normative order, sovereignty has not yet moved towards a new regional centre. From this view, the Union is neither an international organization as conventionally understood, nor is it becoming an ordinary state possessing a monopoly of law-making and law-enforcing powers. As Majone notes, 'the EU has no legislature but a legislative process in which different institutions . . . have different parts to play.'[40] But equally puzzling remains its legal and constitutional physiognomy; for some, it still rests on a dynamic system of international treaty-based rules, whilst others prefer to speak of an incipient constitutional system driven by aspirations akin, yet not identical, to traditional state-building – a constitutional order *in statu nascendi*, if not *ex proprio vigore*.[41] Moreover, although the Union exceeds the Deutschian notion of 'pluralistic security-community', it has failed to meet the sociopsychological conditions identified by the older functionalist school for any substantive, albeit not *toute entière*, transfer of public loyalties to international institutions, or those linked to the building of a neofunctionalist-inspired 'political community' along the lines depicted by Haas (see Chapter 2).[42]

Accordingly, the Union remains an integrative venture whose final destination is yet to become discernible. Attributes like 'partial polity', 'part-formed political system' and the like clearly demonstrate the lack of confident scholarly assertion,[43] whilst rendering the whole enterprise 'a challenge to the continuing separation of international relations from political science [especially the domain of comparative government]'.[44] But even without taking into account the series of neologisms invented over time to capture the distinctive properties that make up its governance structures, the intermeshing of federal principles, confederal structures and consociational processes render the European polity far from comprehensible. To argue simply, however, that the Union is a political phenomenon *sui generis* – often referred to as the n = 1 problem[45] – and should only be examined through the lenses of new conceptual paradigms or *ad hoc* theoretical interpretations runs the risk of complying with undisciplined and often ill-founded formulations. At the same time, there is also the danger of perpetuating its present stance in the grey, 'in-between' area of 'normal interstate' and 'normal intrastate relations' as the two extreme poles of an analytical continuum on which political systems are conventionally located.[46] Herein lies perhaps the greatest intellectual challenge facing the contemporary student of European integration: to transcend the long-standing dichotomy between state-centric and federalist approaches to European integration and concentrate on the theoretical study of more likely intermediate outcomes whose format may differ from 'the forms of political domination that we are used to dealing with'.[47] In other words, the aim is to direct our analytic *foci* to the conceptualization of 'the transient results of an ongoing process, rather than the [imagined] definitive product of a [presumed] stable equilibrium'.[48] For what is more likely to emerge from this complex, historically unprecedented and contentious (due to its multi-actor character) process of European polity-formation will differ markedly both from the constitutional properties attributed to a conventional federal state, however decentralized in constitutional or operative terms, and the type and range of policy competences, legislative powers and administrative responsibilities delegated to an average international organization.

But what terminology can we best employ to arrive at a realistic image of the Union, given that the latter qualifies, according to Ruggie, as a 'multi-perspectival polity'?[49] Of what conceptual and analytic value, or indeed continuity, would such a vocabulary be, given that events outstrip theory or, in Hallstein's words, that 'as language precedes grammar, so politics precedes political theory'.[50] As Wessels recently put it:

> In debating controversial views on the nature, legitimacy and prospects of the EU, one sensation might become more and more dominating: we are confronted with realities and challenges that might be outside our traditional categories. We may be in a situation similar to how de Tocqueville described the United States of the nineteenth century: [t]he human mind invents things more easily than words; that is why many improper terms and inadequate expressions gain currency . . . Hence a form of government has been found which is neither precisely national or federal . . . and the new word to express this new thing does not yet exist.[51]

Keeping in mind Schmitter's view of the Union as 'the most complex polity that human agency has ever devised',[52] the question remains: where does the present European polity fit in the range of (pre)existing forms of political organization? In the hope of linking this question to the systemic complexity of the Union, the following is in order.

To start with, Wallace notes that the constituent governments have now created:

> a constitutional system which has some state attributes, but which most – or all – of its constituent governments do not wish to develop into a state, even while expecting it to deliver outcomes which are hard to envisage outside the framework of an entity which we would recognise as a (federal) state . . . The retreat from a federal objective for the European Community [EC], while retaining a constitutional agenda which implied the need for a federal state-framework, has left a shadowy area at the centre of EC construction . . .[53]

Likewise, Adonis observes: 'It is fashionable to talk of a "democratic deficit", but that is but one aspect of a more chronic malaise: constitutional chaos.'[54] In this context, Sbragia asserts that it is perhaps more useful to think of the Community as 'an ongoing experiment in fashioning a new structure of governance, one that accepts a great deal of cultural diversity as well as incorporating politics based on the state-society model *and* politics based on relations between governments'.[55] Behind this statement lies the notion of symbiosis between the Union and the member state polities, adding credence to those adopting cooperative federalism as a model for conceptualizing the political system of the Union, as well as to Taylor's understanding of the constitutional implications of the symbiotic process for the changing conditions of state sovereignty (see Chapter 5).[56]

Drawing on federal theory, McKay notes that regional integration in Europe 'is a movement towards federation which has indigenous rather than external roots, over which there is near unanimity among elites and which has already produced real results in terms of the delineation of power between national and supra-national (or federal) authorities'.[57] Moravcsik, for his part, by developing a state-centric theory of liberal intergovernmentalism, describes the Union as a regime that makes inter-state bargaining more efficient, whilst enhancing the autonomy of national leaders;[58] a definition that is close to Puchala's earlier understanding of the Community as a multi-level 'system of managed interdependence'.[59] Further, while Wallace places the regional polity between an international regime and a fully fledged political system,[60] Webb takes it to denote 'a partially-integrated policy-making system at the regional level'.[61] Writing on the inadequacy of classical statist, intergovernmental and federal forms of polity, Keohane and Hoffmann have visualized the evolving European reality as 'an elaborate set of networks, closely linked in some ways, partially decomposed in others, whose results depend on the political style in the ascendant at the moment'.[62] Another interesting classification is Scharpf's conception of the Community as a 'joint-decision system', where the pathology of public policy-making is conditioned by a 'systemic tendency towards sub-optimal substantive solutions'.[63] Recognizing that the effectiveness and implementation of common policies are greatly influenced by what Taylor called the 'interdependence trap', Scharpf argues that the regional system 'seems to have become just that "middle ground between cooperation among nations and the breaking of a new one"'.[64] Although this issue is examined in greater detail in Chapter 6, it is important to note that progress towards the formation of a constitutive European polity and, by extension, the making of a transnational civic demos as its main legitimizing referent should not be equated with the possibility of a new form of regional nationhood.

At this point, three further attempts at conceptualizing the Union warrant our attention, for they reveal the difficulties in projecting alternative integration outcomes. They include: Wessels's fusion thesis, Caporaso's international state thesis and Schmitter's concepts of 'condominio' and 'consortio'. Wessels's analysis projects a macro-political view of European integration, which is characterized by an 'ever closer fusion' of 'public instruments from several levels linked with the respective Europeanization of national actors and institutions'.[65] By stressing the importance of institutionalized patterns of joint problem-solving between national and European governance structures, Wessels makes the integrative project part of the evolution of West European statehood itself: 'it is a crucial factor and dynamic engine of the fundamental changes in the statehood of western Europe'.[66] Arguably, this is a much more complex role than that of merely 'rescuing the nation state' along the lines suggested by Milward.[67] Likewise, by 'fusion' is meant more than merely a 'horizontal pooling of sovereignties' as understood by Keohane and Hoffmann.[68] Rather, 'it means a "merger" of public resources located at several "state"-levels for which the "outside world", i.e. the average European citizen but also many experts, cannot trace the accountability, as responsibilities for specific policies are diffused.'[69] This particular interpretation of 'fusion' as a merger process chimes well with the properties of the German system of 'interlocking' federalism or *Politikverflechtung*. In fact, the latter forms part of Wessels's explanatory variables for the patterns of political systemic growth and differentiation in the Union. Although Wessels does not deny the impact of supranational institutions on integration outcomes, or their influence in shaping the perceptions of national actors, his analysis makes it clear that it is 'the rational pursuit of changing national interests' that constitutes a major characteristic and driving force for the stable growth of the Union from a dynamic macro-political view.[70] As Church has remarked, Wessels's thesis 'seeks to explain how states failing to control their situation, turn to supra-nationality to do so . . . The result is a fusion of internal and external affairs into a messy federalism.'[71]

In an illuminating macro-institutional analysis that fits a 'post-ontological' stage of EU studies, i.e., the emphasis being on explaining process and outcome, rather than categorization, Caporaso throws light on the character of the Union from the perspective of different 'forms of state'.[72] He develops an understanding of the common system as an 'international state', which he defines as 'an international structure of governance based on the extrusion of certain political activities of its constituent units'.[73] Being critical of the view that equates the emergence of European authority with a direct loss of national autonomy, Caporaso encourages EU scholarship to focus on 'the ongoing structure of political authority and governance'; that is to say, the complex interaction of economic and political relations among the component states that are mediated by the central institutions.[74] Drawing on three stylized state forms – the Westphalian, the regulatory and the postmodern – as 'conceptually possible expressions of political authority organized at the national and transnational levels',[75] Caporaso notes that each of these forms captures a significant part of the evolving EU reality. After clarifying that his analysis represents a 'comparative exploration of three metaphors rather than a test of three theories', he argues that the first ideal state form helps us to perceive regional integration as 'a re-enactment of the traditional processes of state-building from the seventeenth through to the twentieth centuries'; the second encourages us to think of the Union as 'a supranational state specializing in the control and management of international externalities'; the third directs us to understanding the regional system as a 'polymorphic structure' that lacks a strong institutional core, is increasingly fragmented, has no clear public sphere, and where 'process and activity become more important than structure and fixed institutions'.[76] Caporaso's 'post-ontological' account of the emerging European polity as an international state – itself a novel instance of social formations, interests and interactions embedded in an international structure of governance – approximates more to the regulatory and postnational state forms, than to the Westphalian state model.

Finally, Schmitter's examination of 'some alternative futures for the European polity', through the projection of novel forms of political organization, constitutes a welcome contribution to the debate.[77] Rejecting the idea that the Union will be 'a "re-run" of the processes and policies that earlier made the nation state the predominant political institution of Europe', Schmitter argues that the Union, presently lacking, *inter alia*, a locus of clearly defined authority, a central hierarchy of public offices, a distinct sphere of competence, a fixed territory, an exclusive recognition by other polities, an overarching identity, a monopoly over legitimate coercion and a unique capacity to impose its decisions, 'is well on its way of becoming something new'.[78] What might this 'new' entity be? Two possible suggestions from Schmitter, presented as ideal types, warrant our attention. The first is the idea of 'consortio' defined as 'a form of collective action . . . where national authorities of fixed number and identity agree to co-operate in the performance of functional tasks that are variable, dispersed and over-lapping'.[79] In it, the segments retain their respective territorial identities and 'accept positions within a common hierarchy of authority, but pool their capacities to act autonomously in domains they can no longer control at their own level of aggregation'.[80] According to Schmitter, however, a less imaginative, but most probable trajectory of the transnational polity is the emergence of a 'condominio' based on 'a variation in both the territorial and the functional constituencies'.[81] Schmitter explains:

> Instead of a Eurocracy accumulating organizationally distinct but politically co-ordinated tasks around a single centre, there would be multiple regional institutions acting autonomously to solve common problems and produce different public goods . . . their dispersed and overlapping domains . . . could result in competitive, even conflictual, situations and would certainly seem inefficient when compared with the clear demarcations of competence and hierarchy of authority that (supposedly) characterize existing nation states.[82]

Writing some thirty years ago, Haas came to a conception of European political order similar to the condominio-type outcome, which he termed 'asymmetrical authority overlap' in comparison to other, more state-like possible outcomes such as 'regional state'. According to this multivariate integration scheme,

> authority is not proportionately or symmetrically vested in a new centre; instead it is distributed asymmetrically among several centres, among which no single dominant one may emerge, though one might imagine subtypes of this dependent variable involving various degrees of centralized authority. The ensemble would enjoy legitimacy in the eyes of its citizens though it would be difficult to pinpoint the focus of the legitimacy in a single authority centre; rather the image of infinitely tiered multiple loyalties might be the appropriate one.[83]

Such a conception, which arguably alerts the analyst to the potential implications of the newly incorporated 'flexibility' clause into the formal treaty framework (see Chapter 5), resembles Lindberg and Scheingold's understanding of a possible end-situation along the lines of an ambiguous pluralistic system,[84] as well as Streeck's more recent projection of the European polity developing into *'a collection of overlapping functionally specific arrangements for mutual coordination among varying sets of participating countries'.*[85]

In their effort to capture the complexity, pluralism and hybridity of the Union, since its political system displays a 'bafflingly mixture' of federal and intergovernmental properties, Bellamy and Castiglione have recently employed a neo-republican approach under the heading of 'democratic liberalism' that is based on 'a pre-liberal conception of constitutionalism that identified the constitution with the social composition and form of government of the polity'.[86] Democratic liberalism, by bringing the constituent groups of a political system into an equilibrium with one another, aims 'to disperse power so as to encourage a process of controlled political conflict and deliberation [as a way of filtering and channeling preferences] . . . moving them thereby to construct and pursue the public good rather than narrow sectional interests'.[87] Under this neo-Roman conceptual scheme, the European polity is defined as a 'mixed common-wealth' along the lines suggested by MacCormick, within which the subjects of the constitution are not homogeneous, but rather a mixture of political agents who share in the sovereignty of the composite polity.[88] Bellamy and Castiglione explain: 'The polycentric polity that is therefore emerging is a definite departure from the nation state, mainly because it implies a dissociation of the traditional elements that come with state sovereignty: a unified system of authority and representation controlling all functions of governance over a given territory.'[89]

Informed by an associative understanding of contemporary European governance, this pluralist depiction of the European polity as a heter-archical order within which sovereignty is dispersed across and between a variety of actors and public domains, and where a 'balanced constitution'

emerges as the ultimate protective mechanism against the danger of domination, is fully in line with Tarrow's definition of the Union as a 'composite polity': 'a system of shared sovereignty, partial and uncertain policy autonomy between levels of governance, and patterns of contention combining territorial with substantive issues'.[90] In particular, Tarrow's conceptualization largely draws on the work of historian W. te Brake, and particularly his study of the formation of 'composite states' in early modern Europe, between 1500 and 1700, where people 'acted in the context of overlapping, intersecting, and changing political spaces . . . '.[91]

Reflecting on the differentiated character of the EU system, Schmitter offers a general conceptual justification for applying such a terminology to the study of the European polity: 'We are familiar with the properties of states and intergovernmental organizations . . . but we would have to go far back in European history to recapture a more diverse language about political units.'[92] Indeed, scholars often turn to the past for insights and categories of analysis to get their bearings in a present that is in flux. Rethinking the present in light of the past is a productive way not only of sparking scholarly imagination, but also of searching for important and intriguing questions. This is especially true when the question of 'time' is addressed in a creative manner, as in the logic of 'analogical reasoning' for the study of processes that evolve through different phases not dissimilar to those that other processes have previously undergone.[93] Analogical reasoning permits the transfer of assumptions and ideas from a familiar phenomenon to a less familiar one, providing the necessary cognitive resources for theoretically informed comparative investigations.[94] By using the more familiar as a representational base for the less familiar, the argument goes, we acquire a hypothesis to be tested.[95] In this sense, past experiences can be taken, *ceteris paribus*, as functional analogies of more contemporary developments. Although this line of inquiry may lead to some approximation of EU reality with images of pre-existing political organization, thus helping integration theorists to familiarize with and even simplify an otherwise nebulous image of European polity-formation, it is equally instructive to recall King, Keohane and Verba's advice that scholars would learn a lot if they could re-run history with every-thing constant, save for an 'investigator-controlled explanatory variable'.[96] Some further methodological points merit our attention here (see also Chapter 4).

When conducting comparative research we are advised to select cases that are as similar as possible (rather than merely familiar to the researcher), and then find a crucial difference between them so as to set the limits of comparison. Harris explains: 'We should not compare apples with oranges just because both are fruits, but apples of one sort with apples of another sort.'[97] Inevitably, however, there exists a 'trade off' between similarity and differentiation. As Dogan and Pelassy argue, 'at times comparativists . . . will tend to look for differences in contexts that are roughly similar, or . . . will try to find analogies in contrasting political systems.'[98] Central to the above *problematique* is what Teune calls the 'equivalence across systems' for the purposes of construct validity and measurement.[99] The components and properties of the systems compared should at least indicate some equivalence to avoid the danger of engaging in creative comparisons that are nevertheless meaningless due to their initial lack of equivalence. This applies to a related methodological issue defined by Sartori as the 'travelling problem';[100] namely, when concepts in cross-systemic comparisons 'travel a very long distance'.[101] Be that as it may, McKenzie is right to observe that 'the problem is not whether to compare but how to organise comparison'.[102] All the above point to the different uses of language and traditions of conceptual history; to diverse approaches to concept-building and ways of interpreting concepts that rest on different normative qualities; and to distinct modes of conceptualization and means of determining our perceptions of reality.

Other terms to be found in the *acquis académique* as means of conceptualizing the political and/or constitutional physiognomy of the Union include: proto-federation, confederance, concordance system, network governance, quasi-state, *Staatenverbund*, meta-state, market polity, managed *Gesellschaft*, nascent *Gemeinschaft*, regional regime, federated republic, sympolity, confederal consociation and so on. Arguably, most of these attributes mark a shift away from vertically defined end-products of integration such as political community, federal state, constitutional union, supranational centre and the like, whose inadequacy, according to Haas, lies in the fact that 'they foreclose real-life developmental possibilities'.[103] Writing on the heuristic nature of neologisms as a means of approximating an existing reality to non real-life counterparts, Harrison notes that such hypothetical integration outcomes are 'mere provisional points in the future on which analytical attention may be fixed'.[104] Accordingly, whether these attributes are 'trapped in a state-oriented mode of thinking'[105] – and let us immediately note that statist analogies are partly justified on the grounds that, at some stage of analysis, one cannot but employ concepts that originally aimed at explaining the ontology of the (national) state – they only capture part of a rather more complicated reality. If anything, therefore, the above definitions suggest that the question of what exactly the Union is and is not is still to be sorted out. This, however, does not obviate the question why a 'conceptual consensus' or even convergent (as opposed to merely compatible) conceptual understandings are yet to emerge about the Union's ontological conundrum. A plausible answer is that the process of conceptualizing the political entity that is currently emerging in Europe rests both on different 'polity-ideas', incorporating different visions of regional political order, and on contending normative orders suggesting different ideal-type orientations for the European polity – the result being that such discursive and substantive differentiation and variability account for different 'structures of meaning'.[106]

Hardly surprisingly, then, integration scholarship is still in search of a legitimate model of collective governance as the basis for the future of the

EU. Such a challenging task, which will most likely result in a 'polygamous affair' encompassing different strands of the relevant literature, is compounded further by the very 'betweenness' of the Union, presently hovering 'between politics and diplomacy, between states and markets, and between government and governance'.[107] This, in Sbragia's view, 'will stimulate scholars of politics within unitary states and federations to rethink what they have so far taken as givens'.[108] But Puchala is less inclined to share such optimism. He states: 'European integration will for the foreseeable future continue to be an ongoing social scientific puzzle.'[109] The following points support the latter prophecy. Although from a state-centric view the Union rests on the separate constitutional orders of states, the European Court of Justice (ECJ) has ruled that the founding treaties already represent a 'Constitutional Charter'.[110] Further, consensus-seeking practices in the Council of Ministers are employed more often than not, even when the treaties formally require resort to majority rule. Similarly, the European Parliament (EP) performs functions that even the member state legislatures would be jealous of, yet the lack of its controlling and legislative powers *vis-à-vis* the EU's executive bodies suffices to support the philology of a 'democratic deficit'. Also, Union citizenship has been hailed by some as a step toward the formation of a transnational demos – itself a product of a normative commitment to civic engagement – whilst others have argued that this new *status civitatis* has more to do with the free movement of people within a single economic space than with the construction of a common civic identity based on a substantive corpus of democratic rights. Moreover, whereas an increasing array of policy competences are being brought into the multi-sector system, and having a significant impact upon domestic institutions, their *locus decidendi* remains closer to the domain of state agents. A final point is in order: enshrined in the Treaty on European Union (TEU) as a mechanism for the allocation of concurrent competences, subsidiarity has opened the way for two separate lines of development: the protection of state autonomy against excessive regional centralization and the extension of transnational legislative authority (see Chapter 6). Let us then pose the same question Puchala did almost three decades ago: 'Where do we go from here?'

Given the various conceptual and analytical difficulties involved in reaching an authoritative statement on the political and constitutional nature of the Union, we suggest that instead of placing undue emphasis on the peculiarities of its defining properties, it is perhaps more profitable to examine those aspects of its political organization which can be paralleled, with a greater or lesser degree of accuracy, with already familiar models of governance. This is the view taken in Chapter 5, where the political system of the Union is defined along the lines of a confederal consociation. In general, a new thesis will not only have to take into account pre-existing theoretical classifications, but will also have to use them constructively in order to substantiate its findings both theoretically and empirically. Groom makes the point well: 'There must be acknowledgement of the old Europe, but also a realisation that in building a new one, there are many original aspects that do not fit easily into the customary conceptual frameworks of integration theory.'[111]

The thesis put forward here is that we are currently witnessing the reversal of the Mitranian logic of international integration: instead of 'form follows function', it is increasingly the case that the structural properties of the system dictate both the pace and range of joint integrative schemes.[112] Accordingly, the extension of the 'scope' (range) and 'level' (depth) of integration do not necessarily coincide, let alone act in a mutually reinforcing way. Since the coming into force of the 'policy-generating' Single European Act (SEA) (1987), the 'polity-creating' TEU (1993) and the 'system-consolidating' Treaty of Amsterdam (AMT) (1999), there is evidence to suggest that both the functional scope (new policy arenas) and territorial scale of integration may well be extended, if not at the expense of the level of integration (ways of management), without either altering the locus of sovereignty or having any significant impact on the way in which the central institutions exercise political authority. The extension of qualified majority voting (QMV) in the mid-1980s on largely non-conflict-prone areas (Article 100A EC) and the introduction of a complex co-decision procedure in the early 1990s (Article 189b EC) illustrate this point well. And so does the sensibly arranged reform package agreed in Amsterdam in June 1997, resembling an exercise in system consolidation (or regime maintenance) rather than polity transformation (see Chapter 5). But let us now turn to the way in which the process of theorizing the European condition has evolved through time.

Theorizing the European condition

As already suggested, there are various ways of examining an inherently interdisciplinary object of study – arguably, as many as the constitutive bodies of theory that compose it. The process of European integration, revolving around the three-pillar structure of the Union – a structure which managed to survive any ambition to communitarize its two intergovernmental components at the June 1997 Amsterdam Summit – is a good case in point. For since the early days of the process, students of integration have applied a variety of approaches in order to develop a better understanding of what the European 'body politic' looked like in the many different stages of its political and, in the wider sense of the term, constitutional evolution. And yet, as Church suggests, 'there has been no resolution of the theoretical enterprise'.[113] Indeed, despite the many promising theoretical departures over the years, only a few concrete theoretical arrivals have been achieved.

Drawing on the genealogy of EU theory-generation – i.e. its intellectual context – different traditions of international relations theory (ranging from pluralist paradigms of interstate behaviour to neorealist interpretations of state-centric preferences and power), coupled with a plethora of 'middle-range' theories from comparative politics and public policy analysis (seeking to link the domestic and international arenas of the European polity as a system of governance), seem to have exhausted the analytical spectrum within which the study of European integration can bear fruit. This is far from being the case, however, especially if one subscribes to Rosamond's optimism about the current state of EU theory-building:

> There is no doubt that 'integration theory' (if it can be called that any more) is in a good state of health. It was not always so, and the recent phase of theoretical reflexivity and innovation owes much to the spillover into EU studies of creative thinking across the political sciences . . . European integration may well be a totally unique enterprise without either historical precedent or contemporary parallel, but it is a ready source for comparative study in some of the most emerging and lively social science currently going on.[114]

Despite, however, the recent 'comparativist turn' in EU studies (see Chapter 4),[115] intergovernmentalism – or modified schemes of cooperative interstate behaviour in the form of 'confederance', 'cooperative con-federalism' or 'confederal consociation'[116] – has survived the tides of supranationalism and regional centralization. A crucial implication of this is that the political system of the Union has not developed 'a new base of sovereignty' capable of transcending the sovereignty of its component state/citizen parts, contrary to earlier neofunctionalist and federalist predictions. Put differently, the current interplay between coordinated interdependencies and diffused political authority suggests that the Union, despite the fact that it has long out-reached mere international organization status, is not part of a linear process towards a federal end. Rather, European integration is about the preservation of those state qualities that allow the participating collectivities to survive as distinct constitutionally organized polities, whilst engaging themselves in a polity-formation process that transforms their traditional patterns of interaction. In both historical and political terms, this process amounts to the qualitative transformation of the West European community of states from a group of 'warring nationalities' to the most advanced scheme of voluntary and peaceful regional integration the world has ever witnessed. But such a profound structural transformation should not carry with it the assumption of the end of the nation-state in the 'new' Europe.

More specifically, the joining together of distinct historically constituted polities through a politics of accommodation, institutionalized compromise and an informal culture of consensus-building at the highest political level – all of which correspond to the Union's consociational nature – is part of a wider political evolution that poses no direct challenge to the constitutional conditions of sovereignty itself (see Chapter 5). The latter has simply acquired, through intense formal and informal interaction, a new cooperative dynamic of its own within highly institutionalized frameworks: it is by no means subsumed either by a new political 'centre', or by 'a new "hierarchy"', in which the dominant form of regulation is authoritative rule',[117] or even by a quasi-governmental structure 'that approximates a realistic image of a modern state'.[118] In brief, the Union has not, at least in its present form, taken us 'beyond the nation-state' and towards a postnational state of play.[119] In line with the above observations, and as a general description of the Union's *modus operandi*, comes an unambiguous statement that appeared in *The Economist* on 4 March 2000: 'Inter-governmentalism, as the jargon goes, is what counts.'[120]

Doubtless, schemes of supranational integration were of considerable potential during the formative years of the regional process, dominating the domestic policy arena of the then Community. That was a period when Hallstein's progressive presidency of the newly founded Commission aimed at projecting a new structure of managing the affairs of the Community's nascent regime. Later, however, this trend was replaced by a more balanced relationship between the Community's expansionist ambitions and practical intergovernmental realities. In fact, that was the beginning of what has been termed, after the Luxembourg Accords of 29 January 1966, the 'Second Europe': a transition stage leading to the Hague Summit of December 1969, in turn hailed as the first significant *relance* of the integration process after a period of 'hard' intergovernmentalism. The third integrative stage came about only a few years later, with the institutionalization of the European Council at the 1974 Paris Summit. This top political institution was expected to provide the leadership needed to move the Community towards higher levels of political integration, acting at the same time as a protective mechanism for sensitive (and often non-negotiable) national interests. Such a development signalled the inception of what was to be termed by Taylor the 'Third Europe': a qualitatively different phase from the pre-1974 one, characterized by a more favourable version of intergovernmentalism as a method of promoting integration. The final product of this stage – itself a 'compromised structure' between federal, confederal and consociational governance (see Chapter 4) – projected a symbiotic arrangement between domestic and regional political dynamics.

This brings us to another question contemporary theorists ought to raise: to what extent, if any, are the core theories of integration still capable of offering any sense of direction to the future evolution of the European polity? Whereas functionalism focused on the role of inter-national functional agencies as a means of establishing a 'working peace system' based on the notion of 'technical self-determination' within a largely 'aterritorial' policy environment; neofunctionalism on the internal dynamics of a 'self-regulated pluralistic society' of organized interests, multiple spillovers and patterns of elite socialization; and federalism on large-scale constitution-making – they all focused on questions of 'who governs?' and 'how?' That is to say, on the relationship between national and regional dynamics; joint decision rules; control of the integrative agenda; how policy is pursued at different levels of governance; whether the Union is capable of resolving internal crises and so on. In doing so, these formative integration theories have failed to ask an equally important question: 'who is governed?'

This question has recently prompted a significant 'normative turn' in EU studies, inaugurating a debate that in many respects follows the constructivist discourses in international relations theory.[121] In this context, the European polity is seen as an entity of 'interlocking normative spheres', none of which is privileged.[122] Or, as Laffan put it, 'a harbinger of trends in political and economic order, locked as it is between modernity and postmodernity'.[123] From a combined neo-constitutionalist and post-statist perspective, i.e. what in recent methodological parlance amounts to a normativist 'meta-discourse' (see Chapter 6) – the Union is portrayed as an emerging 'heterarchical space' that combines unity and multiplicity, transcends pre-existing boundaries and projects a pluridimensional configuration of authority.[124] This largely metatheoretical trend directs our research *foci* towards the understanding of a striking paradox: although the Union is often projected as a firmly enough established collective entity where traditional notions of representative and responsible government are losing their once powerful appeal, it does exhibit a notable potential for democratic self-development through the conception of novel forms of legitimate governance and patterns of institutionalized shared rule.

Particularly since the mid-1990s, the Union has shown a growing tendency to transcend issues of market integration and regulation, and touch upon 'sensitive areas of state authority', to the extent that European regionalism has been described as 'the only regionalism in the international system where there is an attempt to democratize politics above the level of the state, to mark a decisive shift from diplomacy to politics'.[125] Hence, the depiction of the Union as a polity or system of governance casts doubt on what Dahl calls 'the continuing adequacy of the conventional solution'.[126] This assertion chimes well with a point made by Kohler-Koch that European governance 'is not just determined by the structural properties of the EC system but also influenced by actors' perceptions of legitimate organising principles'.[127] Interestingly, the idea of a 'network arrangement' embracing the member state governments, subnational authorities, and the Commission seems to lie behind President Prodi's vision/strategy for the future of European governance.[128] 'Governing through networks', therefore, may well become the Commission's next integrative slogan, if not practical political blueprint, adding credence to those who view the Union as a multi-level policy arena assisted by effective regulatory mechanisms that promote a mode of governance based on collective problem-solving.

Although some of these issues are explored in Chapter 4, it is worth pointing out that the greatest challenge confronting the model of network governance and its various combinations of policy synergies among different public and private actors is the level of support it will enjoy by the general public and the means through which the institutions of the larger polity will open up new participatory opportunities for civic governance to endure. For the Europeanization of domestic public policy to enjoy a meaningful level of social legitimacy by the constituent demoi, it is imperative that the emerging forms of governance are accompanied by more civic-oriented processes of EU polity-building: effective governance for the management of a regional liberal economic order based on output-legitimacy – determined by the system's problem-solving capability[129] – will be but a poor substitute for the democratic norms embedded in the political constitution of good governance in relation to a demos. Technocracy and integration may have started as mutual reinforcements during the formative years of the regional process, but have ended in conflict, if not in an acute discrepancy between the strategic choices of Europe's governing elites and the political sentiments of the member state publics.

The many different phases of European integration, and subsequent theoretical approaches devoted to their explanation, point to the assumption that the formation of a European polity, as distinct from the making of a new regional state (a superordinate form of government beyond the nation-state) or, conversely, of a classical confederal union (a loosely institutionalized society of states), resembles an asymmetrical and often analytically incongruent synthesis of academic (sub)disciplines. As a result, different theoretical perspectives on European integration and the role and influence of state or Community institutions have become clear sites of intellectual, and sometimes even personal, contestation. Writing on the growing antithesis between intergovernmentalists and institutionalists, Puchala notes that EU theorizing 'has recently evolved into a full-scale, hard-fought debate . . . with contenders jumping upon one another's attributed weaknesses while disregarding one another's insights'.[130] It is interesting, but not surprising, that some thirty years earlier, Lindberg was reaching a similar conclusion:

> As a contributor to the European integration literature I have more and more come to feel as if I were excavating a small, isolated portion of a large, dimly-perceived mass, the contours of which I could not make out. I know that there are others digging there too, for I can sometimes hear them, but we seldom meet or see each other, and we have seldom organized so as to combine our efforts.[131]

This is reflective of what Jørgensen calls 'my discipline is my castle', which in turn resembles the kind of tribalism depicted by Knudsen in his portrait of 'the parochial scholar' in European international studies: 'so my project has been, in part, an imperfect search through a jungle of small specialities in different disciplines. Most of us are in reality victims of this kind of incomplete communication . . . The European tendency is for each specialist to stick to his own corner.'[132] More recently, Bulmer has expressed a similar concern: 'We may end up with a bewildering set of policy cases explained by a further array of analytical frameworks so that the "big picture" of integration is lost from view.'[133] A rather different account, however, is offered by Pentland, who makes the case against 'the integration of integration theory':

> it would seem potentially more useful to identify, acknowledge and sharpen the fundamental differences between various approaches, so that they can be tested through confrontation in the empirical world. Through this procedure scholars may in time converge on the most useful approach . . . by drawing the disorderly collection of approaches we now have into recognizable lines of battle, we can at least suggest where the most important points of contact will be.[134]

Given the remarkable profusion of theories, approaches, paradigms and wider intellectual orientations in the study of European integration, as well as the level of mutual incomprehension that often pervades among competing lines of inquiry, the question is how ought we to appreciate the relevance and limitations of the theoretical *acquis*? A good start is to examine the formative discourses on the form and functions, structure and process, scope and level of the regional arrangements. For it is this 'first wave' of theorizing European integration that provided an archetypal 'laboratory' of concepts and ideas on which subsequent theories were allowed to draw and expand.

Notes and references

1   L. Mjøset, 'Understanding of Theory in the Social Sciences', ARENA Working Papers, WP 99/33, 1999, p. 10.
2   Ibid.
3   H. J. Laski, *A Grammar of Politics*, London: Allen and Unwin, 1938.
4   R. J. Lieber, *Theory and World Politics*, London: Allen and Unwin, 1973, p. 3.
5   D. Collier, 'The Comparative Method', in A. Finifter (ed.), *Political Science: The State of the Discipline*, Washington, DC: American Political Science Association, 1993, p. 113.
6   C. Tilly, 'Relational Origins of Inequality', Columbia University, mimeo, 4 March 2000, p. 14. By kind permission of the author.
7   Ibid.
8   Ibid.
9   Ibid.

10 A. Rapopport, 'Various Meanings of "Theory"', *American Political Science Review*, 52, 1958, p. 981; quoted in Lieber, *Theory and World Politics*, p. 8.

11 Lieber, *Theory and World Politics*, p. 9.

12 A. J. R. Groom, 'The Setting in World Society', in A. J. R. Groom and P. Taylor (eds), *Frameworks for International Co-operation*, London: Pinter, 1990, p. 3.

13 D. J. Puchala, 'The Integration Theorists and the Study of International Relations', in C. W. Kegley and E. Wittkopf (eds), *The Global Agenda: Issues and Perspectives*, New York: Random House, 1984, p. 198.

14 P. Taylor, *International Co-operation Today: The European and the Universal Patterns*, London: Elek, 1971, p. i.

15 R. O. Keohane and S. Hoffmann, 'Conclusions', in W. Wallace (ed), *The Dynamics of European Integration*, London: Pinter, 1990, p. 284; quoted in C. H. Church, *European Integration Theory in the 1990s*, European Dossier Series, No. 33, University of North London, 1996, p. 8.

16 Church, *European Integration Theory*, p. 8.

17 B. Rosamond, *Theories of European Integration*, Basingstoke: Macmillan, 2000, p. 5.

18 Groom, 'The Setting in World Society', p. 3.

19 For more on this see R. M. Unger, *Knowledge and Politics*, New York: Free Press, 1975, pp. 12–16.

20 Church, *European Integration Theory*, p. 9.

21 Ibid, p. 8.

22 Ibid.

23 G. Allison, *Essence of Decision: Explaining the Cuban Missile Crisis*, Boston: Little Brown, 1971, p. 253, quoted in L. Cram, *Policy-making in the European Union: Conceptual Lenses and the Integration Process*, London and New York: Routledge, 1997, p. 2.

24 D. W. Hamlyn, *Metaphysics*, Cambridge: Cambridge University Press, 1995, p. 31.

25 Groom, 'The Setting in World Society', p. 3.

26 Taylor, *International Co-operation Today*, p. 149.

27 Rosamond, *Theories of European Integration*, p. 4.

28 G. Stoker, 'Introduction', in D. Marsh and G. Stoker (eds), *Theory and Method in Political Science*, Basingstoke: Macmillan, 1995, p. 17; quoted in Rosamond, *Theories of European Integration*, p. 4.

29 R. Bellamy and D. Castiglione, 'Building the Union: The Nature of Sovereignty in the Political Architecture of Europe', *Law and Philosophy*, 16, no. 4, 1997, pp. 421–45.

30 P. Taylor, *The European Union in the 1990s*, Oxford: Oxford University Press, 1996, p. 97.

31 C. Pentland, *International Theory and European Integration*, London: Faber and Faber, 1973, p. 189.

32 Lieber, *Theory and World Politics*, p. 4.

33 Quoted in ibid., p. 9. For the original argument, see T. S. Kuhn, *The Structure of Scientific Revolutions*, Chicago: University of Chicago Press, 1962, p. 15.

34 A. P. Branch and J. C. Øhgaard, 'Trapped in the Supranational–Intergovernmental Dichotomy: A Response to Stone Sweet and Sandholtz', *Journal of European Public Policy*, 6, no. 1, 1999, p. 124. For a similar discussion, see W. Mattli, 'Explaining Regional Integration Outcomes', *Journal of European Public Policy*, 6, no. 1, 1999, pp. 1–27, especially pp. 4–7.

35 W. Wessels, 'The Amsterdam Treaty in View of the Fusion Theory', paper presented to the British International Studies Association, University of Leeds, 15–17 December, 1997, p. 12.

36 B. Laffan, 'The European Union: A Distinctive Model of Internationalization', *Journal of European Public Policy*, 5, No. 2, 1998, p. 238.

37 B. Laffan et al., *Europe's Experimental Union: Rethinking Integration*, London and New York: Routledge, 1999, pp. 15–24.

38 Ibid., p. 39.

39 For definitions of the terms, see M. Forsyth, *Unions of States: The Theory and Practice of Confederation*, Leicester: Leicester University Press, 1981, pp. 1–16.

40 G. Majone, 'The Regulatory State and its Legitimacy Problems', *West European Politics*, 22, no. 1, 1999, p. 18.

41 F. Snyder, *General Course on Constitutional Law in the European Union*, Collected Courses on the Academy of European Law, VI, I, 1998, pp. 51–2; quoted in R. Bellamy and D. Castiglione, 'The Normative Turn in European Union Studies: Legitimacy, Identity and Democracy', mimeo, 1999, p. 2. By kind permission of the authors.

42 See respectively, K. W. Deutsch et al., *Political Community and the North Atlantic Area*, Princeton, NJ: Princeton University Press, 1957; D. Mitrany, *A Working Peace System*, Chicago: Quadrangle, 1966 (first published in 1943); and E. B. Haas, *The Uniting of Europe: Political, Social and Economic Forces 1950–1957*, London: Stevens, 1958.

43 A. M. Sbragia, 'Thinking about the European Future: The Uses of Comparison', in A. M. Sbragia (ed.), *Euro-Politics*, Washington, DC: The Brookings Institution, 1992, pp. 13 and 257.

44 T. Christiansen, 'European Integration between Political Science and International Relations Theory: The End of Sovereignty?', EUI Working Paper no. 94/4, 1994, p. 10.

45 For more on this, see the discussion by M. A. Pollack and J. Caporaso in the *ECSA Review*, 10, no. 3, 1997.

46 On the distinction between these concepts, see Forsyth, *Union of States*, pp. 10–16.

47 P. C. Schmitter, 'Examining the Present Euro-polity with the Help of Past Theories', in G. Marks et al. (eds), *Governance in the European Union*, London: Sage, 1996, p. 14.

48 Ibid, p. 6.

49 J. G. Ruggie, 'Territoriality and Beyond: Problematizing Modernity in International Relations', *International Organization*, 47, no. 1, 1993, pp. 139–74.

50 Quoted in Pentland, *International Theory*, p. 106.

51 W. Wessels, 'An Ever Closer Fusion? A Dynamic Macropolitical View on Integration Processes', *Journal of Common Market Studies*, 35, no. 2, 1997, p. 292. For de Tocqueville's original argument, see A. de Tocqueville, *Democracy in America*, New York: Harper and Row, 1969, p. 157. The first volume of *Democracy in America* was published in French in 1835 and the second in 1840.

52 See P. C. Schmitter, 'Some Alternative Futures for the European Polity and their Implications for European Public Policy', in Y. Mény et al. (eds), *Adjusting to Europe: The Impact of the European Union on National Institutions and Policies*, London and New York: Routledge, 1996, pp. 25–40.

53 W. Wallace, 'Theory and Practice in European Integration', in S. Bulmer and

A. Scott (eds), *Economic and Political Integration in Europe: Internal Dynamics and Global Context*, Oxford: Blackwell, 1994, p. 274.

54 See A. Adonis, 'Subsidiarity: Myth, Reality and the Community's Future', House of Lords Select Committee on the European Communities, London, June 1990, p. 11.

55 A. M. Sbragia, 'The European Community: A Balancing Act', *Publius*, 23, no. 3, 1993, p. 24.

56 See respectively E. J. Kirchner, *Decision Making in the European Community: The Council Presidency and European Integration*, Manchester: Manchester University Press, 1992, pp. 10–14; S. Bulmer and W. Wessels, *The European Council: Decision-making in European Politics*, London: Macmillan, 1988, pp. 8–11; and P. Taylor, *International Organization in the Modern World: The Regional and the Global Process*, London: Pinter, 1993, pp. 80–111.

57 D. McKay, 'On the Origins of Political Unions', paper presented at the 2nd ECSA–World Conference, Brussels, 4–6 May 1994, p. 6.

58 A. Moravcsik, 'Preferences and Power in the European Community: A Liberal Intergovernmentalist Approach', *Journal of Common Market Studies*, 31, no. 4, 1993, p. 507.

59 Quoted in C. Webb, 'Theoretical Perspectives and Problems', in H. Wallace et al. (eds), *Policy-making in the European Community*, Chichester: John Wiley, 1983, p. 36, and n. 22, p. 40.

60 W. Wallace, 'Less than a Federation, More than a Regime: The Community as a Political System', in Wallace et al. (eds), *Policy-making in the European Community*, p. 410.

61 Ibid., p. 406.

62 Keohane and Hoffmann, 'Conclusions', p. 282.

63 F. W. Scharpf, 'The Joint-decision Trap: Lessons from German Federalism and European Integration', *Public Administration*, 66, no. 3, 1988, p. 265.

64 Ibid., pp. 257 and 242. Cf. W. Wallace, 'Europe as a Confederation: The Community and the Nation-state', *Journal of Common Market Studies*, 21, nos. 1–2, 1982, p. 67; P. Taylor, 'Interdependence and Autonomy in the European Communities: The Case of the European Monetary System', *Journal of Common Market Studies*, 18, no. 4, 1980, p. 373; and S. Hoffmann, 'Obstinate or Obsolete? The Fate of the Nation State and the Case of Western Europe', *Daedalus*, 85, no. 3, 1966, p. 910.

65 Wessels, 'An Ever Closer Fusion?', p. 273.

66 Ibid., p. 274.

67 Ibid. Cf. A. S. Milward, *The European Rescue of the Nation State*, Berkeley, CA: California University Press, 1992.

68 Wessels, 'An Ever Close Fusion?', p. 274. Cf. R. O. Keohane and S. Hoffmann, 'Institutional Change in Europe in the 1980s', in R. O. Keohane and S. Hoffmann (eds), *The New European Community: Decisionmaking and Institutional Change*, Boulder, CO: Westview Press, 1991, p. 13.

69 Wessels, 'An Ever Closer Fusion?', p. 274.

70 Ibid., p. 275.

71 Church, *European Integration Theory*, p. 35.

72 J. Caporaso, 'The European Union and Forms of State: Westphalian, Regulatory or Post-modern?', *Journal of Common Market Studies*, 34, no. 1, 1996, pp. 29–52.

73 Ibid., p. 33.

74 Ibid.

75 Ibid., p. 29.

76 Ibid., pp. 35, 39 and 45. On the idea of a European regulatory state, see J. Majone, 'The Rise of the Regulatory State in Europe', *West European Politics*, 17, no. 3, 1994, pp. 77–101.

77 Schmitter, 'Some Alternative Futures', p. 25.

78 Ibid., p. 26.

79 Ibid., pp. 30–1.

80 Ibid., p. 31.

81 Ibid.

82 Ibid.

83 E. B. Haas, 'The Study of Regional Integration: Reflections on the Joy and Anguish of Pretheorising', *International Organization*, 24, no. 4, 1970, p. 635. Quoted in R. J. Harrison, *Europe in Question: Theories of Regional International Integration*, London: George Allen and Unwin, 1974, p. 204.

84 L. N. Lindberg and S. A. Scheingold, *Europe's Would-be Polity: Patterns of Change in the European Community*, Englewood Cliffs, NJ: Prentice-Hall, 1970.

85 W. Streeck, 'Neo-voluntarism: A New European Social Policy Regime?', in G. Marks et al. (eds), *Governance in the European Union*, London: Sage, 1996, p. 70.

86 R. Bellamy and D. Castiglione, 'Democracy, Sovereignty and the Constitution of the European Union: The Republican Alternative to Liberalism', EurCit Working Papers, no. 99/1, 1999, p. 11.

87 Ibid.

88 See N. MacCormick, 'Democracy, Subsidiarity, and Citizenship in the "European Commonwealth"', *Law and Philosophy*, 16, 1997, pp. 331–56.

89 Bellamy and Castiglione, 'Building the Union', p. 443.

90 S. Tarrow, 'Building a Composite Polity: Popular Contention in the European Union', Institute for European Studies Working Paper, no. 98/3, Cornell University, 1998, p. 1.

91 W. te Brake, *Shaping History: Ordinary People in European Politics, 1500–1700*, Berkeley, CA: University of California Press, 1998, p. 278.

92 Schmitter, 'Examining the Present Euro-Polity', p. 2.

93 On this type of analysis, see D. H. Helman (ed.), *Analogical Reasoning*, Dortrecht: Reidel, 1988.

94 L. R. Novick, 'Analogic Transfer: Processes and Individual Differences', in Helman (ed), *Analogical Reasoning*, p. 125.

95 M. Landau, 'On the Uses of Metaphors in Political Analysis', *Social Research*, 28, 1961, pp. 334–5.

96 G. King et al., *Designing Social Inquiry: Scientific Inference in Qualitative Research*, Princeton, NJ: Princeton University Press, 1994, p. 82.

97 P. Harris, *Foundations of Political Science*, 2nd edn, London: Hutchinson, 1976, p. 71.

98 M. Dogan and D. Pelassy, *How to Compare Nations: Strategies in Comparative Politics*, Chatham: Chatham House, 1984, p. 127. Cf. A. Przeworski and H. Teune, *The Logic of Comparative Social Inquiry*, New York: Wiley-Interscience, 1970.

99 H. Teune, 'Comparing Countries: Lessons Learned', in E. Oyen (ed.), *Comparative Methodology: Theory and Practice in International Social Research*, London: Sage, 1990, pp. 53–4.

100 G. Sartori, 'Comparing and Miscomparing', *Journal of Theoretical Politics*, 3, 1991, pp. 243–57.

101 B. G. Peters, *Comparative Politics: Theory and Methods*, London: Macmillan, 1998, p. 86.

102 W. J. McKenzie, *Politics and Social Science*, Harmondsworth: Penguin, 1967.

103 Haas, 'The Study of Regional Integration', p. 610.

104 Harrison, *Europe in Question*, p. 203.

105 M. Jachtenfuchs et al., 'Which Europe? Conflicting Models of a Legitimate European Political Order', *European Journal of International Relations*, 4, no. 4, 1998, p. 417.

106 Ibid., p. 411.

107 Laffan, 'The European Union', p. 236.

108 Sbragia, 'Thinking about the European Future', p. 267.

109 D. J. Puchala, 'Institutionalism, Intergovernmentalism and European Integration', *Journal of Common Market Studies*, 37, no. 2, 1999, p. 330.

110 In asserting the constitutional status of the Treaty, the ECJ has stated that 'the EEC Treaty, albeit concluded in the form of an international agreement, none the less constitutes the constitutional charter of a Community based on the rule of law'. See Opinion 1/91, Draft Agreement on a European Economic Area, 1991, ECR I-6084. This brings to the fore two ways of viewing the Treaty framework: as a 'formal' constitution (referring to the Treaty text as such) and as a 'material' constitution (derived from successive ECJ's rulings). For more on this distinction, see W. Sauter, 'The Economic Constitution of the European Union', *The Columbia Journal of European Law*, 4, no. 1, 1998, esp. pp. 30–4.

111 A. J. R. Groom, 'The European Community: Building Up, Building Down, and Building Across', in Conference Proceedings, *People's Rights and European Structures*, Manresa: Centre Unesco de Catalunya, September 1993, p. 47.

112 See D. N. Chryssochoou, *Democracy in the European Union*, London and New York: I. B. Tauris, 1998, p. 245.

113 Church, *European Integration Theory*, p. 37.

114 Rosamond, *Theories of European Integration*, p. 197.

115 S. Hix, 'Approaches to the Study of the EC: The Challenge to Comparative Politics', *West European Politics*, 17, no. 1, 1994, pp. 1–30.

116 C. H. Church, *The Not So Model Republic? The Relevance of Swiss Federalism to the European Community*, Discussion Papers in Federal Studies, no. FS93/4, University of Leicester, 1993; S. Bulmer, 'The European Council and the Council of the European Union: Shapers of a European Confederation', *Publius*, 26, no. 4, 1996, pp. 19–42; D. N. Chryssochoou, 'Democracy and Symbiosis in the European Union: Towards a Confederal Consociation?', *West European Politics*, 17, no. 4, 1994, pp. 1–14.

117 Keohane and Hoffmann, 'Conclusions', p. 281.

118 Ibid., p. 279.

119 Whether or not the logic of EU power-sharing arrangements is best explained through a theory of institutional delegation (pooling of sovereignty) or through the lenses of a federalist-inspired surrender of state competences (transfer of sovereignty), the most compelling evidence for the lack of European sovereignty *per se* is that European citizens are recognized as 'sovereign' only within their national polities. This begs the question of

developing an effective European 'civic competence' to counterbalance the largely state-oriented configuration of power and authority in the regional political system (see Chapter 6).

120 *The Economist*, 4 March 2000, p. 56.

121 See, *inter alia*, E. Adler, 'Seizing the Middle Ground: Constructivism in World Politics', *European Journal of International Relations*, 3, no. 3, 1997, pp. 319–63; J. T. Checkel, 'The Constructivist Turn in International Relations Theory', *World Politics*, 50, no. 1, 1998, pp. 324–48; T. Hopf, 'The Promise of Constructivism in International Relations Theory', *International Security*, 23, no. 1, 1998, pp. 171–200; and A. Wendt, *Social Theory of International Politics*, Cambridge: Cambridge University Press, 1999.

122 Z. Bańkowski et al., 'Guest Editorial', *European Law Journal*, 4, no. 4, 1998, pp. 337–40.

123 Laffan et al., *Europe's Experimental Union*, p. 189.

124 N. Walker, 'Sovereignty and Differentiated Integration in the European Union', *European Law Journal*, 4, no. 4, 1988, p. 357.

125 Laffan, 'The European Union', pp. 247, 249.

126 R. A. Dahl, 'The Future of Democratic Theory', Estudios Working Papers, no. 90, 1996, p. 13.

127 B. Kohler-Koch, 'The Evolution and Transformation of European Governance', paper presented at the Sixth Biennial ECSA–USA Conference, Pittsburgh, Pennsylvania, 2–5 June 1999, pp. 16–17.

128 *The Economist*, 4 March 2000, p. 56.

129 F. W. Scharpf, *Governing in Europe: Effective and Democratic?*, Oxford: Oxford University Press, 1999.

130 Puchala, 'Institutionalism', p. 318.

131 L. N. Lindberg, 'The European Community as a Political System', *Journal of Common Market Studies*, 5, no. 4, 1967, p. 345.

132 O. F. Knudsen, 'The Parochial Scholar: Barriers to Communication in European International Studies', *NUPI Notat*, no. 140, 1991, p. 8; quoted in K. E. Jørgensen, 'Studying European Integration in the 1990s', *Journal of European Public Policy*, 3, no. 3, 1997, p. 490.

133 S. Bulmer, 'New Institutionalism, the Single Market and EU Governance', ARENA Working Papers, no. WP 97/25, 1997, p. 1.

134 Pentland, *International Theory*, p. 16. Cf. B. Rosamond, 'Mapping the European Condition: The Theory of Integration and the Integration of Theory', *European Journal of International Relations*, 1, no. 3, 1995, pp. 391–408.

PART TWO

THEORIES

2

Formative Theories: Structure *v.* Process

Introduction

This chapter focuses on the principal intellectual tools employed by students of international integration to enrich our understanding of the then nascent institutional structures of the Community system. In large measure, such an investigation was informed by a functionalist, process-driven understanding of the nature of international integration. In this context, the usefulness of functionalist and neofunctionalist theory becomes easily apparent. Equally crucial, however, is to evaluate the contribution of federalist theory to an alternative view of European integration that placed greater emphasis on the end-product of the process, in the form of a formal constitutional settlement at the larger level. Finally, transactionalism was of great importance to the first wave of theorizing the Community, for it offered a distinctive pattern of thought about international community-building. Notwithstanding their particular concerns with description, explanation and prediction, these theories together shaped the early discourse on European integration, yielding new and valuable insights into the development of international theory itself.

Functionalism

Functionalism purports to explain why collective action in specific, functionally linked areas of cooperation is a more attractive option than unilateral state action: group involvement in peaceful problem-solving schemes, supported by the necessary technical expertise, becomes a real option for human governance. Nationalism and international anarchy are treated as sources of the fragmentation of the world community into rival territorially centred groups, obstructing the creation of a 'working peace system' based on the advancement of public welfare. Mitrany explains: 'peace will not be secured if we organize the world by what divides it.'[1] The functionalist remedy he proposed was non-coercive international community-building centred on the resolution of human conflict and the satisfaction of basic welfare needs through 'a smooth-running rational technocracy' that would transcend any dogmatic territorial considerations, or what Pentland terms 'the divisive and self-perpetuating jealousies of the nation-state system'.[2] Rosamond summarizes the functionalist thesis well:

> throughout his work, Mitrany declared himself to be an adamant social scientist and thought his purpose to be the avoidance of normative dogma in the production or prescriptions for future human governance ... For Mitrany, the starting point should not be a question about the 'ideal' *form* of international society, but about what its essential functions should be.[3]

Mitrany's understanding of 'the integrative dynamic', Taylor notes, 'is the learning process of citizens who are gradually drawn into the co-operative ethos created by functionally specific international institutions devoted to the satisfaction of real welfare needs'.[4] At the level of individuals, this implies that 'creative association in ... problem-solving provides a learning-situation in which participants are gradually weaned away from their allegedly irrational nationalistic impulses toward a self-reinforcing ethos of cooperation'.[5] Linked to this elaborate action process is a notion of integration whereby individuals develop a greater awareness of their mutual needs (and interests) and are prepared to transfer their loyalties, albeit function by function, to the nascent common institutions. More important perhaps is the implicit normative assumption that 'there is – or ought to be – no political loyalty *per se* which transcends the sum of functional loyalties'.[6] Yet, the relationship between functionalism and community or *Gemeinschaft*, along the lines suggested by Tönnies in the late nineteenth century (see below),[7] is one that has not been explicitly demonstrated by Mitrany or other like-minded functionalists. Haas, however, has argued that 'it is precisely our hope that functional sociology can show how *Gesellschaft* [or society] can develop into *Gemeinschaft*', whilst noting that 'community is immanent in the evolutionary logic of [the Mitranian] action process . . . '.[8] The basis of the functionalist hypothesis suggests that as individuals gradually identify with the problem-solving capacity of the new agencies, a popular consensus will emerge on what functions should be performed by the latter and what needs should be served first. The next logical step involves the development of habits of cooperative interaction among individuals that indicate, alongside the functionalist reorganization of international society, 'a sense of the "whole" or *Gemeinschaft*'.[9]

In large measure, the organic process of social learning, attitudinal change and community growth by functional association – directed against the outmoded forms of state governance – is furthered by what is called 'management committee government', reflecting Mitrany's inherent distrust of traditional assembly controls or 'government by politicians' over complex policy-making. Guided by the quest to watch closely for the 'relation of things', Mitrany's political science makes the case for replacing old-style, non-specialist assemblies by new forms of representation and ways of obtaining public control such as 'functional' assemblies composed of experts whose technical knowledge would guarantee greater and better efficiency in supervising governmental actions. In *The Functional Theory of Politics*, he reiterates that 'no one would share in power who did not share in responsibility' and that 'the functional structure could be made a union of peoples . . . directly concerned in any specific function, by giving them functional representation'.[10] Mitrany's underlying rationale is that 'in acquiring formal representative status, [pressure groups] also assume a corresponding democratic responsibility'.[11] No doubt, however, that this form of democracy – labelled by Mitrany himself as 'working democracy', as opposed to 'voting democracy' – is seen by those who perceive the institution of parliament as the focal point of public accountability as a major hindrance to established notions of representative and responsible government. At the same time, it exemplifies a functional model of politics situated between democracy and technocracy, according to which the art of government is dissociated from any rigid adherence to a 'set' political ideology, as opposed to 'a "way" of thinking': the central tenet of Mitrany's conception is a kind of pragmatic or 'service politics' which, although it does not dispense with the idea of power *per se*, it focuses more on the role and welfare functions of administration, as well as on the peaceful settlement of social conflicts.[12]

As for the functionalist conception of 'union', it is part of an evolutionary process of achieving functionally specific objectives, and not of a deterministic situation leading, either immediately or necessarily, towards a federal state or even a state-like entity. Like other theories of international integration, the end-product remains deliberately vague, although some form of a larger, but flexible, constitutional framework is not dismissed outright. One reason for this is that, according to Mitrany's philosophy, 'form follows function', in that the actual needs of the integrative system will determine the structural properties of the larger association. In his words: 'The nature of each function tells precisely the range of jurisdiction and the powers needed for its effective performance.'[13]

Notwithstanding the Mitranian philosophy of technocratic social engineering, it would be false to assume that functionalist theory perceives federalism as an uncontrolled homogenizing force eroding national diversity and identity. Rather, it maintains that it is in the interests of the integration process itself to proceed in an incremental, piecemeal fashion, as opposed to a federalist 'head-on' approach to European unity, for fear that a federal surrender of state sovereignty would be too big a political sacrifice for national governments on the altar of their unification. In addition, federation is seen by Mitrany as a rather inflexible political arrangement, as well as a type of political organization that could increase, rather than transcend, existing divisions at the societal level, by resulting in a territorial realignment. In a nutshell, such an arrangement would reproduce at a larger scale territorially defined authority structures. The above line of reasoning is intimately linked to the functionalists' distrust of an allegedly irrational, dysfunctional and increasingly obsolete nation-state, and a general perception of international integration as 'the gradual overlaying and eventual elimination of the state-system by an administrative network which better serves human needs in what is assumed to be an emergent global community'.[14] As Mitrany wrote as early as 1932:

> That we are going through a crisis in political outlook is evident: one cannot put it down to a decline in political fervor, like the decline in religion, for the surge towards the 'good society' and so the wrestling with politics is more than ever with us. Rather the crisis is one of political confusion . . . from trying to work an epochal change in social direction with the outworn ways and forms of the individualist-nationalist period.[15]

The key concept of the functionalist method is identified in the perception of a common interest among the various actors involved in the integration process, as well as a propensity to non-coercive means of rationalist problem-solving. Technical bodies such as the Tennessee Valley Authority or various United Nations specialized agencies are good cases in point. Technical cooperative arrangements were seen as vital for the European region to develop the necessary machinery to produce common policies and decisions, not least following the turbulent 1930s and 1940s. Thus, the pursuit of common tasks was linked from the outset to the creation of international institutions possessing a responsibility of their own, albeit limited in scope. As Kitzinger points out, the main difference between functionalists and federalists was that, whereas the former were preoccupied with defining the 'general interest', first, and then finding common answers to common problems, the latter sought joint action as a means of obtaining more effective central institutions.[16] As a result, the functionalists sought 'to set up only that minimum of political institutions that was indispensable in order to direct the common action that was most urgently required'.[17] Supranationalism, as applied in a specific regional context, producing a larger-scale territorial authority, is thus perceived as a potential source of replicating nationalist sentiments at a level beyond the nation-state. As mentioned earlier, Mitrany treated the idea of a European supranational state with maximum suspicion due to its perceived inability to nurture a conflict-free mode of transnational order.

Being confined to technical and economic areas, functional integration does not postulate the creation of a new sovereign power at a higher level. Instead, by trying to eschew politics, in terms of depoliticizing communal issues rather than being inherently apolitical in itself, it presents no immediate challenge to the sovereignty of states. Put differently, states continue to exist as identifiable entities.[18] As Taylor argues:

> the functionalist approach, indeed, allows the view that there is no point at which the state would *necessarily* lose its sovereignty, in the sense that power would now need to be finally transferred, or that the state would lose its legal right to act, if it so wished, against the wishes of the functional agency.[19]

In particular, the 'functional imperative', as the basic law governing the evolution of the European integration process, rejected the inevitability of constitutional requirements and fixed divisions of functional and political authority, and instead focused on problems which, although they cannot really be ignored, cannot be solved separately by each government acting alone. This has been termed by Albertini as the 'unitary trap'.[20]

There seems to be a globalizing, cumulative effect in the functionalist thesis: once problems are recognized as common, or at least not essentially differentiated by the relevant community of actors, and solutions to these problems may arise from collective rational thinking, then there is a tendency to expand such cooperative behaviour to other relevant spheres of action. Does Mitrany's logic, however, necessarily avoid being trapped in the domain of conventional politics, where interests and preferences are largely shaped by traditional party political discourse and electoral considerations? The answer is that, despite certain elements of 'technical self-determination' embedded in the functionalist method, the Mitranian thesis does not always evade parameters of this kind. Another crucial point about the political aspects of the functionalist logic to international integration is that functionalism is about the application of carefully examined, but not necessarily politically structured, strategies for transcending (national) territorial boundaries in tackling issues of a technical nature. International institution-building, in this respect, becomes conditional upon the (functionally determined) needs of the system, rather than the preferred lines of action to be taken by states according to their narrowly conceived territorial interests. In fact, such is the antithesis between functionalism and nationalism (or even statism), that Pentland suggests that '[t]he integration of mankind will thus come about not through, above or beyond, but despite, the nation-state.'[21]

But it is not always easy to distinguish between 'non-territorial' and 'territorial' politics in the context of contemporary European governance, especially when a variety of actors pursue different, albeit not necessarily antithetical, interests and are motivated by different culturally defined and historically diverse traditions. In principle, not 'apolitical' but 'aterritorial' is a more appropriate term to describe the internal logic of Mitranian functionalism, which is above all a theory about the functions of international society based on the principle of technical self-determination, reliance on non-coercive means of international community-building and an inherent mistrust of formal constitutional prescriptions of power-sharing as instruments for the advancement of human governance. This is clearly reflected in Mitrany's view of the uses of political science itself, since it must become 'an instrument devoted . . . to the service of human progress'.[22] In conclusion, Mitrany's main concern is how to transcend and eventually replace territorially based structures of decision-making with task-oriented international functional agencies, leading towards an integrated world system: a global society working on the basis of an 'interwoven network of cross-national organizations . . . meeting all human needs and responding to technological change'.[23]

Federalism

Federalism is very important as a theory of integration because of:

Federalism as a theory of integration is much more relevant to the study of the European polity than is often confessed. And this for a number of reasons: its increased concern with the dialectics of power-sharing in a compound political setting; its emphasis on in-built democratic arrangements linking different levels of governmental authority; its often flexible interpretation of the sovereignty principle; its focus on constitutional issues including individual and collective liberties; its emphasis on legislative representation within a bicameral structure and the allocation of competences among different policy domains; and its deeper concern about how to organize in a mutually reinforcing way the concurrent demands for 'unity in diversity'. But federalism does not emanate either from a single corpus of theory or from a grand constitutional design that can be transplanted from one federal system to another without losing its internal (or systemic) relevance and cohesion. Rather, there may well be different but equally federal sets of principles and structures composing a federal polity, which nevertheless need to be seen in a wider symbiotic perspective: a creative co-existence of distinct but constitutive units.

Notwithstanding the fact that no less than 267 different definitions of federalism were recorded by 1988,[24] definitions of 'federation' – as the formal expression of federal principles in the organization of the polity – are less abundant. Elazar and his research team have performed a useful service by defining federation as 'a compound polity compounded of strong constituent entities and a strong general government, each possessing powers delegated to it by the people and empowered to deal directly with the citizenry in the exercise of those powers'.[25] In this context, federalism aims to reconcile the parallel demands for greater political union – but not necessarily unity – of the whole (federal polity) with adequate constitutional guarantees for the parts (territorially defined subunits). Or, for 'unity without uniformity and diversity without anarchy'.[26] Thus, the appropriateness of federal arrangements 'would appear to lie in those instances where the existence and vigour of the forces that press both for wider unity and for autonomous regional diversity are relatively balanced'.[27] The striking of such a delicate balance between self-governance and shared rule emerges as the strongest catalyst for achieving overall 'federal cohesion' – itself a precondition for federations to survive the test of time. In Forsyth's words: '[Federal structures] establish a union but they simultaneously guarantee autonomy, and they fix or settle ratio or balance between the two.'[28] Or, as Robinson puts it, '[Federalism] is based on the existence of regional differences and recognizes the claims of the component areas to perpetuate their individual characters.'[29] According to Watts, it is equally important to distinguish between 'constitutional form' and 'operational reality' and study both constitutional law and the politics of a federation if we are to gain an understanding of the federal process, for in many federal systems 'political practice has transformed the way the constitution operates'.[30] He then makes the point that, although some federal constitutions recognize non-territorial constituent units, 'the constitutional distribution of power among *territorial* units is by far the most common pattern among federations'.[31] In any case, democratic representation becomes a crucial factor for the political viability of federal systems. This assertion also highlights the importance of accommodating territorial and non-territorial claims in nascent federal structures operating alongside the traditional nation-state such as the Union, based on systems of common management across an ever-expanding range of policy arenas.

Moreover, the representation of the people, either as a whole (when taken as a single demos) or as parts (when taken as a plurality of demoi) becomes the prior object of the federation.[32] 'What is distinctive about federations', King notes, 'is not that "the people" are viewed as sovereign, but that the expression of this sovereignty is tied to the existence and entrenchment of regional, territorial entities.'[33] In fact, 'one of the characteristics of federalism that flows from its popular base is the reduction of the question of political sovereignty to an incidental one', with the federal principle representing 'an alternative to (and a radical attack upon) the modern idea of sovereignty'.[34] Consequently, there are two possible but not antithetical ways of perceiving 'the people': as united and as diverse; a duality which 'for the life of the federation, is implicitly inexpugnable'.[35] In both equations, however, it is the federal demos as a whole, rather than primarily the dominant political elites representing the interests of each constituent unit, that is to be served by the central arrangements.

Although federations 'represent a particular species in which neither the federal nor the constituent units of government are constitutionally subordinate to each other',[36] they encompass considerable variation in purposes, identities, cultural traditions, financial resources, political and constitutional symmetry, organizational logic, conflict-resolution mechanisms, constitutional amendment procedures, power-sharing arrangements, as well as in the means of protecting the constitution. Yet, democratic representation of all participating units emanates as a common defining property. The crucial point here is not so much about creating direct links between different levels of government, but rather about establishing concrete and accessible avenues of communication between the federal demos and the central political institutions. In speaking of such 'levels' one might assume that they are sharply separated from each other, 'like boxes piled on top of one another'.[37] In reality, however, these different levels are never thus sharply divided. But if one considers that in most federal systems the central authorities are free to exercise considerable power over the federal demos as a whole, it is easy to explain why these direct links are central to the democratic legitimacy of the federal polity. In this sense, also, power and responsibility need to be seen as being mutually supportive, serving the interests of the collective citizen body, rather than as a competitive tussle for political authority between the federal and state governments.

Unlike a unitary state model, the degree of democratic participation in a federal system is linked to the extent to which legislative autonomy has been conferred on each participating collectivity by the constitution, either in terms of direct self-rule or in the form of 'reserved powers'; that is, powers not delegated to the federal government. Thus, public participation in the affairs of the federation is intrinsically woven into the degree of autonomous action granted to each level of government in which the demos exercises its sovereign rights. Further, the extent to which democratic diversity, or 'a co-ordinated expression of it',[38] can be maintained without endangering the political cohesion of the federation as a whole is conditioned by the ability of the central arrangements to produce viable constitutional equilibria. Indeed, the intersection or 'synergy' between federalism and democracy passes through the capacity of the compound polity to generate a common commitment to federal unity, a kind of mutual loyalty or *Bundestrue*, whilst safeguarding the continued existence and autonomy of the subunits. This implies that the idea of federation emerges as a living, pluralist and organic political order which 'builds itself from the grounds upwards'.[39] In Elazar's words: 'Federalism

must be considered a "mother" form of democracy like parliamentary
democracy or direct democracy.'[40] In short, federalism might be defined as
a multi-level political arrangement based on a constitutional system of
delegated, reserved and/or shared powers between relatively autonomous,
yet interrelated, structures of government whose multiple interactions aim
to serve the sovereign will of the federal demos.[41] But let us now turn to
the application of federalist designs to European unity and appreciate the
diversity of their logic.

With the postwar circumstances in Western Europe corresponding,
in Bowie's words, 'to those which often in the past have led nations
to undertake the initial steps towards federation', the federal solution
emerged as an inspiring remedy for Europe's multiple organizational
problems.[42] At the same time, the interposition of a central authority
beyond pre-existing boundaries acquired, mainly thanks to Italian federalist thinking, the status of a desirable political ideology. Although the
ideal of a united Europe predated the specific postwar attempts, what
makes them unique is that 'the unity concept moved into the foreground
of popular thinking with both an emotional and practical appeal'.[43] Deeply
shocked by the suicidal effects of nationalism, the federal impulse to
postwar European unity arose as an attractive alternative to a challenge
that, in Bowie's words, 'went to the very foundations of social existence'.[44]
Far from conceiving the nation-state as an *a priori* fact of existence, but
rather as 'a historic accident', the federalists proposed its transcendence by
a process of 'rational federal development'.[45] As a 1944 Draft Declaration
by the European Resistance Movement put it: 'Federal Union alone can
ensure the principles of liberty and democracy in the continent of Europe.'[46]
Following this somewhat teleological line of argument, any federal
surrender of sovereignty seemed better than allowing the European state
system to consolidate itself once more, especially after its 'great moral and
material bankruptcy'.[47] Reflecting upon the 1944 Ventotene Manifesto,
Bosco writes: 'The real cause of international anarchy was seen as "the
absolute sovereignty of national States", which is the source of power-
politics in the international sphere and of totalitarianism in the national
one.'[48] Similarly, Spinelli has argued that the nation-state had become 'a
compass which has ceased to give any bearings'.[49] These statements
provided the moral justification for early federalist designs. In brief, it
seemed as though the choice for European nations was one between
federalism (as a form of polity conducive to democratic peace and stability)
and anarchy (as a state of affairs conducive to nationalism and civil
or international war), rather than between the former and some form or
measure of regional interstate cooperation.

The federalists have also made their case by stressing the inability
of states to provide new means of popular participation, and that an
unprecedented 'legitimacy crisis' had shaken their once powerful
structures: a deep-rooted structural crisis which prompted them to look
above the nation-state itself as a means of resolving its acute legitimacy

problems. Underlying these criticisms is a higher political purpose, amounting to the belief that 'new loyalties will arise in direct conflict with the nation-state',[50] opening up much wider horizons than those afforded by the latter. This is exactly what European federalists had in mind: that these multiple pressures on the nation-state would lead to the recognition that new democratic arrangements would have to be devised so as to meet the challenges of the postwar era. Spinelli, for instance, had strongly opposed the idea proposed by national governments of a 'partial' European union (in the form of a limited-purpose confederal partnership) without first creating a democratic infrastructure upon which common institutions would be based. In this sense, federalism provided the means not only to overcome the structural crisis of the nation-state itself, or even 'to transform the very essence of national statehood into a larger loyalty going beyond its territorial affinities',[51] but also a powerful stimulus to the extension of the democratic process.

Whatever the title ascribed to the envisaged polity, it was widely recognized that it would have to strike a balance between interdependence and autonomy, democracy and efficiency and, above all, unity and diversity. To convince the European peoples of the merits of federalism as a means of safeguarding their cultural and political traditions, the federalists stressed the representative character of the central institutions. It was maintained that the latter should be left free to exercise the political authority conferred on them by a written constitution in direct relation to the European public without having to rely upon the convergence of short-term national interests for the formulation of common policies and the taking of joint decisions. Herein lies federalism's greatest contribution to the cause of European unity: the projection of an 'inclusive' political community based on the democratic functions of government.

Writing on the strategic aims of the Federalist Movement, Levi refers to 'the objective of changing the character of exclusive communities which nation-states have and unify them in a federal community thus transforming them into member states of the European Federation, in such a way that they can coexist peacefully though maintaining their autonomy'.[52] It was believed that federalism would encourage democratic diversity by establishing a system of coordinated but independent spheres of authority based on a division of powers among state and federal agents. According to this, the member state legislatures would hold their executives accountable to their respective publics, whilst a European legislature would act as a potential barrier against the danger of central executive dominance. Resting on a 'firm constitutional structure', the main powers of the federation were to lie in the sphere of defence, foreign affairs, commerce across state lines, international exchange, communication and, in Pinder's words, 'enough tax to sustain the necessary expenditure'.[53] On the whole, the envisaged pattern of federal–state relations was closer to the dualistic model of classical federalism, requiring a constitutional separation of policy responsibilities between state governments and the general government, rather than to a system of shared rule based on concurrent competences, which were seen at the time as a potential source of internal disputes.

It soon became evident, however, that if the federal project were to be crowned with success it would have to overcome national governmental resistance to an immediate relinquishing of state sovereignty to a federal polity. The solution to this problem came from Spinelli, who proposed a strategy based on a campaign of public persuasion for the drafting of a federal constitution. This task was to be carried out by a directly elected European Constituent Assembly.[54] The justification for Spinelli's 'constituent method' lay in the belief that such an assembly was the only acceptable body to transform the possibility of popular participation in the affairs of the federation into political reality. The constitution was to be based on a declaration of fundamental rights, democratic institutions and the separation of powers: it was believed that a balanced structure of national and federal competences based on the principle of dual federalism would preserve national identity and diversity in a way compatible with the democratic ethos. Thus, it was agreed that the federation should have limited but real powers, with the remaining spheres of competence resting on state jurisdiction. In short, the gist of the federalist thesis was that 'federalism is the only international democratic bond which can create a reign of law among nations', as well as the only possible means for enlarging 'the sphere of democratic government from the ambit of the state to that of a group of states'.[55] As most federalists have acknowledged, however, the difficulty of the task lay not so much in convincing the European peoples of the need for a political federation, but in convincing them that they, rather than their national governments, must create it. In the end, the dialectic between popular consciousness-raising and rationalist persuasion by governmental elites failed to bring about the envisaged results, something that directs our attention to the very limitations of European constitution-making itself.

The first real test for the idea of creating a European federation came with the convention of the 1948 Hague Congress. Yet, its end-product, in the form of the Council of Europe, did not live up to federalist expectations. Rather, it represented 'a triumph of the unionists'.[56] As the federal movement was losing whatever popular appeal it initially displayed, an alternative method of institutional development began to consolidate its strength, known as Monnet's 'functional federalism'. Being functionalist in conception but federalist in prospect, this approach represented a new, albeit modest, integration philosophy. Convinced that European unification was not interested in 'end-situations' as in evolutionary processes, the functionalists criticized the federal alternative for being totally impractical and idealistic, 'offering', in Harrison's words, 'merely the prospect of the unattainable'.[57] Instead, by recognizing that integration had nothing to do with formal constitutional engineering, the functionalists stressed the point that Europe could not be unified 'by a stroke of the constitutional lawyer's pen'.[58] In particular, they criticized the federalists for being advocates of an immediate objective that was largely overtaken by a naïve sentimentalism, deceiving themselves with the illusion of radical political change. Likewise, Spinelli's pathway to European unification was viewed as over-ambitious and legalistic, resting on the fallacious assumption that the termination of the war had also signalled the 'withering away of the nation state'. In general, federalist projects were believed to be consciously undermining the necessary gradual nature of integration in order to achieve a rigid constitutional settlement in Europe, thus losing sight of the imperatives of 'functional incrementalism' as a feature central to the viability of the regional process.

The early school of European federalism, by relying heavily on the American federal experience, seemed to have undermined the *sui generis* character of postwar European integration. In their unrestrained passion for a united Europe, Beloff asserts, federalists were misguided in looking to the US pattern for a promising analogy.[59] In Albertini's words: 'as a new form of the modern state, federalism is an American product. But the United States of America had not to overcome historically constituted nations to constitute itself.'[60] By contrast, the federal conception of Europe failed to recognize that its vision was not the primary goal for a sufficient number of Europeans. Likewise, its federal democratic principles did not acquire sufficient persuasive power to win the confidence of national governments and mobilize accordingly the political elites. Finally, a third line of criticism, this time of the relationship between federalism and the role of institutions, comes from Rosamond: 'Institutions matter, either as human creations to inaugurate a transnational federalist legal order, or as advocates shaping mass ideational change in favour of federation as a preferred structure of governance.'[61]

But it would be unjust not to reiterate the commitment of European federalists to a more democratic process of European political union, and their opposition to an essentially utilitarian form of interest-convergence among national governmental actors as a structural precondition for any substantive public loyalty transfers. Indeed, European federalists have unequivocally maintained that the institution of parliamentary democracy (in the form of representative and responsible government) was too closely related to Europe's political culture to be denied at a level beyond the traditional state. Finally, it was they who first stressed the importance of linking the idea of a formal European constitution with the democratic legitimacy of the envisaged federal polity based on the principles of segmental autonomy and diversity, and a bicameral system of government.

Transactionalism

The approach developed by Deutsch and his research team in their examination of the North Atlantic Area represented a shift in emphasis from
earlier theoretical work on international integration to a more empirically
oriented framework of analysis. Rosamond makes the point well when he
argues that transactionalism 'grew out of a conscious effort by social
scientists to bring about a formal separation of theory from practice'.[62]
Or, as put by Pentland, 'in the work of Deutsch . . . there flows a strong
stream of rationalistic optimism of social science . . . '.[63] Transactionalism
represented a systematic attempt to capture the dominant character of the
relationship between international integration (largely seen as a process of
community-formation) and social communication (changes in patterns
of transactions), by focusing on the conditions which may bring about a
large-scale 'sociopsychological community'. In particular, Deutsch defines
integration as 'the attainment of a "sense of community" and of institutions
and practices strong enough and widespread enough to assure, for a "long
time", dependable expectations of "peaceful change" among its population'.[64] By 'peaceful change', a theme central to Deutsch's analysis, is meant
'the resolution of social problems, normally through institutionalized
procedures, without resort to large-scale physical force'.[65] The idea here
is that political integration, and with it the emergence of a new type of
international system based on peace and security, could be achieved
through processes of mutual transactions, cultural flows and social learning
that change the attitudes and behaviour of individual citizens and
contribute to the gradual growth of community or, indeed, a collective
consciousness.

Social learning is particularly crucial, for as Deutsch wrote in *Nationalism
and Social Communication*, successful (political) integration depends on 'a
historical process of social learning in which individuals, usually over
several generations, learn to become a people'.[66] It thus becomes the central
integrative dynamic of international community-building to the eventual
formation of a people 'who have learned to communicate with each other
and understand each other well beyond the mere interchange of goods
and services . . . '.[67] According to Deutsch, 'a people' comes into being
through the development of complementary habits and facilities of communication, which would in turn allow for the qualitative transformation
of 'previously separate units into components of a coherent system'.[68]
Prominent in his argument lies the idea of peaceful problem-solving
through the intensification of avenues of communication among nations
(non-state international exchanges). This he calls a 'security community': a
framework of social interactions within which war would eventually
become in the relevant region both unthinkable and impractical. Deutsch's
notion of 'security community' could take the form of being either 'pluralistic' (where no formal/legal merger has occurred among the constituent
units) or 'amalgamated' (where the component parts have been formally

incorporated into a higher authority). However, Deutsch never really implied that there was an automatic forward linkage between these two types of political organization. As Lijphart has rightly pointed out, Deutsch's theorizing is also of importance due to the fact that it 'disputes the axiomatic character of the relationship between war and anarchy'.[69]

Deutsch was not particularly concerned with the institutional config-uration that the integration process would bring about, or for that matter with processes of formal institutional change. Nor was he generally interested in the allocation of authoritative power among different levels of political decision-making. His research focused on the sociopsychological aspects of international community-formation, which was seen as a result of increased and 'mutually responsive' transactions. But it would be unfair to the logic of his approach to present the developments in transactions solely as an indicator of international community-building. Taylor explains: 'It is also important to point out that it is the range and quality of changes in transactions that constitutes an indicator of community: too frequently Deutsch's ideas are criticized on the mistaken assumption that he sees *particular* transactions as *equivalent* to developing community.'[70] The end-situation of integration would take the form of an identifiable community of citizens – i.e. a people – through a process of social learning. Although such an outcome would take a long time to materialize, in fact several generations as Deutsch himself suggested, what is important is that the 'uniting parts' would start to develop 'a sense of community' based on the power of common identities, shared values and belief-systems, a common perception of their destiny, and that certain norms and habits of societal interaction would emerge from the range and intensity of informal contacts. Community feelings, and the emergence over time of a 'community of values' at the larger level of aggregation, were thus seen as the result, rather than the cause, of closer links among the participating units.

The distinction made by Deutsch between 'pluralistic security community' and 'amalgamated security community' warrants our closer attention. The former was expected to produce a 'sense of security' among the relevant populations, whereby the resolution of conflicts through violent means would be replaced by mutually acceptable methods for their peaceful settlement. It was the particular attitudes of the actors involved that would create a certain culture of cooperation which, through the forging of further and closer communicative links among them, would make resort to war highly unlikely. On the other hand, Deutsch's idea of 'amalgamated security community' was a more advanced form of political community or *Gemeinschaft*. In this type of association, as opposed to the more 'instrumental' notion of *Gesellschaft* (or society), one may perceive the embryo of a genuinely 'constitutive' community: 'a community that would constitute the very identity of the individuals'.[71] *Gemeinschaft* is generally regarded as a stable form of association that best suits the prospering of mutually responsive relations on the grounds that the individuals forming it have developed to a sufficient degree a 'sense of community' – also known as 'community spirit' or 'community of attachment' – strong enough to overcome and even transcend any potentially divisive issues which may arise as integration proceeds. Equally, where the 'community spirit' is less intense and profound, it can be said that the integrative system will find it much more difficult to cope with internal social and political disputes. From this view, then, the *'Gemeinschaft* factor' appears to constitute one of integration's indispensable 'common spheres'.

Although no actual society or institution will ever conform completely to Tönnies's theoretical selections,[72] since they are conceptual entities representing two ideal types of social organization, Deutsch was aware of the fact that a sociopsychological community would have to be based on 'a sense among the individuals forming it of belonging together, of having common loyalties and values, of kinship', so that the tasks performed within its structures stem from 'a feeling of contributing something worthwhile to the good of the whole'.[73] Thus, a *Gemeinschaft* is something qualitatively distinct and presumably higher than the numerical sum of the private well-being of its members. In this type of society, people associate themselves together because they think of their relationships as valuable in the dual sense of being important as an end both *in* and *of* itself. Thus, it is perceived as an internal, living and organic 'collective entity' – organic in terms of being considered and conceived in relation to its parts[74] – whose 'norms of order' are based upon 'concord', as opposed to a *Gesellschaft* which rests on a contractual arrangement or 'convention'. Resting on relationships of mutual affirmation of a *federative* kind, the members of a *Gemeinschaft* gradually develop strong feelings of 'togetherness', 'we-ness' or even 'oneness', to the eventual framing of a collective consciousness. Accordingly, they are bound together by symbiotic relationships, think of their collective existence as dominating their respective individualism and perceive their close association as a means of improving their domestic conditions of living. An entity which is formed through this positive type of relationship points to 'a lasting and genuine form of living together', as opposed to its counterpart form of 'human *Gesellschaft*' which is considered as a mere co-existence of people independent of each other.[75] In short, whereas the 'common sphere' of a *Gesellschaft* rests on the concept of contract, with its 'secret' lying in 'a rational coming together of ends that remain individual',[76] that of a *Gemeinschaft* rests on the concept of 'one people'; its 'secret' lying in an internally oriented relationship developed among its members, rather than in an artificial fusion of private wills. Also, in *Gemeinschaft*-like relationships, the ensemble of individual wills mutually direct each other towards an 'equilibrium of forces', with authority not being viewed as an all-powerful decision-making centre, but rather as a dialectical process of structuring civic relations within a socially legitimized environment.

Deutsch's sociological approach focused more 'on description and was more cautious about predicting the dynamic links between the various stages of the integration process'.[77] This distinguishes him from neo-functionalist analysis and the premium it places on forward linkages. Being interested in the early stages of community-formation and the relationship between different conditions of the integrative process, Deutsch's analysis is also easy to distinguish from the early federalist school of thought and its emphasis on the constitutional prerequisites of European unification. In fact, Taylor notes, 'Deutsch's pluralistic security community contains no common decision-making centres . . . but in some ways it is highly integrated.'[78] Institution-building, therefore, is not treated in mainstream Deutschian analysis as an end in itself or, from a methodological perspective, as a primary indication that integration has actually taken place. Rather, the emphasis is on a different level of analysis: the development of a sense of community at the popular level. In this, Deutsch shares a common belief with the older functionalists: the higher the level of sociopsychological community and, hence, of consensus in society, the greater the progress towards the integration of the segments into a larger purposive whole – i.e. 'a community of attitudes and values' – and the less controversial the process of transferring crucial decision-making powers to a new centre.

Deutsch's political science and particularly his contribution to international pluralist theory have been widely acknowledged by students of international politics and nation-building alike. His theoretical work arguably set in train innovative research programmes on both sides of the Atlantic 'that guided scholars away from the narrow domain of inter*state* interaction to the study of the relations between *societies and peoples* more generally'.[79] More recently – and against the background of a post-Cold War international system – a renewed interest in the study of the conditions that are conducive to the development of security communities has emerged, following the work of Adler and Barnett.[80] But in contrast to Deutsch's ponderous reliance on behavioural patterns and 'measurable' or 'quantifiable' indices of societal exchanges and communication – largely through techniques of quantitative, social scientific research based on aggregate data, content analysis and the use of information theory – their approach emphasizes 'the sociological origins of transactions and . . . the processes of social learning and communicative action that produce mutual identification [and trust] among actors'.[81]

In conclusion, Deutsch's pluralistic approach to international integration and the peaceful formation of international political communities represented an attempt to 'transcend the atmosphere of "political realism"'[82] in an era dominated by the politics of superpower rivalry and acute ideological confrontation between liberal and communist values (that were also greatly exacerbated by discontinuous communication between the two power blocs). In doing so, Deutsch's innovative research laid the foundations for a credible alternative to mainstream realist analysis, whose ontological stance portrayed states as more concerned with clashing interests, strategic interaction, security alliances, means of coercion, relative power and relative gains, viewing the conduct of international politics as resting on a plethora of *Machtpolitik* games among power-hungry, antagonistic and egocentric state actors 'pursuing self-help policies under conditions of anarchy'.[83]

Neofunctionalism

Neofunctionalist theorizing is often mistakenly associated with Monnet's 'functional federalism'. The latter term has been employed as an analytical tool to explain the composite character of Monnet's gradualist approach to European unity, amounting to a rather eclectic synthesis of elements of functionalism and neofunctionalism, without however being fully in accord with either of them. Neofunctionalism, therefore, should not be hastily classified as being – conceptually or otherwise – in limbo between functionalist and federalist approaches to international integration. Although it does share some important elements of both (from functionalism the centrality of transnational actors, and from federalism that of the central institutions), it has developed its own intellectual arsenal and integrative logic, subscribing to certain principles and values of transnational interaction, patterns of regional institution-building and styles of collective decision-making. In defence of this view comes a crucial line of demarcation between neofunctionalism and other integration theories: its essentially abstract conception of politics and/or the political, since these are taken as inherently conflictual processes not in the traditional sense of the accretion of authoritative power, but rather in terms of 'the allocation of basic values in the community'.[84] Conflict itself becomes, to borrow a phrase, the 'circulatory dynamic' of the (ideally) integrated political system. Another important distinction, Pentland incisively asserts, is that whereas the older functionalist school declares 'an unabashed preference for administration over politics, the neofunctionalists create . . . a blend of the two, but a blend in which there remains an administrative flavour to "politics"'.[85] It is fair, therefore, to suggest that the contribution of neofunctionalist theorizing has been unique in the field of regional integration studies.

In particular, inspired by an American school of liberal pluralist thinking initially led by Haas,[86] but also influenced by behavioural political science (since politics itself is ultimately about the behaviour of competing actors), neofunctionalism decisively inserted the element of conflict in the analysis of the European regional process, as well as that of forward linkages among different, yet interrelated, policy arenas. Procedural mechanisms were seen as decisive, whereas the idea of a sociopsychological consensus at the popular level, a variable indirectly linked to Mitrany's philosophy of international functionalism, was not taken as a structural prerequisite for the transfer of decision-making authority to a new regional centre. Rather, such a consensus, which in a way corresponds to the idea of a less polarized form of society, emerges as a latent property and/or a consequence of successful elite socialization: the process by which influential actors of policy- and decision-making from different national settings learn to work with each other within a larger management system. In this context, a process of bureaucratic interpenetration, usually referred in the literature as *engrenage,* emerged as the dominant *modus operandi* of the regional political system. The idea is that different actors decide to shift their focus on collaborative action to the point that competences – functional, jurisdictional or other – become blurred, identities overlap and loyalties co-exist. Mutual reinforcement is a key to understanding the logic of neofunctionalist 'spillover' in functionally or politically related policy domains or issue areas. Progressively, the neofunctionalist argument goes, there would be a convergence of demands among national governments and a propensity for further integrative action, facilitated by the new central authorities. In general, the drive of integration is the expansive logic of spillover, whereby 'a given action, related to a specific goal, creates a situation in which the original goal can be assured only by taking further actions, which in turn create a further condition and a need for more, and so forth'.[87] The spillover effect may take three different forms: functional (referring to technical pressures leading towards further sector integration), political (as a result of intensive levels of elite socialization and of gradual convergence of interest/expectations), and cultivated (through the active role of the central bureaucracy as agent of integration).

An essential part of the neofunctionalist strategy was the identification of the Community method as the new *modus operandi* of the general system. Such a 'method' consisted, *inter alia*, of high levels of elite socialization, joint lobbying activities by organized interests, the Commission's right of legislative initiative, the involvement of national governments in complex negotiations at the European level and a certain culture on the part of the Commission for upgrading the wider Community interest. It was not accidental, then, but no less ironic for a theory based on the idea of 'non-ideological' politics, that in the formative stages of the Community's development, neofunctionalism acquired the status of an ideology in Brussels. As Milward and Sørensen put it, 'the theory's technocratic elitism appealed strongly to European Community officials who naturally saw the extensive theorizing about the workings of the Community as a confirmation of their historical role as guardians of European integration processes.'[88] This line of argument chimes well with Monnet's philosophy of European unification since 'neofunctionalism . . . provides relatively rigorous formulation of the means of political integration developed *ad hoc* by Jean Monnet and his colleagues in the 1950s.'[89] Likewise, Monnet's gradualist and highly pragmatic method was fully in accord with Haas's famous dictum that 'functional integration requires pluralism'.[90]

Taken as a process rather than a condition, the end-situation of the regional experiment remained a deliberately open-ended one. Even Haas's definition of political integration as 'the process whereby political actors in several distinct national settings are persuaded to shift their loyalties, expectations, and political activities to a new centre, whose institutions possess or demand jurisdiction over the pre-existing ones',[91] leaves much to be desired from a teleological, let alone organizational, point of view. In particular, the envisaged end-situation is a new 'political community' along the lines of a supranational pluralist polity, within which 'specific groups and individuals show more loyalty to their central political institutions than to any other political authority'.[92] A more cautious approach to the end-product is offered by Lindberg, who defines it as 'a legitimate system for the resolution of conflict, for the making of authoritative decisions for the group as a whole'.[93] In conceptual terms, therefore, attributes like 'supranational authority', 'regional state', 'federal union' and the like add rather little to the precise constitutional form and/or structure of the envisaged 'political community'. Perhaps the only relatively discernible outcome of European integration in neofunctionalist terms is the creation of what Harrison called a 'self-regulating pluralist society whose unity and stability rests on mutual adjustment between groups following accepted norms'.[94]

The reason for this general reluctance by neofunctionalists to identify a clearly defined terminal state of integration can be traced in the logic of the theory itself: having stressed the idea of an inner compulsion towards further integrative action, since 'the creation of common institutions would set in motion a process for the accumulation of wider functions',[95] it would be too risky an endeavour to reach any authoritative conclusion on the political properties of the envisaged regional polity. At the same time, it would foreclose potentially significant conceptual possibilities for the development of Community politics and structures of collective decision-making. From early on, also, neofunctionalist writings would go as far as to declare that the very incompleteness of the European project would create the need for new central arrangements and, in time, for a directly elected regional parliament to ensure democratic control over the larger, and by then superimposed, European 'political community'. But it is equally true that direct democratic legitimacy was not viewed as a prime requisite for entrusting the new central institutions with the political management of the larger entity, nor was it taken as a fundamental deficiency of the Community system *per se* to reach a dynamic equilibrium. European integration in general, and the dynamics of political change in particular, could accordingly be sustained by a predominantly utilitarian (interest-fulfilling), rather than affective/identitive (emotional), support by the relevant community of citizens. That is to say, by an abstract, non-politicized, passive and output-oriented 'permissive consensus'.

Neofunctionalists, by abandoning the central integrative role of attitudinal change, while exhibiting a strong normative commitment to elite-driven political integration, placed the emphasis on a 'procedural consensus' about the institutional rules of the game: they stressed 'the psychology of elites in an integration process ideally culminating in the emergence of a new political system . . . '.[96] Further, they conceptualized integration as resulting from what Haas called an 'institutionalized pattern' of interest politics.[97] Such concentration on system-wide institutional developments within a liberal pluralist setting entailed important implications for their conception of sovereignty, in that the latter could be strengthened by an expanding legal competence.[98] Moreover, it was crucial for the common regional system to operate under conditions of economic and political pluralism, driven by the expansive, if not deterministic, logic of integration. The latter, once in train, was expected to transcend and eventually replace pre-existing nation-state structures with a new form of pluralist regional polity. Implicitly at least, neofunctionalists envisaged the development of a supranational state composed of a highly interactive community of transnational actors.

But the important element remained firmly confined to the process of integration itself: successive spillovers would bring together previously unconnected policy arenas and demand a change in both the behavioural and operational attitudes of the 'relevant elites'. In this respect also, the Commission, in its function as a collegiate body, was to occupy the major role in European policy change. It was assigned the task of acting as the motor of the integration process, the source of integrative initiatives, and the centre of technical expertise for launching joint projects of a supranational character. The point here is that the Commission, in contradistinction to its predecessor (High Authority), was given a wide range of policy competences to influence, together with the Council, the common legislative process and significantly involve itself in the process of setting the Community's policy agenda. This was especially true before the establishment (or formal institutionalization) of the European Council at the 1974 Hague Summit and the increasingly influential role and dynamism of the Council Presidency thenceforth.

Although neofunctionalism stressed the importance of 'conflict' in the integrative system, it failed to distinguish clearly between the scope and level of integration. The former refers to the range of common functional arrangements in the form of different policy areas that become part of the region's integrative corpus. That is to say, specific functions that are commonly managed at the larger level of aggregation. On the other hand, level refers to the ways in which the functional areas are managed, the involvement of supranational institutions in shaping common policies and, crucially, the extent to which these institutions are capable of exercising political authority independently of the component polities. Neofunctionalist thinking assumed that the scope and level of integration are mutual reinforcements: the more you bring new areas of policy action into the common framework, the greater the involvement and, subsequently, the influence of supranational institutions. But consequent amendments to the original treaties point in the opposite direction – for a number of reasons (see also Chapters 4 and 5).

In the case of the SEA, although there existed a feeling of accomplishment among European leaders for overcoming some of the obstacles towards further (negative) market integration, greater majority rule-making, increased parliamentary involvement and more attention to issues of economic and social cohesion, the level of integration was not fundamentally altered to take the system closer to a supranational political community. At the same time, the scope of integration was significantly advanced to include new areas of transnational cooperation. A similar view may be adopted for the TEU and the Amsterdam reforms which, taken together, did not alter in any fundamental sense the locus of sovereignty from national authorities to common institutions of governance. Doubtless, both treaty revisions added to the dynamics of 'ever closer union', a preambular clause that still remains poorly defined, but not to the formation of a federal political system or some form of regional state, whose constitutional properties present a direct threat to the sovereignty of the component state polities. A similar point is made by Taylor with reference to the continuous extension of QMV since the mid-1980s:

> [QMV] did not mean that the federalizing majority could now impose itself on the more cautious states; it did mean, however, a rather more subtle exercising of national sovereignty. The new arrangements meant that a new balance of restraints and powers had to be found for both the dissenting and the assenting states.[99]

Neofunctionalist theorizing has also been criticized for:

- projecting a supranationally biased image of Community arrangements and dynamics;
- underestimating the role of 'summit diplomacy' in putting together complex package deals;
- overestimating the role of the Commission as policy initiator and more generally of the Community Method;
- disregarding the indirect impact of successive enlargements on joint decision-making and the functional scope of integration;
- overstressing the influence of organized interest association activity at EU level;
- oversimplifying the relationship between politics and economics;
- offering an elite-driven explanation of the Community's internal workings;
- not taking into account 'the logic of diversity' argument;
- lacking operational referents;
- paying little attention to the likelihood of alternative integration outcomes;
- being overtaken by events, especially after the first major constitutional crisis of the Community in the mid-1960s;
- underestimating the viability of national polities and the endurance of their respective constitutional spheres;

- failing to distinguish between 'low politics' (low-priority areas like economic and technical cooperation) and 'high politics' (high-priority areas like foreign policy and defence);
- ignoring the high levels of issue/functional interdependence in the global economic arena and of changes in the international political system (factors exogenous to the regional policy environment).

ignore global

Church has summarized the debate on the validity of the theory by asserting that its 'predictions proved empirically wrong . . . the states of western Europe did not lie down and let supranationality walk over them'.[100] But he is equally right to point out that neofunctionalism, despite some overrated predictions about the dynamics of integration, 'was the first really deep and complex explanation of the Communities'.[101] Moreover, one has to remember that the most constructive line of criticism of the theory came neither from constitutional federalists nor from mainstream intergovernmentalists, but from neofunctionalist writers themselves, most of all by Haas in the mid-1970s.[102] And given the intellectual richness embedded in this elaborate exercise in self-inspection, one is compelled to acknowledge that neofunctionalism has performed a valuable service to the theoretical study of contemporary international organization. More important perhaps, in line with the older functionalist school, neofunctionalist writings have both encouraged and inspired political science research 'to move away from state-centricity and power politics',[103] and direct its *foci* to units of analysis that are either consistently ignored or generally dismissed as irrelevant by the dominant realist school of international politics.

Above all, however, neofunctionalism represented the first systematic attempt to offer a general theory of regional integration, remaining to this day an indispensable referent not only for theorizing the European experience, but also for the comparative study of other regional unions or processes of regionalization. The next chapter examines the state of integration theory during the Community's consensual phase – from the 1965 constitutional crisis to the *relance* of European integration in the mid-1980s leading to the SEA – when the acclaimed supranationalism of the classical Community Method, at least in the neofunctionalist explanatory system, seemed to have run out of momentum.

Notes and references

1 D. Mitrany, *A Working Peace System*, Chicago: Quadrangle, 1966, p. 68.
2 C. Pentland, *International Theory and European Integration*, London: Faber and Faber, 1973, p. 70.
3 B. Rosamond, *Theories of European Integration*, Basingstoke: Macmillan, 2000, p. 32.
4 P. Taylor, 'The Concept of Community and the European Integration Process', *Journal of Common Market Studies*, 12, no. 2, 1968, p. 86. Others, like Hirst, are partly in favour of these views insofar as 'different forms of representation are not seen as a substitute for representative democracy, but rather as a supplement to it'. See P. Hirst, *Associative Democracy: New Forms of Economic and Social Governance*, Cambridge: Polity Press, 1994, pp. 16–17.
5 Pentland, *International Theory*, p. 84.
6 Ibid.
7 See F. Tönnies, *Community and Association*, trans. and supplemented by C. P. Loomis, London: Routledge and Kegan Paul, 1974.
8 E. B. Haas, *Beyond the Nation-state: Functionalism and International Organization*, Stanford: Stanford University Press, 1964, p. 26.
9 Pentland, *International Theory*, p. 84.
10 D. Mitrany, *The Functional Theory of Politics*, London: Martin Robertson, 1975, p. 119.
11 Ibid., p. 261.
12 For more on this, see J. Eastby, *Functionalism and Interdependence*, Lanham: University Press of America, 1985, p. 14. For the original argument, see D. Mitrany, *The Progress of International Government*, New Haven, CT: Yale University Press, 1932, p. 256.
13 Mitrany, *Working Peace System*; quoted in Pentland, *International Theory*, p. 69.
14 Pentland, *International Theory*, p. 83.
15 Mitrany, *Progress*, p. 247; quoted in Eastby, *Functionalism*, p. 15.
16 U. Kitzinger, 'Time-lags in Political Psychology', in J. Barber and B. Reeds (eds), *European Community: Vision and Reality*, London: Croom Helm, 1973, p. 13.
17 Ibid.
18 This point is analysed further in P. Taylor, 'Functionalism: The Approach of David Mitrany', in A. J. R. Groom and P. Taylor (eds), *Frameworks for International Co-operation*, London: Pinter, 1990, p. 132.
19 Ibid.
20 Quoted in A. Bosco, 'What is Federalism?', paper presented at the Second ECSA–World Conference, Brussels, 4–6 May 1994, p. 15.
21 Pentland, *International Theory*, p. 81.
22 Mitrany, *Progress*, p. 176; quoted in Eastby, *Functionalism*, p. 19.
23 Pentland, *International Theory*, p. 70.
24 T. Conlan, *New Federalism*, Washington, DC: The Brookings Institution, 1988, p. xxiv; quoted in C. Bolick, 'European Federalism: Lessons from America', Occasional Paper no. 93, London: The Institute of Economics Affairs, 1994, p. 9.

25 D. J. Elazar et al., *Federal Systems of the World: A Handbook of Federal, Confederal and Autonomy Arrangements*, 2nd edn, London: Longman, 1994, p. xvi.

26 R. L. Watts, 'Federalism, Regionalism, and Political Integration', in D. M. Cameron (ed.), *Regionalism and Supranationalism: Challenges and Alternatives to the Nation-state in Canada and Europe*, London: The Institute for Research on Public Policy, 1981, p. 10.

27 Ibid., p. 13

28 M. Forsyth, 'Political Science, Federalism and Europe', Discussion Papers in Federal Studies, no. FS95/2, University of Leicester, 1995, p. 12.

29 K. Robinson, 'Sixty Years of Federation in Australia', *Geographical Review*, 51, no. 1., 1961, p. 2. Quoted in A. Murphy, 'Belgium's Regional Divergence: Along the Road to Federation' in G. Smith (ed.), *Federalism: The Multiethnic Challenge*, London and New York: Longman, 1995, p. 75.

30 R. L. Watts, *Comparing Federal Systems*, 2nd edn, Montreal and Kingston: McGill-Queens University Press, 1999, p. 14.

31 Ibid.

32 P. King, 'Federation and Representation', in M. Burgess and A–G. Gagnon (eds), *Comparative Federalism and Federation*, New York: Harvester Wheatsheaf, 1993, pp. 95–6. Cf. P. King, *Federalism and Federation*, London: Croom Helm, 1982, pp. 88–95.

33 King, 'Federation and Representation', p. 96.

34 D. J. Elazar, *Exploring Federalism*, Tuscaloosa: University of Alabama Press, 1987, pp. 108–9.

35 King, 'Federation and Representation', p. 96.

36 Watts, *Comparing Federal Systems*, p. 7.

37 Carl J. Friedrich, *Trends of Federalism in Theory and Practice*, London: Pall Mall Press, 1968, p. 3.

38 R. J. Harrison, *Europe in Question: Theories of Regional International Integration*, London: Allen and Unwin, 1974, p. 43.

39 M. Burgess, 'Federalism as Political Ideology: Interests, Benefits and Beneficiaries in Federalism and Federation', in Burgess and Gagnon (eds), *Comparative Federalism*, p. 149.

40 D. J. Elazar, 'Federalism', in S. M. Lipset (ed.), *The Encyclopedia of Democracy*, Vol. II, London: Routledge, 1995, p. 475.

41 On this issue, see D. N. Chryssochoou, 'Federalism and Democracy Reconsidered', *Regional and Federal Studies*, 8, no. 2, 1998, pp. 1–20.

42 R. R. Bowie, 'The Process of Federating Europe', in A. W. Macmahon (ed.), *Federalism: Mature and Emergent*, Garden City, NY: Doubleday, 1987, p. 497.

43 Ibid., p. 496. For an account of past attempts to unite Europe, see S. D. Bailey, *United Europe: A Short History of the Idea*, London: National News-Letter, 1948.

44 Ibid., p. 497. Bowie writes: 'As important as its economic and political decline was the spiritual malaise that affected much of its population'; see *Europe in Question*, p. 495.

45 Harrison, p. 45.

46 As quoted in U. Kitzinger, *The European Common Market and Community*, London: Routledge, 1967, pp. 29–33.

47 Kitzinger, 'Time-lags', p. 8.

48 A. Bosco, 'The Federalist Project and Resistance in Continental Europe', in A. Bosco (ed.), *The Federal Idea*, Vol. II: *The History of Federalism since 1945*,

London and New York: Lothian Foundation Press, 1992, p. 52. See A. Spinelli and E. Rossi, *Il Manifesto di Ventotene*, Pavia, 1944, pp. 19–20. Cf. M. Albertini, 'The Ventotene Manifesto: The Only Road to Follow', in L. Levi (ed.), *Altiero Spinelli and Federalism in Europe and in the World*, Milano: Franco Angeli, 1990, pp. 127–40.

49 A. Spinelli, 'European Union and the Resistance', *Government and Opposition*, April–July 1967, pp. 321–9, quoted in G. Ionescu (ed.), *The New Politics of European Integration*, London: Macmillan, 1972, p. 2.

50 Ibid., p. 25.

51 L. Levi, 'Altiero Spinelli, Mario Albertini and the Italian Federalist School: Federalism as Ideology', in Bosco (ed.), *Federal Idea*, Vol. II, p. 214.

52 L. Levi, 'Recent Developments in Federalist Theory', in Levi (ed.), *Altiero Spinelli*, p. 62. Cf. Watts, 'Federalism, Regionalism, and Political Integration', p. 4.

53 J. Pinder, 'The New European Federalism', in Burgess and Gagnon (eds), *Comparative Federalism*, p. 45.

54 S. Pistone, 'Altiero Spinelli and a Strategy for the United States of Europe', in A. Bosco (ed.), *The Federal Idea*, Vol. I: *The History of Federalism from the Enlightenment to 1945*, London and New York: Lothian Foundation Press, 1991, pp. 351–7. See also M. Burgess, 'Federal Ideas in the European Community: Altiero Spinelli and European Union', *Government and Opposition*, 19, no. 3, 1984, pp. 339–47.

55 Bosco, 'What is Federalism?', p. 2.

56 D. de Rougemont, 'The Campaign of European Congresses', in Ionescu (ed.), *New Politics of European Integration*, p. 25.

57 Harrison, *Europe in Question*, p. 48.

58 Ibid.

59 Beloff has asserted that 'what one is struck with is not the parallel . . . but the immensity of the difference.' He concludes: 'those who believe in furthering European unity must seek elsewhere than in American federalism.' See M. Beloff, 'False Analogies from Federal Example of United States', *The Times*, 4 May 1950. Cf. R. MacFarquhar, 'The Community, the Nation-state and the Regions', in B. Burrows et al. (eds), *Federal Solutions to European Issues*, London: Macmillan, 1978, pp. 17–24.

60 Quoted in Bosco, 'What is Federalism?', p. 13.

61 Rosamond, *Theories of Europe Integration*, p. 29.

62 Ibid., p. 23.

63 Pentland, *International Theory*, p. 35.

64 K. W. Deutsch, *Political Community and the North Atlantic Area*, Princeton, NJ: Princeton University Press, 1957, p. 5.

65 Pentland, *International Theory*, p. 31.

66 K. W. Deutsch, *Nationalism and Social Communication: An Inquiry into the Foundations of Nationality*, 2nd edn, Cambridge, MA: MIT Press, 1967, p. 174.

67 Ibid., p. 91.

68 K. W. Deutsch, *The Analysis of International Relations*, Englewood Cliffs, NJ: Prentice-Hall, 1971, p. 158.

69 A. Lijphart, 'Karl W. Deutsch and the New Paradigm in International Relations', in R. L. Meritt and B. M. Russett (eds), *From National Development to Global Community: Essays in Honor of Karl W. Deutsch*, London: Allen and Unwin, 1981, p. 236 (233–51). Quoted in P. Willetts, 'Transactions, Networks

and Systems', in Groom and Taylor (eds), *Frameworks for International Co-operation*, p. 257.

70 P. Taylor, 'A Conceptual Typology of International Organization', in Groom and Taylor (eds), *Frameworks for International Co-operation*, p. 18.

71 C. Mouffe, *The Return of the Political*, London: Verso, 1993, p. 61.

72 E. Kamenka, Bureaucracy, Oxford: Blackwell, 1989, p . 81.

73 P. Taylor, *The Limits of European Integration*, New York: Columbia University Press, 1983, p. 3.

74 Tönnies, *Community and Association*, p. 160. Cf. R. M. MacIver, *Community: A Sociological Study*, London: Macmillan, 1936, pp. 22–8. MacIver states: 'A community is a focus of social life; an association is an organisation of social life . . . but community is something wider and freer than even the greatest associations'; see p. 24.

75 Tönnies, *Community and Association*, pp. 38–9.

76 Kamenka, *Bureaucracy*, p. 79.

77 P. Taylor, *International Co-operation Today: The European and the Universal Patterns*, London: Elek, 1971, p. 7.

78 Ibid., p. 10.

79 Rosamond, *Theories of European Integration*, p. 45.

80 E. Adler and M. Barnett, 'Security Communities in Theoretical Perspective', in E. Adler and M. Barnett (eds), *Security Communities*, Cambridge: Cambridge University Press, 1998, pp. 3–28.

81 Rosamond, *Theories of European Integration*, p. 169.

82 Pentland, *International Theory*, p. 59.

83 R. O. Keohane and J. S. Nye, 'Introduction: The End of the Cold War in Europe', in R. O. Keohane et al., (eds), *After the Cold War: International Institutions and State Strategies in Europe, 1989–1991*, Harvard, MA: Harvard University Press, 1993, p. 2.

84 Pentland, *International Theory*, p. 108.

85 Ibid., p. 111.

86 E. B. Haas, *The Uniting of Europe: Political, Social and Economic Forces 1950–1957*, London: Stevens, 1958.

87 L. N. Lindberg, *The Political Dynamics of European Economic Integration*, Stanford: Stanford University Press, 1963, p. 9.

88 A. S. Milward and V. Sørensen, 'Interdependence or Integration? A National Choice', in A. S. Milward et al. (eds), *The Frontier of National Sovereignty: History and Theory 1945–1992*, London and New York: Routledge, 1993, p. 3.

89 D. Mutimer, 'Theories of Political Integration', in H. J. Michelmann and P. Soldatos (eds), *European Integration: Theories and Approaches*, Lanham: University Press of America, 1994, p. 33.

90 Haas, *Beyond the Nation-state*, p. 450.

91 Haas, *The Uniting of Europe*, p. 16.

92 Ibid., p. 5.

93 Lindberg, *Political Dynamics*, p. vii.

94 R. Harrison, 'Neo-functionalism', in Groom and Taylor (eds), *Frameworks for International Co-operation*, p. 145.

95 Haas, *The Unity of Europe*, p. 5.

96 Taylor, *Limits of European Integration*, p. 7.

97 Haas, *Beyond the Nation-State*, p. 35; quoted in Taylor, 'Concept of Community', p. 87.

98 Taylor, *Limits of European Integration*, p. 17.

99 P. Taylor, *The European Union in the 1990s*, Oxford: Oxford University Press, 1996, p. 87.

100 C. H. Church, *European Integration Theory in the 1990s*, European Dossier Series, no. 33, University of North London, 1996, p. 20

101 Ibid.

102 E. B. Haas, *The Obsolescence of Regional Integration Theory*, Berkeley, CA: Institute of International Studies, 1975.

103 A. J. R Groom, 'The Setting in World Society', in Groom and Taylor, *Frameworks for International Co-operation*, p. 10.

3

The Consensual Phase:
Autonomy through Control

Autonomy through control

At a time when neofunctionalism was losing its original appeal, with Haas critically refining his earlier formulations on the automaticity of the spillover effect, a sense of renewed theoretical excitement was set in train by other approaches, focusing more on international cooperation than regional integration *per se*; confederalism, regime theory, the interdependence school and the concordance systems approach being among the most prominent. Although confederalism is not usually classified as a theory of European integration, it offers a general framework for understanding the state-centric properties of the regional process and the relationship between the Community and the state as a limited but meaningful partnership that safeguards national autonomy through a consensual form of governance. Like federalism, the confederal phase of the Community's evolution during the 1970s and early 1980s reflected the search for 'unity in diversity'. Unlike federalism, however, its focus was not on the possibilities but rather on the limits of regional constitutionalization and community-building. International regime theory brings into the debate the question of whether institutions really matter in processes of internationalized governance. The proliferation of extra-treaty arrangements since the early 1970s, alongside the preferred pattern of policy interaction for greater coordination but not harmonization, is a good case in point. The interdependence school, on the other hand, portrays a more dynamic system of increased inter-connectedness, both functional and structural in nature, which sets the pace and to a certain extent the limits of the integrative process. It reflected the mood of the deteriorating international economic environment at the time and the need for pragmatic policy responses to structural changes in the political economy of Western Europe and the changing conditions of market forces more generally. The logic of interdependence became distinct from that of regional integration since the management of complex relations among states and societies does not necessitate the setting up of supranational agencies and institutions. Finally, the concordance systems approach was developed by Puchala in an attempt to throw light on what contemporary international integration really is. His aim was to transcend the biases that were inherent in the conventional approaches to the study of international integration in Europe and elsewhere, and assess the prospects for the emergence of a genuine consensus not only among states, but more crucially between states and peoples.

For all their respective differences, these theoretical perspectives represent a fairly discernible second wave of theorizing about the politics of the Community in the 1970s against the background of a turbulent international economic environment, a dynamic tension between auton-omy and interdependence, and the prospects for effective and coordinated action in multiple policy arenas. At the same time, they represent alternative modes of conceptualizing the Community system that challenge the determinism and teleological confidence of early neofunctionalist writings. The mood of that period was captured by Hoffmann's 'logic of diversity' thesis, emphasizing the propensity of international systems 'to produce diversity rather than synthesis among the units', as well as the extent to which domestic and global pressures are conducive to centrifugal tendencies rather than a convergence of national interests and expectations.[1] Hoffmann's argument was that the expansion of integrative tasks to conflict-prone areas, where state autonomy is at stake, would undermine the operational capacity of the supranational method to produce a profound consensus among the member state executives over the definition of a common interest. Instead, Hoffmann asserted that only in 'low politics' areas, which exclude foreign and security policy, would states be willing to engage themselves in advanced cooperative schemes. His philosophy was epitomized thus:

> In areas of key importance to the national interest, nations prefer the certainty, or the self-controlled uncertainty, of national self-reliance, to the uncontrolled uncertainty of the untested blender . . . The logic of diversity implies that, on a vital issue, losses are not compensated by gains on other (and especially not on other less vital) issues . . . The logic of integration deems the uncertainties of the supranational functional process creative; the logic of

diversity sees them as destructive past a certain threshold: Russian roulette is fine only as long as the gun is filled with blanks.[2]

Hoffmann's state-centric analysis was suggestive of the limits of supranational integration in the political sphere through the classical Community Method and of the causes responsible for activating national reflexes towards the reassertion of state autonomy. Such limitations were confirmed some twenty years later by Taylor, who stated that 'the challenges to sovereignty were successfully resisted and the central institutions failed to obtain the qualities of supranationalism.'[3] As Claude succinctly puts it, 'Supranationality has contrived no genuine escape from sovereign states.'[4] A similar conclusion underlies Lindberg and Scheingold's overall assessment of central competence expansion in the 1960s.[5] Despite the occurrence of 'upward' shifts in certain economic policy areas, the general pattern of development was disappointing as compared to earlier neofunctionalist predictions, heading for what Schmitter calls a 'protracted equilibrium'.[6]

It was largely due to the increased scepticism with which international scholarship viewed the development of the Community in the 1970s that an alternative paradigm in the discipline began to consolidate its strength. It is best captured by the term 'creative intergovernmentalism', turning the Community into what Streeck describes as 'a mutual insurance arrangement for nation-states under rising interdependence'.[7] At the heart of this reciprocal process, which is part of a state-centric conception of Community politics, lies a belief in the continued centrality of states in processes of collective governance and with it the importance of joint consensual rule for the political viability of the regional system. But this particular trend in theory development should not be equated with the 'crude intergovernmentalism' that prevailed between the striking of the Luxembourg Accords and the *relance* of integration following the Hague Summit in December 1969. For that period represented a transition phase from a narrow interpretation of interstate bargaining, where consensus-building became more closely related to the practice of blocking integrative initiatives of a progressive nature – i.e. the kind of realist state-centrism advanced by Hoffmann in the mid-1960s – to a stage of consolidation resting on a more favourable version of (institutionalized) intergovern-mentalism as a method of managing Community business. In short, the retention of national autonomy through a state-controlled process of integration epitomized the operational ethos of the Community throughout the 1970s and up to the mid-1980s.

Confederalism

Just as a federal state differs essentially from a unitary one, so does a confederation differ from a federation. Whereas the latter is based on a constitutive act that gives birth to a higher, superordinate legal order, a confederation or 'union of states' is based on a *foedus* (covenant or agreement) among sovereign states. It thus represents a 'contractual union of states' in which the participants voluntarily decide to band together by way of 'mutual agreement' in order to transform their existing patterns of relations into something akin, yet not identical, to the internal relations of one state.[8] But, as Riker rightly points out, '*foedus* is also *fides* or trust'.[9] This is of crucial importance to the life of both federal and confederal systems since the constituent units have entered into a special kind of arrangement about the organization of common government based on mutual confidence. Classic examples of confederations include the Swiss Confederation (officially termed the *Confoederatio Helvetica*, 1291–1798 and 1814–1848), the United Provinces of The Netherlands (referred to as the Dutch Republic, 1579–1795), the American Confederacy (1781–89) and the German Bund (1815–66).[10] A classic premodern confederation is the ancient Greek Sympolities (otherwise known as the Greek Amphyctionic Leagues).[11]

Sharma and Choudhry have epitomized the distinction between confederation and federation as follows: 'a confederation is a loose union over confederating independent states, whereas a federation is a union deriving its authority from the citizens of the union'; 'a confederation is the outcome of an agreement or treaty made generally for a specific period . . . whereas a federation is the result of a true constitution supreme over all other instruments from which both [levels of] government[s] . . . derive their respective powers'; 'in a confederation, the powers of the common body or authority are narrow and extremely limited, whereas in a federation the powers of the general government are wider, largely exclusive, and capable of being exercised through its own agencies'; 'in a confederation, the units are free to dissociate themselves from the union, whereas in a federation the units are united with the general government on a co-operative basis'; 'in a confederation the units retain their sovereignty, whereas in a federation the authority of government is shared by them with the general government'; and 'in a confederation the general government is subordinate to the regional governments, whereas in a federation the general government co-exists with the regional governments and is independent from them'.[12] Elazar adds yet another useful distinction: 'A confederation is not built on the traditional tripartite separation of powers and three-fold set of constitutional arenas. Its separation of powers is much looser, usually based on a four-fold separation of institutions and up to four or five arenas with their own constitutional standing.'[13] Moreover, Lister argues that in a confederation 'the relationship between central and regional governments is reversed since confederal treaty-constitutions are designed to protect the latter from the risk of subordination, and the treaty aspect of the basic law is strictly maintained',[14] whereas in a federation, according to Wheare's classic dictum, central and regional governments 'are not subordinate one to another, but co-ordinate to each other'.[15] In summary, and according to Watts,

> The difference between the federal and confederal forms lies in the fact that in federal systems, the central institutions are free to exercise responsibilities assigned to them under the constitution in a direct relationship with the electorate, while in confederal systems the central agencies, operating as delegates of the regional governments, are dependent upon them for agreement to common policies.[16]

From a different perspective, in the case of the confederation, a plurality of previously independent states gives way to a 'treaty-constituted political body',[17] in which 'the condition of "the last say"',[18] to borrow Dahl's terms, rests with the partners to it, rather than with an independent authoritative entity having a monopoly of legislative and coercive powers. Hence, Forsyth views confederation as being 'far more directly a contractual creature than the normal state', manifesting itself not as 'the constituted unity of one *people* or *nation*, but a unity constituted by *states*'.[19] He explains:

> the constitution of a confederation is not, by definition, the unilateral act of *one* people . . . considered as a homogeneous entity . . . a confederation is formed precisely because a nation or people in this sense is not deemed to exist, because the sense of identity and thus of trust between the citizens of each member state does not run to that depth.[20]

Unlike a federation, whose purpose is, according to Duchacek, 'either to create one nation out of many or to preserve a nation by a timely recognition of its inner diversity',[21] the purpose of a confederation is to establish a special order of unity among states without depriving them of their statehood.[22] Forsyth also makes the point that the union does not abolish the (identity or functions) of the component parts, 'but rather exists alongside them': union members retain both the right and power to act internally either in the form of making law, or by exercising powers that have been reserved in certain domains, or through discretionary action.[23] The same applies when the confederating states delegate specific governmental functions and even authority to the institutions of the union; such functions, however, in contrast to federal systems, can then be reclaimed by the states.

In practice, a confederation takes the form of a 'half-way house' between 'normal interstate' and 'normal intrastate relations' with the constituent units reserving the right of self-determination: 'it is a union that falls short of a complete fusion or incorporation in which one or all the members lose their identity as states'.[24] Or, as defined by Elazar, 'Several pre-existing polities joined together to form a common government for strictly limited purposes . . . that remains dependent upon its constituent polities in critical ways and must work through them.'[25] This type of union, similar to a 'mutual pact' among self-determining polities, signifies a 'joint agreement to be independent'.[26] Forsyth explains: 'The contract which lies at its base is not a contract to abide by the will of the majority regarding the government to which all shall be subordinate, but simply a contract between equals to act henceforth as one.'[27] This is not to imply that a confederation possesses merely a 'legal' personality of the type of 'conventional' international organizations; rather, it is capable of developing a 'real' personality of its own: 'an original capacity to act akin to that possessed by the states themselves'.[28] At a more specific level, the underlying characteristic of a confederation as 'a system of governments' is that it provides the component parts with a variety of opportunities to achieve mutually advantageous cooperation without, however, resigning their individual sovereignty to a single government. This is better achieved once 'a certain threshold of intensity has been reached in the relationships between states',[29] as legally and politically equal centres of authority, rather than between them and a single federal government.

According to the German political theorist von Treitschke, a confederation 'is recognised by international law as an association of sovereign States, who have bound themselves together, without resigning their independence, to further certain common goals'.[30] 'Consequently', he concludes, 'the members of a Confederation exercise their natural *liberum veto*.'[31] In other words, although confederations may have a considerable freedom in determining their internal organizational structures, 'they cannot as organisations make general rules or measures which are directly binding upon the states that create them'.[32] Forsyth's remark on the subject sharpens this point: 'Thus the individual states must give their express assent, or at the very least withhold their express dissent during a fixed period, before a convention, treaty, or any kind of general resolution made within or by an interstate organization becomes binding upon them.'[33] All in all, confederations do not fundamentally challenge, at least in constitutional terms, the legal capacity of the constituent units to determine the fate of their own polities. In this context, the idea of a 'condominium of powers' in which the management of certain policy areas are voluntarily put into a limited but joint pool of sovereignty (as the power to produce publicly binding decisions) does not conflict with the above description.[34]

Forsyth also argues that 'the permanence accorded to a confederation is more than merely the standing "disposability" of the institutions of the typical international organisation.'[35] Instead, 'it is a profound locking together of states themselves as regards the joint exercise of fundamental powers', driven by a common determination to prevent hegemony and, hence, a monopoly of power.[36] Accordingly, confederation can also be seen as a *process* by which a group of separate states commit themselves by a treaty of union to mutually beneficial interaction, which may well extend beyond the traditional patterns of international cooperation. And since it aims to reconcile the concurrent demands for preserving the sovereignty of the parts, and with it the integrity of their populations, and for maintaining high levels of coordination amongst them, this model is indeed capable of embracing a wide range of institutional possibilities. Thus, it can be conceived, in line with Friedrich's dynamic model, as a 'federation-to-be',[37] or even taken to denote a 'genuine federal body', albeit of a looser kind, in so far as the constituent units become parts of a new whole.[38] Irrespective of whether the analytical dichotomy between the two forms of political organization springs, as Friedrich believes, from 'the quintessence of the static and formalistic approach',[39] the concept of confederation still 'remains a useful part of the federal vocabulary'.[40] After all, as Elazar rightly points out with reference to the American federal experience, '[f]or most of recorded history, federalism meant confederation . . . [which] was considered normative federalism and federation was the newcomer on the block'.[41]

The literature on confederation has influenced a number of scholars over the years in their attempt to classify the defining properties of the Community system. The confederal character of the system has been pointed out by several scholars, as recently summarized by Keohane and Hoffmann: 'If any traditional model were to be applied, it would be that of a confederation . . . since the central institutions are (a) largely intergovernmental, (b) more concerned with establishing a common framework than with networks of detailed regulations, and (c) apparently willing to tolerate a vast amount of national diversity.'[42] Similar descriptions of the Community system are to be found in Forsyth's notion of 'economic confederation'; Brewin's classification of the Community as a 'union of states without unity of government'; Church's application of the term 'confederence' in his comparative study of the Community system and the Swiss polity; Elazar's characterization of the Community as a 'postmodern confederation' – 'a new-style confederation of old states'; Kincaid's synthesis of 'confederal federalism' in his examination of the Union as a system of 'compounded representation'; Lister's account of the Union as a confederal polity responsible for the revival of confederal governance in the modern world, and the present writer's understanding of the Union as a 'confederal consociation' (see Chapter 5).[43]

The justification of the confederal approach to the study of European integration is that the evolution of the Community has been shaped by arduous intergovernmental bargains among sovereign nation-states, as well as by an attempt to accommodate the varying interests of the participating collectivities in a mutually acceptable way, that is, without threatening what they have often perceived as their vital (or even non-negotiable) national interests. In this context, the idea that the transnational entity is based on a system of international treaty rules, rather than a European Constitution 'proper', is also supportive of its essentially confederal character. What this view often fails to take into account is the legal dynamics of integration and the political activism of the ECJ in the process of 'constitutionalizing' the treaties. Yet, it is doubtful whether subsequent amendments to the Treaty of Rome, including the Treaty of Amsterdam, have brought about a higher constitutional order, at least when measured against the constitutional properties of the component state polities. Rather, it seems that the larger political association rests upon the separate constitutional orders of its component parts which, by virtue of their sovereign nature, continue to act as *Herren der Verträge*. The mere fact that formal treaty revisions require the unanimous consent of the member state governments illustrates this point well, as does the fact that the essential components of Europe's quasi-constitutional order are indeed states, rather than a European citizen body in the form of a transnational demos whose members are conscious of their collective civic identity.

At the decision-making level, there is a case to be made against the confederal approach in so far as majority rule applies in the Council. Yet, clear as it may be that states may well be outvoted in a number of policy areas, there is a tendency among national governments to treat the dissenting states with caution when national interests are at stake. Hence the contention that more often than not it is the threat of invoking the right of veto, in accordance with the provisions of the Luxembourg Accords, that has a crucial impact on the negotiating process, often leading to 'package deals' of an accommodationist nature (see Chapter 5). Another point that *prima facie* appears to contradict the application of the confederal approach to the Union is that the EP is the only directly elected international parliament, possessing limited but real co-legislative powers. Again, it may be true that the EP acts as a source of the Union's democratic legitimacy, but it remains far from being regarded as a parliament in the conventional sense since it still lacks the power to initiate legislation, to have a prominent role in setting the Union's legislative agenda, to hold collectively to account the Union's main legislative body (the Council) for its actions or inaction, to elect a single European government, to hold its elections under a uniform electoral procedure, and so on. But more important, perhaps, there is evidence to suggest that the Union is characterized by a fragmented citizen body, rather than a self-conscious European demos, whose members are capable of directing their democratic claims to, and via, the central institutions (see Chapter 6). This is a point that needs to be made in relation to the democratic properties of contemporary federal polities, where a composite demos forms the 'constitutive' power of the federation.

International regimes

International organizations and international regimes were once considered as two sides of the same coin: the former focusing on structural or institutional arrangements, the latter on the norms and principles laid down by these organizations. But international regimes are in effect a subgroup of international institutions, of which international organizations are a more formalized subclass. Young distinguishes between organizations and institutions, as well as between orders and regimes: organizations are 'material entities possessing physical locations (or seats), offices, personnel, equipment, and budgets ... generally posses[ing] legal personality',[44] whereas institutions are 'social practices consisting of easily recognised roles coupled with clusters of rules or conventions governing relations among the occupants of these roles'.[45] International orders are broad structures governing a wide variety of activities of most, if not all, actors in the international system; international regimes are more specific structures governing 'well-defined activities, resources, or geographical areas of only some actors'.[46] Although regimes are distinguished from orders, the two structures are not necessarily mutually exclusive. In fact, it has been argued that international regimes may well have certain orders associated with them, and vice versa. On the relationship, finally, between international regimes and international organizations, Keohane has pointed out that the latter are embedded within the former; hence, they are coterminous in practice since 'much of what they do is to monitor, manage, and modify the operation of regimes'.[47]

More recently, Hasenclever et al. have made a distinction between power-based, interest-based and knowledge-based theories of international regimes.[48] Power-based theories can be also read as 'realist' theories of international cooperation, where power and the distribution of state capabilities can explain both conflict and cooperation. Interest-based theories, considered as part of mainstream regime analysis, emphasize 'the role of international regimes in helping states to realize common interests'.[49] In Claes's words: 'If the observed cooperation is explained by patterns of complementary interests and underlying distribution of power, regimes have no effect and thus, in such cases, theories of international regimes do not contribute to the explanation of cooperation.'[50] Therefore, the focus is on situations where the constellation of actors' interests is such that they can only achieve mutually beneficial outcomes through institutionalized cooperation. Finally, knowledge-based theories stress ideas and knowledge as explanatory variables; the focus here, according to Jervis, is on how 'causal and normative beliefs form perceptions of international problems and thus demand for regimes'.[51]

International regimes justify the separateness of states as constitutionally distinct entities. To borrow from Taylor, 'states do not cease to be states because they are members of a regime.'[52] At the same time, regimes allow states to 'socialize' with each other in a complex web of norms of behaviour, rules and procedures of decision-making that are commonly, if not *ex ante*, agreed upon by the participating units. As Checkel rightly points out, socializing, or its close synonyms like habitualization, schooling, internalization, depersonalization and the like, are key mechanisms that effectively link international institutions and norms to states, or to groups and agents within them.[53] The emphasis is on informal routes of cooperative interstate behaviour, patterned as much on specific interests – although it has been argued that regimes imply 'a form of co-operation that is more than the following of short-run interests'[54] – as on a common tendency to pursue, but not necessarily explicitly set or determine as such, reciprocal objectives.

In general, regimes project a certain image of international cooperation based on an 'inclusive' framework of multiple and, more often than not, complex interactions that reflect a given political reality. At a more specific level, neoliberal institutionalists view international regimes as stemming from attempts by individual actors to achieve control and counteract the inadequacy of their own resources. From this view, fluctuations in their number or strength reflect the calculations of self-interested actors in their efforts to pursue their aims, solve collective-action problems and gain efficiency through voluntary exchanges and contracting. Outcomes depend, *inter alia*, on the ability to implement Pareto-improvements, counteract market failures, reduce transaction costs and overcome conflicts of predominantly self-defined interests. A core question here is how alternative institutional arrangements, including international regimes, might affect the chances of discovering mutual benefits.[55] In the case of the Community system, it could be argued that regime creation, as in the cases of the European Monetary System in 1978 and European Political Cooperation (EPC) in the early 1970s, was directed at setting the limits of acceptable behaviour within a structure of collective but flexible governance that would guarantee a measure of autonomy on the part of national decision-making systems.

Although the influence of American-led international relations scholarship immediately became apparent in the discussion of the Community as an international regime (or a system with significant regime aspects), the concept remained conveniently vague as to embrace a variety of different manifestations concerning the management of complex interdependencies on such diverse issues as money, trade, natural resources, arms control, the management of outer space and seabed, and so on.[56] To such an extent that almost every aspect of intergovernmental cooperation, whether stemming from a treaty-based mandate or from 'extra-treaty' arrangements, can be classified as one type of regime or other. Cox's definition illustrates this point succinctly: '[Regimes] are . . . recognized patterns of practice that define the rules of the game.'[57] And so does Krasner's, according to which regimes are taken to denote 'sets of implicit and explicit principles, norms, rules and decision-making procedures around which actors' expectations converge in a given area of international relations'.[58] In his view, it would be wrong to perceive regimes as ends in themselves, for '[o]nce in place they do affect related behaviour and outcomes. They are not merely epiphenomena.'[59] These premises challenged the structural realist dismissal of international institutions as capable of shaping states' definitions of interests and patterns of interaction: institutionalized governance matters and so does its design. Accordingly, principles, norms, rules and decision-making procedures have an impact on outcomes and related behaviour, thus transcending 'structural orientations [that] conceptualise a world of rational self-seeking actors'.[60] The point being made by Krasner is twofold: first, regimes make a difference, going beyond a realist perspective that reflects calculations of self-interest; second, the relationship between patterned behaviour and convergent expectations is a key to our understanding of international cooperation for these aspects create an environment of 'conditionalised behaviour' that in turn 'generates recognised norms' that transcend national boundaries and nurture a broader social space.[61] After all, institutionalists of all kinds would agree that it is this distinctive pattern of mutual expectations among actors that constitutes the very fabric of a viable regional or international order based on rule-governing state behaviour. In fact, contrary to the structural arguments advanced by realist international theory, regimes are capable of having an independent impact on behaviour and constitute a crucial part of patterned human interaction. The latter assumption is drawn from the Grotian tradition, where 'regimes are a pervasive and significant phenomenon in the international system'.[62]

A somewhat different account of international regimes is offered by Young who defines them as 'social institutions governing the actions of those involved in specifiable activities or sets of activities'.[63] The emphasis in Young's definition is on rules that are translated into 'well-defined guides to action' and on compliance mechanisms with the rules governing the regime. There is a certain procedural bias in this view, in terms of the actors' expected actions 'under appropriate circumstances'.[64] But the regularization of behaviour also implies the creation of patterns of procedure, patterns of compliance to norms and rules, and above all patterns of expectations. Keohane explains: 'What these arrangements have in common is that they are designed not to implement centralized enforcement of agreements, but to establish stable mutual expectations about others' patterns of behavior.'[65] Indeed, norms and principles have a major normative and/or psychological component in that national policy-makers feel that they *should* act in certain ways because they are expected to (and expect others to), whether or not a rule has been formalized by an international treaty. In an influential study that straddled the lines of realist and neoliberalist thinking, Keohane suggested that international regimes are 'institutions with explicit rules, agreed upon governments that pertain to particular sets of issues in international relations'.[66] His 'lean' definition, as opposed to Krasner's, has the advantage of relieving scholars from the burden of justifying their decision to call a given injunction a 'norm' rather than a 'rule'.[67] It should be noted, however, that the term 'international regime' was introduced as early as 1975 by Ruggie to describe 'a set of mutual expectations, rules and regulations, plans, organizational energies and financial commitments, which have been accepted by a group of states'.[68] Not surprisingly, then, much discussion has taken place on the 'consensus definition' of international regimes as well as on the usefulness of the theory itself. The latter has been criticized by Strange as imprecise, value-based, narrow-minded, overemphasizing the static, and being a 'fad'.[69]

Different interpretations of these elusive social constructs come from authors who focus on the norms that regularize the behaviour of primarily but not exclusively state actors and guide their choices. Norms, according to Krasner, constitute 'standards of behaviour defined in terms of rights and obligations'.[70] For others, norms carry social content and are often independent of power distributions; they provide agents/states with understandings of interests and do not merely constrain behaviour. Empirical work along these lines undertaken by constructivist theorists has convincingly demonstrated that norms can have such constitutive effects.[71] The question here is twofold: can norms transcend possible sources of tension among regime actors stemming from the self-interests of governments? If the answer is 'yes', then through which mechanisms of institutional accommodation do actors reconsider their choices and decide to comply with a certain pattern of behaviour that is acceptable to their partners? This is no ontological issue; it is about the flexibility of the regime in question, the way in which it is valued by the involved actors and the means by which the setting of certain norms and rules can facilitate the reaching of agreements on the basis of mutual sensitivity and reciprocity. In a word, what are the limits of consciousness-raising that a regime can generate? These questions have serious theoretical and empirical impli-cations when examining the major political crises in the history of the Community, ranging from de Gaulle's 'empty chair policy' in the summer of 1965, to the budgetary crisis of the early 1980s (centred around the British contribution), to the negative Danish vote on the TEU in June 1992,[72] to the inability of member state governments to reach a normative and procedural consensus on institutional reform during the Amsterdam negotiations in view of further enlargements (see Chapter 5). Notwithstanding their respective differences, a thread common to these notable 'episodes' in the political and constitutional evolution of the Community is that the dis-senting state(s) did not really contemplate the possibility of withdrawing from the regional association (exit option). This, the argument runs, is a clear enough indication that regime analysis still remains an important part of theorizing European integration.[73]

What regime theory found difficult to transcend, however, was the role of national political establishments and decision-making systems in dealing effectively with issues relating to the level of integration, rather than merely its functional scope: the quality of management exhibited by the central institutions. Although the concept could explain why inter-national cooperation does not necessarily take place within an anarchical environment, or even that it creates conditions conducive to structured interactions, regime analysis fell short of explaining the intensity of relations resulting from the integration process, as well as the extent to which the structural properties of the general system – i.e. its treaty-based nature, the reality of mutual vetoes in the Council and so on – can determine the level of the regional arrangements at certain points in time. It may be true that regime theory is capable of accounting for the progressive institutionalization of multilateral relations in specific domains of collective action, but it does not offer any structured analysis of the nature of power-politics and interest differentiation among the participating actors. The conceptual lenses used by regime theory are often part of a normative interpretation of internationalized cooperation since states will play by the rules of the game as set by themselves. Purely political considerations may then become subordinate to a functionalist explanation of collective governance or coordinate policy action, overemphasizing the actors' initial commitments to meeting certain ends.

In particular, where the degree of commitment exhibited by the segments varies according to the stakes involved in the integration process, or in fields of cooperation where governmental activity rests primarily within the domestic arena, regime theory is confronted with a difficult challenge: it has to take account of the more formalistic networks of relations developed by the Community legal and political system, where the influence of non-territorial institutions such as the Commission and the ECJ is of importance. Like interdependence theory, regime analysis is often trapped in a rather dispersed or loose framework of exchanges within the relevant community of actors, undermining the impact of the Community legal or constitutional system on the domestic orders of states, or for that matter the effect of the Community's legislative authority in shaping national patterns of behaviour and limiting the preferred options of national decision-makers, as in the case of state compliance with detailed Community regulations.

Another area of concern is that the Community is too fragmented a system of policy interactions to be treated as a single international regime. Rather, it needs to be differentiated according to the specific conditions of cooperation developed within its various policy arenas. No doubt the introduction of the so-called 'flexibility clause' into the treaty framework sharpens this point (see Chapter 5). Following this line of argument, the Community could be seen as a multilayered structure of partial regimes, encompassing a multiplicity of different norms of behaviour and rules of the game, especially when different legislative procedures apply and determine accordingly the degree of involvement and relevant strategy of the participating actors. As Wallace puts it with reference to the Community budget: 'the difficulties which the Community so far faced in agreeing on the objectives which the budget should serve . . . and the policies and priorities it should support, offer sobering evidence of the incompleteness and incoherence of the partially integrated policy-making system which it represents.'[74] Further, a partial conceptualization of the Community's functional 'policy regimes' is not particularly helpful when assessing its cross-sectional, essentially political properties, i.e. what defines it as a political system, a polity, or even a nascent constitutional order.

The proliferation of extra-treaty arrangements in the 1970s stemmed from a deeper concern on the part of member state executives to reassert a considerable degree of political autonomy in the handling of their internal affairs, within a sensibly arranged framework of interactions. In this respect, regime theory failed to take into account the relationship between the politicization of issues that regional integration produced and the strategy employed by particular state actors to exercise managerial control over the integration process. These deeper concerns have as much to do with implied benefits from collective policy action (or regime maintenance) as with questions of an ideological nature about what form of political organization the Community is allowed or indeed prohibited from taking. In fact, viewing the Community from the relatively modest lenses of regime theory entails the danger of missing important points about the dynamics of formal inter-institutional linkages at the regional level and the way in which domestic politics impinge upon the formulation and implementation of common policies. Perhaps herein lies the strongest critique of regime analysis as applied to the Community system: politicization and grassroots democratic concerns often determine the limits of regime-formation; they provide a clearly defined set of conditions about the legitimation of systems of common management. On the other hand, regime theory claims to possess a plausible answer to the diachronic question of why states cooperate and why they are bound by certain norms of behaviour. Whether international cooperation is an *a priori* objective of states, or stems from a certain idealism on how to overcome collective goods dilemmas, states pursue their interests more effectively by being members of a larger association, for the latter provides a framework for agreement, increases the possibilities of coordinated action, encourages transactions and reduces cheating among states.

Interdependence

'Interdependence' was put forward by students of the Community as a more analytically profitable term than 'integration', partly as a result of the unfulfilled objectives of political union in the mid-1960s, partly because of the dominant role national governments continued to enjoy in the management of Community affairs throughout the 1970s, and partly because of the increased complexity of the global political and economic arena and the subsequent proliferation of actors that cut through the traditional domestic/foreign divide. The gist of the argument was that 'integration' had lost its meaning as a guiding concept and it had become almost impossible to set priorities for solving collective-action problems. Although theoretical agreement among scholars on the meaning of 'interdependence' is not unproblematic,[75] the logic of Community politics could no longer be captured either by the constitutional teleology of orthodox federal theory or by the centralizing prescriptions of neofunctionalist theorizing. These premises were also reflective of the serious political implications that the Luxembourg Accords had on the institutional balance of power within the Community, following de Gaulle's attempt to reinstate nationalism into its workings. They included: first, the preservation of a consensual style of collective decision-making in the Council; secondly, the gradual marginalization of the Commission's influence over the domestic orders of states and a corresponding increase in the managerial capabilities of the Council; and, thirdly, a general belief in the continued centrality of member state governments in the political management of the Community. Soon after the worsening of the international economic conditions following the collapse of the Bretton Woods system and the first oil crisis of the early 1970s, a common thread began to emerge among West European executives for the maintenance and even reassertion of a considerable degree of autonomy in their internal affairs against any potentially ambitious federalist designs, either in the field of institutionalized monetary cooperation or in areas associated with the harmonization – although the preferred term at the time was 'coordination' – of the separate foreign policies of the member states.

By the mid-1970s, the core set of relations determining the management, political or otherwise, of Community business was captured by the concept of interdependence. Webb defines this as 'a condition (of intensive economic exchange) which may influence political relationships but does not necessarily elicit an integrative response from those most affected'.[76] Unlike mainstream neofunctionalist analysis, interdependence theory encapsulates the process of European integration in erratic rather than linear terms, emphasizing 'the loss of control and sense of hopelessness which complex economic interactions can trigger, especially in governments whose fate turns on their ability to safeguard the welfare of their electorates'.[77] In a way, it sets the limits of regional centralization by shifting the emphasis from questions of formal institution-building and constitutional engineering to those concerning the management of pressing realities as a response to the rapidly changing conditions of market forces and the global economy.

Although some scholars emphasize the relationship between positive linkages among national interests, others like Keohane and Nye stress the costs or constraints imposed on states: 'the reciprocal (although not necessarily symmetrical) costly effects of transactions'.[78] As Taylor notes, these authors tend to accept the organizing principles of the *Gesellschaft* model of society since they are more concerned with procedures for realizing interests that are thought to be separately defined by competitive actors 'rather than the question of whether interests are compatible, or reflect a consensus, which would be central in the alternative *Gemeinschaft* approach'.[79] In the latter case, interdependence is expected to act as a learning process, with the realization of mutual interests preceding the procedural arrangements: states may thus learn to identify common interests and act collectively upon them. The point Taylor makes is that in the *Gesellschaft*-oriented, pluralist accounts, 'interdependence is to be tested in the opportunities it creates to exert power by exploiting the "sensitivity" or "vulnerability" of partners'.[80] Here, the strength of the partnership is tested in relation to one actor's vulnerability against another actor's threat. From this perspective also, the following useful scholarly parallel is drawn:

> the interdependence theorists are the most recent intellectual heirs of Thomas Hobbes. The modern equivalent of the Leviathan, however, is not a superior international power which compels the citizens in their own interest to refrain from war, but rather a procedural device such as the 'régime'. Subjects are seen to accept the rules of the régime because it is only by doing this that they obtain their separate interests, as Hobbes' citizens accepted the Leviathan, so that they could establish order which was otherwise unobtainable.[81]

The application of interdependence theory to European integration studies in the 1970s produced less concern about the conceptualization of the Community within clearly defined boundaries of institutional development, diverting attention from the oft-raised question of whether the Community should follow an intergovernmental or federal path, to questions dealing more immediately with the implications of policy coordination for the efficiency of the regional system. Policy outputs, in other words, were seen as much more interesting clusters of analysis – at both micro- and macro-levels – as compared to abstract models of collective governance with ideologically determined rules of political organization. Institutionalization, at least as a means of realizing political objectives, becomes of secondary importance to the student of interdependence: national governments may well achieve a considerable level of policy coordination and even organizational cohesion without being represented in a highly institutionalized system of governance that is either primarily controlled or significantly influenced by supranational agencies. In this sense also, by dismissing any deterministic projections of supranational integration in the European region, interdependence theory deviates both from mainstream neofunctionalist analysis as well as from federalist-driven macro-political aspirations. Webb explains: 'Interdependence seems to be the answer for scholars and politicians who wish to keep their options open on the evolution of the EC.'[82]

On the other hand, there is a common denominator where interdependence analysts converge when referring to the internal dynamics of the Community system: namely, the practice of mutualism in the management of complex relations that result in a policy 'mix': a variety of costs and benefits to the participating (interdependent) units. From this view, the theory may be able to explain some, albeit certainly not all, aspects of the various negotiating games being played between national governments, transnational actors and non-territorial central institutions. The emphasis here is placed on a perceived diffusion of decision-making power among the major actors involved in the regional process and on expected utilitarian outcomes of intense interrelationships in essentially non-conflict-prone areas, where state and non-state actors pursue their strategic choices in view of pressing socio-economic problems stemming from functional and to a lesser extent structural or institutional interdependence. Hence, 'transnational coalitions' take shape within the Community's multilayered setting, impinging with considerable rigour upon the European policy process. Whether interdependence theory was a forerunner of what is now referred to as multi-level governance (see Chapter 4), it did direct attention to examining 'the multi-actor complexity of the [Community] system'.[83] Moreover, by transcending the 'end-product dilemma' evident in mainstream approaches to European integration – i.e. federation, confederation, political community, supranational authority and so on – this school of thought claims to offer a pragmatic, ideologically free alternative to the study of the politics and economy of the Community regime. This is something that supranationalism, the argument has it, cannot claim by its very nature. To borrow again from Webb: '[Interdependence] encourages the analyst to focus on the policy issues first and foremost rather than be diverted by the particular and frequently parochial institutional problems which infiltrate and obscure the policy debate in Brussels.'[84]

A fair amount of criticism directed at the interdependence school centres around the basic, and arguably hard-won, political properties of the Community system: the role and influence of its supranational institutions *par excellence*; the dynamics of institutional spillovers and forward linkages leading to further institutionalization at the larger level of aggregation; and the actual impact of 'extra-treaty' arrangements on the working conditions of joint decision-making, especially when sensitive issues are or appear to be at stake for a particular state or group of states. The list could be extended to cover inter-institutional relations, bargaining practices among state actors, issues of large-scale jurisdictional competence, the constitutional implications of Community law for the domestic legal orders of states and so on. These issues, often due to their controversial nature, are dealt with more explicitly by *political* theories of regional international integration.

But more important, perhaps, interdependence should be seen as only one side of the coin. The other is the principle and practice of autonomy on the part of national political authorities. The interplay between the two has produced, as many theorists may have rightly expected, a 'flexible equilibrium' or even 'multiple flexible equilibria' in the liberal pluralist tradition, where structural (mainly systemic) properties were in a position to determine and at the same time be influenced by the quality of functions performed by state agents (ways of management), be they bureaucrats, administrators or government representatives. Without wishing to simplify an inevitably complex reality based on open-ended processes that often produce unintended consequences, the problem confronting the interdependence approach is that it relies primarily on horizontal interactions whose decisional outcomes – i.e. the process of regulating a policy arena where cooperative action applies – are based on a set of authoritative rules reached by joint decisions but applied vertically to the domestic orders of states. Thus, a functionalist understanding of the sovereignty principle, as part of the interdependence vocabulary, is in need of further clarification. Related to this is the question of whether interdependence is part of the integrative process – i.e. whether it constitutes only a particular stage of it – or a condition that can motivate states to take measures towards the preservation of their autonomy. This refers to what Taylor calls the 'interdependence trap' since 'there are circumstances in which actors might be expected to resist increases in coordination from a particular level because it is seen as generating a net loss of values at an accelerating rate'.[85] The general assessment is that, throughout the 1970s, the states tended to resist the growth of common rules (regime-strengthening) which detracted from their capacity to control integration in view of developments in the wider international political economy.

At a larger level, but with important implications for the theoretical value of interdependence to the study of international organization, one may detect the following line of criticism. Whether or not 'interdependence is the denial of independence',[86] an issue that has not escaped the scrutiny of international scholarship, Willetts is right to argue that, '[i]f the concept is to make any contribution to theory-building, it must mean more than the loose idea of connectedness'.[87] Applied to the Community framework, an important distinction should be made between 'activity' and 'influence' following an essentially pluralist conception of Community politics as a system (or regime) of multiple, competing and mutually dependent actors. In this light, interdependence theory may well explain why higher levels of interaction occur among competing actors – i.e. in dealing with issues of negative integration to create an open economic space – but does not really go as far as to tackle the more crucial issue of how political power is organized within highly interdependent systems, and when the result of increased and complex interconnectedness is reduced to mere activity with no significant policy implications.

Ideally, in a system of highly interdependent relations, territorially demarcated boundaries become of secondary importance to the expected fruits (or non-costs) of concerted action. Yet, in the case of the Community system, the management and, more accurately, the exercise of managing these relations rests closely with executive-centred elites who are often willing to compromise the wider interest – resulting from the dictates of interdependence itself – so as to avoid the danger of intersegmental confrontation. Here, consensual politics prevails in the form of unanimous (or near-unanimous) decisions in the Council, despite the fact that specific treaty provisions may formally require a different course of procedural (decisional) action. Put differently, interdependence does not guarantee that rational decisions prevail between actors who find themselves in the middle of a difficult political dilemma: to strengthen the cooperative ethos of the regional arrangements or to resort to autonomous action when faced with ideological or party political pressures. In fact, the latter may be part of a single political package, as has often been the case in the long history of interstate bargaining within the Community.

What interdependence theory cannot properly address, therefore, is the question of explicitly political choices made by dominant governing elites about the nature and extent of their involvement in joint cooperative schemes. This is something that, much to the detriment of supranationalist-driven aspirations about the Community's political or constitutional future, state-centric approaches to European integration are better equipped to deal with (see Chapter 4). In conclusion, interdependence theory places Community politics in a wider pluralist perspective of postindustrial relations, whilst diverting attention from a structured analysis of hierarchical conceptions of the integrative system to a much more diffused and even fragmented structure of European policy coordination, transnational coalition-formation and regional economic management.

Concordance systems

Almost thirty years have elapsed since Puchala's celebrated linking of the Community with the story of the elephant and the blind men. Although part of the wider analytical framework of the interdependence school, Puchala's 'new thinking' about contemporary international integration is worth exploring in its own right, offering at the same time a thorough critical evaluation of conventional integration models. Indeed, in an attempt to break away from the classical theses of federalism and inter-governmentalism, Puchala discussed international integration in terms of 'what it really is and is actually leading to'.[88] As he wrote: 'No model describes the integration phenomenon with complete accuracy because all models present images of what integration could be or should be rather than what it is here and now.'[89] His main concern was that pre-existing accounts of international integration were characterized by conceptual confusion, yielding 'artificial, untidy results', whilst stressing respectively the indispensability of national political systems or that of the common central institutions. As a result, normative theoretical preferences had exhausted the intellectual efforts of scholars, depriving the integration process of a descriptive model capable of conceptualizing its distinctive properties, functions and dynamics. The message Puchala tried to convey was clear: 'We must . . . stop testing the present in terms of progress toward or regression from hypothetical futures since we really have no way of knowing where or how contemporary international integration is going to end up.'[90] He thus saw the need for a new model based on the premise that 'international integration could very well be something new'.

Puchala argued his case against the analytical validity of conventional approaches to the study of international integration such as federalism, functionalism, nationalism and what he called 'old-fashioned power politics'. His criticism also reflected the state of theorizing the European experience in the early 1970s, when the Community's workings were characterized by a more favourable version of intergovernmentalism, but where no clear model of integration or, for that matter, a wider conceptual consensus had emerged among its students. Puchala was critical of the limited, predominantly economic nature of the Community at the time, as well as of the autonomy of the Commission in representing the wider European interest detached from the separate interests of the component states. His understanding of the West European system also challenged the mainstream federalist approach since progress towards further integration was being equated with movement towards a central European government and the extent to which national political authorities had relinquished their sovereignty to an emerging federal state. In this context, the question he asked was 'to what extent does participation in an international integration arrangement actually enhance rather than undermine national sovereignty?'[91] – a question which remained largely unanswered by European federalists.

But Puchala was also critical of the view that equates international integration with nation-building processes. The point he made was that West European integration does not even closely approximate to a model of political evolution where the measurement of its 'progress' or 'success' is conditioned by the extent to which the parts that are being integrated move towards 'the social and cultural assimilation of [their] nationalities'.[92] In this respect, Puchala was sceptical of the applicability of the 'nationalism model' in the study of international integration, arguing that such an approach lacked evidence of progress towards the envisaged process of assimilation among diverse peoples. In his view, students applying the 'nationalism model' were asking the wrong questions: 'about people-to-people interactions and transactions, about similarities and differences in peoples' life styles, value systems and cultural norms, and especially about their attitudes toward one or another and attendant perceptions of "we-ness"'.[93] For Puchala, the more interesting question to pose was about the relationship between peoples and their national governments, and between the former and international organizations and processes.

In his equally critical approach to Mitrany's functionalism, Puchala questioned the extent to which this sectoral approach, for all its validity in locating the sources of international cooperation and the role of transnational (non-governmental) actors, had actually worked in the way that the functionalist model had originally been intended. The point he made here was that in internationally integrating systems, '[l]eadership, initiative and prerogative have by and large remained with national governments',[94] rather than with newly formed technocratic agencies, large bureaucratic entities and non-governmental actors. Moreover, functionalist theorizing failed to predict the importance attached by national governments to the pursuit of 'welfare' objectives, as opposed to merely 'power' relations at the regional level. Equally, Puchala dismissed the functionalist claim about non-political aspects of international cooperation, arguing that no such issues really exist in interstate relations. He also pointed to another deficiency of the functionalist design, instead of being primarily pre-occupied with sector-to-sector task expansion: 'there is possible expansion in the *political system* brought into being when functional sectors are integrated internationally'.[95] Finally, he was concerned with the normative/hypothetical aspects of mainstream functionalist analysis since the end-product of integration would resemble a 'functional federation' or some sort of 'multi-sector merger'. Functionalism in the Mitranian tradition failed, in Puchala's view, to ask 'how international cooperation is in fact achieved during international integration in the very course of international politics'.[96] It has been 'partially strait-jacketed' by its own integrative assumptions.

Last in his 'critical list' came the realist school of international politics, perceiving international integration as 'power politics'. This traditional international relations approach fails to understand what the phenomenon is all about, for it views integration as 'a process of mutual exploitation wherein governments attempt to mobilize and accumulate the resources of neighbouring states in the interests of enhancing their own power'.[97] Such an account emphasizes the self-interests of national governmental elites who understand international integration as an instrument for the accumulation of greater power, or as 'international marriages of convenience, comfortable for all partners as long as self-interests are satisfied . . . '.[98] The point advanced by realist thinking is that international integration never really gets 'beyond the nation-state', but rather merely stays confined within the dictates of international diplomacy, leading eventually towards disintegration: the participating actors are 'destined for divorce the moment any partner's interests are seriously frustrated'.[99] Puchala has also argued that political realists are so convinced that in the arena of international integration the game is played by classical international relations rules – as set by traditional state actors themselves – that they never ask 'whether actors committed to international integration may be pursuing any other than the traditional inventory of international goals – autonomy, military security, influence and prestige'.[100] In brief, 'by assuming that international politics remains the same "old game" and that international integration is but a part of it',[101] the realist thesis failed to take into account the possibility, if not reality, that international integration arrangements may in the end define the self-interests of states, rather than vice versa.

So, with what did Puchala propose to replace the existing deficiencies in international integration analysis? His answer was that '*contemporary international integration can best be thought of as a set of processes that produce and sustain a Concordance System at the international level*.'[102] This he defined as 'an international system wherein actors find it possible consistently to harmonise their interests, compromise their differences and reap mutual rewards from their interactions'.[103] Harrison notes: 'Donald Puchala has given another name and definition [concordance system], virtually devoid of regional implications, to the rather nebulous dependent variable which embraces the many alternative "mixes" which may eventuate.'[104] Such a system of 'co-operatively interacting states' is based on the harmonization of the actors' interests and on mutually beneficial interactions. The role of the nation-state remains central in the integration process but at the same time the institutions of the larger system possess their own organizational and operational logic. A concordance system may include actors from different organizational levels or governmental arenas without producing a system of hierarchical authority structures. Rather, 'each of the actors remains semi-autonomous . . . all are interdependent, and all interact in pursuit of consensus that yields mutual rewards.'[105] It is a complex international pluralist system characterized by high levels of institutionalization and various organizational networks, where international interactions are mainly channelled through bureaucratic, rather than diplomatic means: 'a system of relations among sovereign states and separate peoples'.[106]

In the concordance system, problem-solving and conflict regulation are facilitated via 'institutionalized, constitutional, precedential or otherwise standardized, patterned procedures which all actors commit themselves to use and respect'.[107] But it is not a state, national or transnational in kind. Rather, it takes the form of numerous functionally specific bodies, without having to rely upon federalist-inspired processes of institutional centralization. More important, political conflict arises from different approaches to international cooperation, mainly in terms of the necessary procedural avenues to be pursued, rather than from 'fundamental incompatibilities in the interests of the various actors'.[108] Hence, conflict may well be one of the system's functional aspects and not, as is often the case in various realist predictions, a move towards disintegration (or de-federation). Another important dimension of the concordance system is the bargaining techniques used by the relevant actors to reach mutually reinforcing outcomes in international negotiations: coercion and confrontation are excluded from the acceptable patterns of international behaviour. Instead, the rules of the system are determined by a 'full information' game, where secrecy and deception are altogether unknown.

International interdependence – along with perceptions of 'national inadequacy' – emerges as a defining property of concordance systems. This does not amount, however, to a negation of the nation-state. Rather, 'nation-states can be preserved as distinct entities only through the international pooling of resources to confront problems that challenge their separate existence.'[109] Likewise, Puchala explicitly states that 'mass populations within the concordance system need not be assimilated into a supranationality.'[110] But they do confer legitimacy upon the system, comply with its authoritative decisional outcomes and, in general, support the integration process. In summary, the theoretical lenses employed by the concordance systems approach focus on aspects of the structural, attitudinal and procedural conditions of international integration, whilst freeing the analyst from normative, hypothetical and ideological interpretations of the integrative phenomenon. Thus, it is a pragmatic approach aimed at revealing the underlying structure of relations between highly inter-dependent units, and the way in which large-scale coordinated projects that are patterned on routinized procedures and standardized codes of conduct transcend the ill-effects of adversarial politics in multiple policy arenas. It is these regime aspects of the concordance system that are mainly responsible for the elimination of competitive tussles for political power among the participants, and the prevalence of positive-sum outcomes in multilateral negotiations.

In conclusion, Puchala's approach to international integration processes attempted a fresh start by exploring the possibilities of consensus-formation, pragmatic politics, patterned procedures, institutionalized compromise, mutual responsiveness and cooperative behaviour. His analysis still remains a valuable contribution to the relevant field, raising serious questions about the ontological properties of the Community as a 'system' conducive to positive-sum governance, as well as about the relationship between the form of international cooperation and the way in which interdependent actors pursue a pragmatic politics of consensus-building as a plausible alternative to the logic of regional nationalism, classical realism, international functionalism and federalism.

Notes and references

1 See B. Rosamond, *Theories of European Integration*, Basingstoke: Macmillan, 2000, p. 76. For the original argument, see S. Hoffmann, 'Obstinate or Obsolete? The Fate of the Nation State and the Case of Western Europe', *Daedalus*, 85, no. 3, 1966, pp. 862–915.

2 Hoffmann, 'Obstinate or Obsolete', p. 882; quoted in G. Marks et al., 'European Integration from the 1980s: State-centric v. Multi-level Governance', *Journal of Common Market Studies*, 34, no. 3, 1996, p. 344.

3 P. Taylor, *The Limits of European Integration*, New York: Columbia University Press, 1983, p. 56.

4 I. L. Claude, Jr, *Swords into Plowshares*, 3rd edn, New York: Random House, 1964, p. 103; quoted in C. Pentland, *International Theory and European Integration*, London: Faber and Faber, 1973, p. 218.

5 L. N. Lindberg and S. A. Scheingold, *Europe's Would-be Polity: Patterns of*

Change in the European Community, Englewood Cliffs, NJ: Prentice-Hall, 1970.

6 P. C. Schmitter, 'Examining the Present Euro-polity with the Help of Past Theories', in G. Marks et al. (eds), *Governance in the European Union*, London: Sage, 1996, p. 10.

7 W. Streeck, 'Neo-Voluntarism: a New European Social Policy Regime?', in G. Marks et al. (eds), *Governance*, p. 66.

8 M. Forsyth, *Unions of States: The Theory and Practice of Confederation*, Leicester: Leicester University Press, 1981, pp. 1–16.

9 W. H. Riker, 'European Federalism: The Lessons of Past Experience', in J. J. Hesse and V. Wright (eds), *Federalizing Europe? The Costs, Benefits, and Preconditions of Federal Political Systems*, Oxford: Oxford University Press, 1996, p. 10.

10 See C. Hughes, *Confederacies*, Leicester: Leicester University Press, 1963; Forsyth, *Union of States*; F. K. Lister, *The European Union, the United Nations and the Revival of Confederal Governance*, Westport, CT: Greenwood Press, 1996.

11 F. K. Lister, *The Early Security Confederations: From the Ancient Greeks to the United Colonies of New England*, Westport, CT: Greenwood Press, 1999.

12 B. M. Sharma and L. P. Choudhry, *Federal Polity*, London: Asia Publishing House, 1967, pp. 11–12. Cf. Taylor, *Limits of European Integration*, pp. 270–5.

13 D. J. Elazar, *Constitutionalizing Globalization: The Postmodern Revival of Confederal Arrangements*, Lanham: Rowman and Littlefield, 1998, p. 213.

14 Lister, *European Union*, p. 22.

15 K. C. Wheare, *Federal Government*, 4th edn, Oxford: Oxford University Press, 1964, p. 2.

16 R. L. Watts, 'Federalism, Regionalism, and Political Integration', in D. M. Cameron (ed.), *Regionalism and Supranationalism: Challenges and Alternatives to the Nation-state in Canada and Europe*, London: The Institute of Research on Public Policy, 1981, p. 12.

17 M. Forsyth, 'Political Science, Federalism and Europe', Discussion Papers in Federal Studies, no. FS95/2, University of Leicester, 1995, p. 16.

18 R. A. Dahl, *A Preface to Democratic Theory*, Chicago: University of Chicago Press, 1956, p. 38.

19 Forsyth, *Unions of States*, pp. 15–16.

20 M. Forsyth, 'Towards a New Concept of Confederation', in Conference Proceedings, *The Modern Concept of Confederation*, European Commission for Democracy through Law, Council of Europe, 1995, p. 64.

21 I. D. Duchacek, *Comparative Federalism: The Territorial Dimension of Politics*, London: Holt, Rinehart and Winston, 1970, p. 233.

22 Lister, *European Union*, p. 35.

23 M. Forsyth, 'The Political Theory of Federalism: The Relevance of Classical Approaches', in Hesse and Wright (eds), *Federalizing Europe?*, p. 38.

24 Forsyth, *Unions of States*, p. 1.

25 D. J. Elazar et al., *Federal Systems of the World: A Handbook of Federal, Confederal and Autonomy Arrangements*, 2nd edn, London: Longman, 1994, p. xvi.

26 Forsyth, *Union of States*, pp. 11, 15–16.

27 Ibid., p. 16.

28 Ibid., p. 15.

29 Forsyth, 'Political Theory of Federalism', p. 37.

30 H. von Treitschke, 'State Confederations and Federated States', Book III, in M. Forsyth et al. (eds), *The Theory of International Relations*, London: Allen and Unwin, 1970, p. 330.

31 Ibid., p. 331.

32 Forsyth, *Unions of States*, p. 13.

33 Ibid., pp. 13–14.

34 On this idea, see A. D. Smith, *National Identity*, Harmondsworth: Penguin, 1991, p. 153.

35 Forsyth, *Unions of States*, p. 15.

36 Ibid. and p. 205.

37 C. J. Friedrich, *Trends of Federalism in Theory and Practice*, London: Pall Mall Press, 1968, pp. 11–12. Friedrich defines federation as 'a union of groups, united by one or more common objectives, rooted in common values, interests, or beliefs, but retaining their distinctive group character for other purposes'; see p. 177. He defines federalism as 'the process by which a number of separate political organizations, be they states or any other kind of associations, enter into arrangements for making joint decisions on joint problems, or reversely the process by which a hitherto unitary political organisation becomes decentralised to the point where separate and distinct political communities arise and become politically organised and capable of making separate decisions on distinct problems'; see C. J. Friedrich, 'Federal Constitutional Theory and Emergent Proposals, in A. W. Macmahon (ed.), *Federalism: Mature and Emergent*, Garden City, NY: Doubleday, 1955, p. 517.

38 M. Forsyth, 'Federalism and Confederalism', in C. Bacon (ed.), *Political Restructuring in Europe: Ethical Perspectives*, London and New York: Routledge, 1994, p. 58.

39 Friedrich, *Trends of Federalism*, p. 82.

40 Forsyth, 'Federalism and Confederalism', pp. 57–8.

41 Elazar, *Constitutionalizing Globalization*, p. 40.

42 R. O. Keohane and S. Hoffmann, 'Conclusions', in W. Wallace (ed.), *The Dynamics of European Integration*, London: Pinter, 1990, p. 279.

43 See respectively, Forsyth, *Unions of States*; C. Brewin, 'The European Community: A Union of States without Unity of Government', *Journal of Common Market Studies*, 26, no. 1, 1987, pp. 1–24; C. H. Church, *The Not So Model Republic? The Relevance of Swiss Federalism to the European Community*, Discussion Papers in Federal Studies, no. FS93/4, University of Leicester, November 1993, p. 15; Elazar et al., *Federal Systems of the World*, p. xvi; J. Kincaid, 'Confederal Federalism and Compounded Representation in the European Union', *West European Politics*, 22, no. 2, 1999, pp. 34–58; Lister, *European Union*; and D. N. Chryssochoou, 'New Challenges to the Study of European Integration: Implications for Theory-building', *Journal of Common Market Studies*, 35, no. 4, 1997, pp. 521–42.

44 O. R. Young, *International Cooperation: Building Regimes for Natural Resources and the Environment*, Ithaca, NY: Cornell University Press, 1989, p. 32; quoted in R. E. Breckinridge, 'Reassessing Regimes: The International Regime Aspects of the European Union', *Journal of Common Market Studies*, 35, no. 2, 1997, p. 174.

45 Ibid.

46 Ibid., p. 13.

47 R. O. Keohane, 'Neoliberal Institutionalism: A Perspective on World
    Politics', in R. O. Keohane (ed.), *International Institutions and State Power:
    Essays in International Relations Theory*, Boulder, CO: Westview Press, 1989,
    p. 4; quoted in Breckinridge, 'Reassessing Regimes', p. 179. Drawing from
    Keohane's analysis, Breckinridge reaches the conclusion that the Union
    represents 'an organization embedded in a regime', and that 'one should
    consider both regime and organizational aspects in order to understand fully
    the European Union . . . especially its influence on states and in comparative
    terms'; see respectively, pp. 185 and 186.
48 A. Hasenclever et al., *Theories of International Regimes*, Cambridge:
    Cambridge University Press, 1997.
49 Keohane, 'Neoliberal Institutionalism', p. 4.
50 D. H. Claes, 'What do Theories of International Regimes Contribute to the
    Explanation of Cooperation (and Failure of Cooperation) among Oil-
    producing Countries?', ARENA Working Papers, no. WP 99/12, University
    of Oslo, 1999.
51 R. Jervis, 'Security Regimes', in S. D. Krasner (ed.), *International Regimes*,
    Ithaca, NY: Cornell University Press, 1983, p. 137.
52 P. Taylor, *International Organization in the Modern World: The Regional and the
    Global Process*, London: Pinter, 1993, p. 3.
53 J. T. Checkel, 'International Institutions and Socialization', ARENA Working
    Papers, no. WP 99/5, 1998.
54 Jervis, 'Security Regimes', p. 173.
55 See, *inter alia*, A. A. Stein, 'Coordination and Collaboration: Regimes in an
    Anarchic World', in S. D. Krasner (ed.), *International Regimes*, pp. 115–40;
    R. O. Keohane, *After Hegemony: Cooperation and Discord in the World Political
    Economy*, Princeton, NJ: Princeton University Press, 1984; and, O. R. Young,
    'International Regimes: Toward a New Theory of Institutions', *World Politics*,
    39, no. 1, 1986, pp. 104–22.
56 O. R. Young, 'International Regimes: Problems of Concept Formation', *World
    Politics*, 32, no. 3, 1980, pp. 331–56.
57 R. W. Cox, 'Social Forces, States and World Orders: Beyond International
    Relations Theory', *Millennium*, 10, no. 2, 1981, p. 128; P. Willets, Transactions,
    Networks and Systems', in A. J. R. Groom and P. Taylor (eds), *Frameworks for
    International Co-operation*, London: Pinter, 1990, p. 202.
58 S. D. Krasner, 'Structural Causes and Regime Consequences: Regimes as
    Intervening Variables', in S. D. Krasner (ed.), *International Regimes*, Ithaca,
    NY: Cornell University Press, 1983, p. 2.
59 Ibid., p. 5.
60 Ibid., p. 6.
61 Ibid., p. 9.
62 Ibid., p. 10.
63 Young, *International Cooperation*, p. 12; quoted in Breckinridge, 'Reassessing
    Regimes', p. 179.
64 Young, *International Cooperation*, p. 16.
65 Keohane, *After Hegemony*, p. 89.
66 Keohane, 'Neoliberal Institutionalism', p. 4.
67 Hasenclever et al., *Theories of International Regimes*, p. 7.
68 J. G. Ruggie, 'International Responses to Technology: Concepts and Trends',
    International Organization, 29, no. 3, 1975, pp. 557–84.

69 See further analysis provided by S. Strange, '*Cave! Hic Dragones*: A Critique of Regime Analysis', in Krasner (ed.), *International Regimes*, pp. 337–54.

70 Krasner, 'Structural Causes', p. 2.

71 For a good treatment of these theoretical and ontological issues, see, *inter alia* M. Finnemore, 'Norms, Culture and World Politics: Insights from Sociology's Institutionalism', *International Organization*, 50, no. 2, 1996, pp. 325–47; P. Katzenstein (ed.), *The Culture of National Security: Norms and Identity in World Politics*, New York: Columbia University Press, 1996.

72 Breckinridge, 'Reassessing Regimes', pp. 181–3.

73 Ibid., p. 183.

74 W. Wallace, 'Less than a Federation, More than a Regime: The Community as a Political System', in H. Wallace et al. (eds), *Policy-making in the European Community*, Chichester: John Wiley, 1983, p. 408.

75 On different interpretations of the term, see P. Taylor, 'Interdependence and Autonomy in the European Communities: The Case of the European Monetary System', *Journal of Common Market Studies*, 18, no. 4, 1980, pp. 370–87.

76 C. Webb, 'Theoretical Perspectives and Problems', in Wallace et al. (eds), *Policy-making in the European Community*, p. 32.

77 Ibid.

78 R. O. Keohane and J. S. Nye, *Power and Interdependence: World Politics in Transition*, Boston, MA: Little Brown, 1977, p. 9.

79 Taylor, 'Interdependence and Autonomy', pp. 372, 373.

80 Ibid., p. 372.

81 Ibid.

82 Webb, 'Theoretical Perspectives', p. 33.

83 Rosamond, *Theories of European Integration*, p. 95.

84 Webb, 'Theoretical Perspectives', p. 34.

85 Taylor, 'Interdependence and Autonomy', p. 375.

86 Keohane and Nye, *Power and Interdependence*; quoted in Willets, 'Transactions, Networks and Systems', p. 271.

87 Willets, 'Transactions, Networks and Systems', p. 271.

88 D. J. Puchala, 'Of Blind Men, Elephants and International Integration', *Journal of Common Market Studies*, 10, no. 3, 1972, p. 268.

89 Ibid., p. 276.

90 Ibid., p. 277.

91 Ibid., p. 271.

92 Ibid.

93 Ibid., p. 272.

94 Ibid., p. 273.

95 Ibid., p. 274.

96 Ibid., p. 275.

97 Ibid.

98 Ibid., p. 276.

99 Ibid.

100 Ibid.

101 Ibid.

102 Ibid., p. 277.

103 Ibid.

104 R. J. Harrison, *Europe in Question: Theories of Regional International Integration*, London: Allen and Unwin, 1974, p. 231.

105 Puchala, 'Of Blind Men', p. 278.
106 Ibid.
107 Ibid., p. 279.
108 Ibid., p. 280.
109 Ibid., p. 282.
110 Ibid., p. 283.

PART THREE

THEORIZING

4

Paradigm Shift: From Policy to Polity

Introduction

The mid-1980s became dominated by claims of a 'neofunctionalist comeback', modified in nature, yet easily discernible in scope.[1] Processes of negative integration at the market level were linked to the development of a wide range of policies, while new pressures towards task expansion were greatly facilitated by an emergent neoliberal consensus among the member state governments. Neofunctionalist spillovers were expected to mark their impact on a difficult transition from a 'Business Europe' to a 'People's Europe'. In overall terms, the functions of the Community political system not only seemed to have produced new expectations for European leaders and publics, but also a new dynamic towards deeper integration through the '1992 project'. Yet, the institutional evolution of the Community was lagging behind its renewed neofunctionalist ambitions. The SEA did not represent too much of a qualitative leap towards a 'self-regulating pluralist society', or even towards significant levels of autonomy on the part of supranational institutions.

Although the then Delors Commission tried to develop an independent strategy both for managing the single market programme and exploiting its enormous publicity, a project supported at the time by even the most 'reluctant' Europeans, the member states once again found ways of resisting any substantive movements towards a profound transformation of the Community's institutional setting. Supranationalism was championed in areas where the states wanted to see progress such as the completion of the single market (even here, there was to be a target date, rather than a legally binding date for its completion); in those areas where national interests seemed to be at stake, as in the context of EPC, intergovernmentalism effectively prevailed as the dominant mode of decision-taking. Moreover, no subsequent alteration of the locus of sovereignty emerged as a result of the coming into force of the Act in July 1987, although it did intensify the level of inter-institutional power-sharing. An equally important line of criticism directed against neofunctionalism came from scholars who argued that the theory did not take into account the wider international setting (exogenous factors) within which political and institutional Community change was to occur.[2]

So, why was neofunctionalism, which remained beneath the surface for some twenty years, presented once again as the leading theory of European integration? One answer is that the SEA was hailed by many observers at the time as opening up new horizons for positive integration. Neofunctionalism was in fact the only theory that could place, if not justify, such claims in a dynamic perspective, linking institutional reform, albeit of a limited nature, to the expansive logic of Community action. After all, the analytical validity of the theory had been linked from the outset with the development of the Community system and now there was a widespread sense of a renewed dynamism in the integration process. In particular, there was a feeling that the single market plan would not allow for any critical drawbacks. Market integration (and its assorted politics of liberalization and deregulation) was now seen not only as a functional imperative, but more importantly as the long-needed integrative project that would accelerate the pace of the regional process by mobilizing the support of political elites, trade unions and the wider business community. At the same time, it was expected that economic integration would sooner rather than later spill over into the institutional sphere. Although new sources of pressure became manifest in many policy areas, neofunctionalist analysis concentrated on the stimulus, rather than the outcome, of envisaged spillovers. Put differently, it focused on the integrative dynamic as opposed to the consequence of the renewed impetus.

More specifically, it was expected that increased trade interdependence would lead, in a somewhat deterministic fashion, to higher levels of monetary integration on the grounds that positive movement in one level of integration would set up problems that could only be resolved at another level. But there was no immediate link, nor was there any automatic mechanism to that end. Instead, much had to rely on the convergence of interests among the dominant governing elites who also had to take into account what further integration would entail for the sovereignty of their respective polities. The crucial question missed by resurgent neofunctionalist thinking was how far Community competences could be extended without raising questions about, on the one hand, the sovereignty and autonomy of states and, on the other, their constitutional relationship to a potentially federalizing European centre. In the end, for all the innovative thinking and entrepreneurial potential of the new Commission, and despite a widespread consensus among national leaders and even the positive mobilization of non-governmental actors (mainly business associations and industry coalitions) around the 1992 project, the level of European integration cannot be said to have been significantly advanced. In fact, the SEA seems to have promoted a new synthesis between state and Community with two important implications for state sovereignty. The first is that a process of system-wide scope expansion need not get in the way of individual state-building projects. Belgium and Spain are good cases in point: the former has been gradually transformed through a series of constitutional reforms from a unitary decentralized state into a fully fledged federation; the latter is increasingly driven by the logic of 'asymmetrical federalism' and what Forsyth calls the process of 'autonomization' to accommodate claims to self-governance by the Autonomous Communities (formally guaranteed in their respective Statutes of Autonomy).[3] Likewise, other member states have recently embarked on a substantive restructuring of their domestic constitutional order. The United Kingdom clearly represents the most striking example of radical constitutional engineering with profound implications for the internal distribution of political authority. The second implication is that first-order decisions, primarily but not exclusively confined to 'high politics' areas, still require the explicit consent of member state executives. This dialectic is termed by Taylor a 'new reconciliation' between state sovereignty and the emergent regional regime.[4] Underlying this thesis is the view that, although treaty change in the mid-1980s may have resulted in a modest rearrangement of jurisdictional lines within the Community, such a rearrangement has followed the same pattern: the joint exercise of authority by state executives has not led, either gradually or automatically, to the erosion of sovereign statehood, but rather has strengthened the capacity of states to promote and in the long run secure a fair share of their interests within the general system, whilst preserving an area of autonomous domestic jurisdiction crucial to their identity as states.

In the same vein, it is difficult to assume that the constituent governments decided to refocus their loyalties, activities and expectations in a classical neofunctionalist fashion to a new regional centre, for no such 'locus of power' came into being with the Act. Nor did the technical characteristics of the vision of a 'Europe without frontiers', nor the utilitarian calculus of 'the cost of non-Europe', nor even the introduction

of QMV in the Council (largely aimed at speeding up Community legislation in areas related to the completion of the single market) and of a new
cooperation procedure upgrading (under certain conditions) the legislative
role of the EP correspond to what neofunctionalists had originally
in mind: the gradual centralization of authoritative decision-making
driven by the internal logic of spillover and, eventually, the emergence of
a new European 'political community'. The Act represented neither a clear-
cut victory of an expansionist Commission over a sovereignty-conscious
Council, nor was it the outcome of a treaty-amending process whose
drafters were conscious at the time of the institutional implications that
treaty reform would generate for the future of supranational governance
in Europe. Likewise, the point made in the literature that with the conclusion of the Act the Community entered into an era of 'mega-constitutional
politics' needs careful qualification.[5] Although the Community's agenda
was henceforth to pay greater attention to institutional issues, and even to
a growing politics of inter-institutional accommodation, no major constitutional transformation was to follow, in terms of a system-wide hierarchy
of norms and rules as the basis for a genuine European sovereignty to
emerge and replace what seemed to be the hallmark of the regional
arrangements: the simultaneous functional and political enmeshment of
'formal institutions of governance and informal processes of exchange'.[6]
Taylor's assessment of the new Community dynamism makes the point
well: 'what is changed is the wish of national legislatures and governments
to do certain things in common, rather than their legal or constitutional
capacity to do them'.[7]

In summary, the Act was the first concrete step towards a comprehensive
strategy of Europeanization capable of producing and sustaining a new
dynamic equilibrium between the Community, the state and an emergent
transnational (civil) society. The real issue was not about sacrificing
national sovereignty on the altar of positive integration, nor was it about
the nurturing of a transcendental 'community of fate' among 'fellow
Europeans', despite the conscious efforts of the Adoninno Committee.
Rather, it was about the institutionalization of new modes of joint decision-
making in areas of common concern. The states were by this time prepared
to give up an outmoded condition of sovereignty for a more pragmatic
interpretation of the sovereignty principle, where systems of collective
management could form the basis of an acceptable political option.
Arguably, this was no different from what had been suggested in the 1975
Tindemans Report on European Union: that states should 'exercise their
sovereignty in a progressively convergent manner'.[8] By the mid-1980s, it
had become clear that the driving force of integration was neither the
rationalist maximization of purely territorial interests, nor the promotion
of a centralized Europe, let alone of a European superstate as Mrs Thatcher,
then British Prime Minister, would have had us believe. Nota bene that
even such a skilful fighter of European federalism had to go down the
road of formal institutional reform for fear of being left outside the realm

of influencing future Community developments. Indeed, the fear of vulnerability in the regional society of states acted as a powerful incentive towards maintaining an active role in the central system (see Chapter 5). A final point made by Forsyth is in order. The decision to retain in the Act, as was earlier the case in the Rome Treaty, an 'action-plan philosophy' to preserve its 'framework character' (against the danger of the detailed legalistic graphomania that international lawyers are so accustomed to) was of particular importance, for it practically meant that 'the Treaty and the amendments do not define completely and finally the obligations agreed by the signatories'.[9]

European polity dynamics

From a phase of integration in the mid-1980s where expected spillovers monopolized the interest of the academic community, the early 1990s brought us into a situation where signs of European polity-formation became manifest: as the range of things that member states had decided to do together had by this time seriously expanded, it became increasingly difficult to dissociate developments at the level of integration from questions of national sovereignty. The outcome of the twin intergovernmental conferences (IGCs) of 1990/91, culminating in the signing of the TEU in February 1992, clearly marked the passage of the Community's evolution 'from policy to polity'. This is not to imply that member state executives decided to be drawn into advanced, let alone uncontrolled, federalist schemes, abandoning their earlier claims to preserve their sovereignty or even to enhance their autonomy. Rather, there was evidence that the TEU brought the new structure closer to being considered as a political system in its own right, with a significant capacity for governance and, crucially, for a 'politics like any other'.[10] In this view, the conception of the Union as a form of polity, as opposed to a transnational policy arena concerned with issues of economic governance, market integration and technical regulation, refers to 'a venue where interested actors pursue their goals and where authoritative actors deliver policy outcomes'.[11] Underlying these new European polity dynamics was a firm commitment to institutional innovation linking together multiple arenas of governance.

An equally important aspect of the life of the polity was the authoritative allocation of values, functional responsibilities and resources among the constituent units through publicly binding decisions. From this perspective, the process of EU polity-building was not driven by aspirations to transcend the sovereign statehood of the component parts, but by the importance of developing a constitutive political space – a new public arena 'within' – through the internalization of new norms and rules about the organization of social and political life in the new polity. It follows that, apart from its profound effects on the domestic order of states, European polity-formation can also be seen as an exercise in enlarging the operation of social engineering while creating new structures of opportunity above the state level, without conforming to the contours of a system-wide hierarchy that is typical of the component polities. This is termed by Laffan et al. as an 'extra-territorial constitutional system' based on a dynamic political process of shared governance that grants citizens additional rights and avenues of politics.[12] It rests on the following logic: 'Political hierarchy and steering are replaced by segmented policy-making in multiple arenas characterized by negotiated governance.'[13] This mode of understanding collective governance in Europe is also supportive of the view that the establishment of the Union gave rise to a 'prismatic political system', in which 'rays of activity and authority are scattered or focused more or less effectively through institutions and social forces'.[14] The general point here is that increased interest in the theoretical study of the EU as a multi-level polity (or system of governance) represented a significant shift in paradigm.

There are at least three good reasons why integration theorists consider the term 'polity' an appropriate point of departure. For one thing, the term is ideologically free both of the insights offered by the less startling micro-analyses of specific policy sectors and of the often inelastic arguments advanced by classical intergovernmentalist and federalist approaches to European integration. Moreover, the term avoids the equally biased interpretations embedded in a supranationalist conception of EU politics and the making of a new regional centre based on a single locus of law-making and regulatory powers. Finally, the term offers a kind of reflective distance from the examination of the Union's ontology, whilst opening a whole range of possibilities for not complying with pre-existing classifications of its internal political arena. But what is really meant by 'polity'? Under the new paradigm, 'polity' referred to a system of institutionalized shared rule whose governance structures were capable of producing authoritative political decisions over a given population and of allocating values in society. The characterization of the Union as an 'emerging polity', compound yet easily identifiable as a collectivity, makes it possible to contemplate the idea of replacing the rather deterministic concept of 'integration' – for it is usually associated with 'a sense of directionality'[15] – with that of 'polity-formation': the making of a large-scale system of mutual governance without the formal legal or constitutional attributes of competence embedded in classical state structures; namely, a polycentric regional order composed of highly interdependent 'polities' operating within a complex policy environment. Integration theory may then be taken as part of a wider intellectual evolution linking the constitutive elements of a compound polity to common management arrangements. What are the theoretical implications that this paradigm shift generates for our understanding of the nascent European 'body politic'? How should we think about its emerging properties?

A first point is that, although 'integration' purports to explain the coming together of previously independent entities under a new political unit regulated by autonomous supranational agencies, 'polity-formation' captures the constitutive nature of European governance. It is around this *problematique* that a 'new governance' agenda has emerged, focusing on the nature, dynamism and sophistication of collective governance structures; new forms of transnational 'synergies' in the everyday management of the European policy process; the extent to which supranational institutions influence the choices of state administrations and even coordinate national expectations; and the role these institutions play in shaping political behaviour, setting norms, generating change and allocating values.[16] The thrust of the argument is that state agents are only one set of actors out of many within a multi-level polity which is, to draw from Elazar's neoteric metaphor, 'cybernetic': it is 'based on multiple arenas, many channels of communication among [actors], and a variety of different mechanisms for mobilizing them to undertake particular courses of actions in place of a single channel'.[17] Whether or not the often polemical exchanges between those subscribing to a state-centric conception of EU politics and those whose faith lies more in an institutionalist account of supranational governance will be replaced by a constructive discourse on the ontological properties of the Union, the paradigm shift from policy to polity certainly made an impact on the process of theorizing the state of European integration at the turn of the century. This shift also reflected an emerging consensus on the analytical potential of the new 'governance discourse' in capturing the systemic and operational complexity of the European polity, as opposed to the more conventional uses of the term 'government'. As Caporaso notes, while the latter refers to the institutions and agents occupying key institutional roles and positions, 'governance' refers to 'collective problem-solving in the public realm', or the way in which relations are governed among governments that reside in constitutive units within a system of dispersed or fragmented political authority.[18]

But let us now turn to some important innovations of the TEU (1993). They may be listed as follows:

- the introduction of a process of parliamentary co-decision granting the EP the right of veto (should its members decide to reject by an absolute majority the Council's position);
- the establishment of Union citizenship conferring a new set of transnational civil and political rights upon member state nationals (see Chapter 6);
- the inclusion of federally inspired principles such as subsidiarity and proportionality;
- the creation of the Committee of the Regions for the representation of subnational units at EU level;
- the extension of QMV in the Council in the areas of public health,

education, consumer protection, trans-European networks, transport, energy and small and medium-size firms;

- the establishment of a specific timetable for the attainment of economic and monetary union (EMU) leading to a single currency;
- the embodiment of new civil arrangements to regulate interstate relations in the areas of policing, visa, asylum, immigration, and so on (replacing and extending the Trevi system which began in 1975);
- and the creation of a 'common' foreign and security policy (replacing and building on the EPC framework).

As for the structure of the newly born Union, Article A TEU reads: 'The Union shall be founded on the European Communities, supplemented by the policies and forms of cooperation established by this Treaty.' The problem here lies in the fact that the above provision is mired in ambiguity. Is the Union actually founded by the new treaty itself, or does it merely consist, as Forsyth legitimately asks, of 'an accretion of policies and cooperation'?[19] Should the latter hypothesis hold, then it raises the question whether a genuine reconstitution of existing arrangements took place, or whether there was a deliberate decision to downplay the federal substance of the Union's *traité constitutif*.[20] A more obvious reading of the Maastricht reforms is that the TEU offered a general umbrella under which the pre-established Communities continued to exist as separate legal entities, with the renamed 'European Community' being the most advanced component of a three-pillar architectural structure complemented by the Common Foreign and Security Policy (CFSP) and cooperation in the fields of Justice and Home Affairs (JHA).

The introduction of the new pillars, by strengthening the confederal properties of the general system, clearly revealed the limits of European supranationalism in still sensitive policy domains. For, the *locus decidendi* of new competences 'pooled' to the central institutions in these sectors was to rest firmly in the hands of the Council, the limited consultative role of Parliament and the Commission notwithstanding. As Taylor puts it, 'The whole was to be consolidated into a single package of activities linked in systems of common management.'[21] If one tries to capture the wider picture, even the extension of QMV was more a result of the new circumstances of mounting interdependence among the states (compounded by strong global liberalizing and deregulatory pressures) than an indication that the West European state was heading towards its own demise. This is an important point, for 'the majority-voting arrangements were primarily an instrument for consensus-building',[22] whilst the underlying principle of the Luxembourg Accords was still politically relevant, no longer in a classical Gaullist fashion, but as a last resort: member state governments would not tolerate the possibility of being regularly outvoted on matters important to their national interests and constituencies. A pattern also emerged that, through their proportional representation in the central institutions and their active participation in transnational agencies that were – at least partly – responsible for the formulation of common policies with potential centralizing effects, national executives retained their capacity to resist or amend policy proposals that they did not approve of.[23] It is instructive, for instance, to note that '[b]etween December 1993 and March 1995 the Council adopted a total of 286 legislative acts but only voted on forty of these acts'.[24]

In a similar context, due to the cautiously designated stages for arriving at joint decisions, the procedures operating within the new intergovernmental pillars resemble an exercise in 'alternative' regime creation: a cooperative venture based upon a commonly agreed set of principles, rules and procedures, elaborate enough to promote a relatively high degree of horizontal interactions among the states, and elastic enough to be wholly consistent with the pursuit of a wide range of segmental interests in EU affairs.[25] As Bulmer and Scott note, 'the two new pillars of the Union constitute an extension of the terrain of inter-state co-operation . . . '.[26] Likewise, Laffan et al. observe that 'institutional roles and decision rules in pillars two and three are designed to limit the role of the Union's supranational institutions and to retain as much national control as possible.'[27] This point is further supported by taking into account the perpetuation of a 'comitology' system which evades proper parliamentary control; the issue of extending the EP's co-responsibility for compulsory expenditure (agriculture); the question of a uniform procedure for European elections; the purely consultative role of the Committee of the Regions; and a wide range of issues relating to the Union's opaque system of decision-making, characterized, *inter alia*, by a lack of clarity, openness and transparency.[28]

According to Article E TEU, the four main institutions of the Union shall exercise their powers 'under the conditions and for the purposes provided for' by the provisions of the treaty, whilst Article N TEU renders all parts of the treaty subject to the same revision rules (see Chapter 5). And since the TEU rests on two different sets of legal mechanisms – the Community Method and intergovernmental cooperation – the extent to which it has provided for a 'single institutional framework' is far from evident. As Demaret notes, 'the dividing line between the two types of mechanisms and between their respective fields of application is, in several instances, less than clear-cut.'[29] Likewise, the wording of Article C TEU that the Union will be 'served by a common institutional framework' deviates greatly from what Forsyth calls 'the classic concept of institutions representing the union', according to which 'a union is represented by a set of institutions, which enable it to act as one within the boundaries of the union, and as one *vis-à-vis* outsiders'.[30] He explains: 'The establishment of these representative institutions . . . is the constitution of the union . . . an act by which reality is given to a common political will, the creation of a distinct political personality . . . which changes the status of the partners.'[31] But even despite these critical notes, the legal maze surrounding the 'letter' – and for some even the 'spirit' – of the TEU arguably raised more questions than it originally sought to answer, thus proving to be 'a source of controversy'.[32]

Reflecting on the ambiguity of the TEU, Wallace notes that 'the terms of Maastricht . . . can be interpreted as easily as making efforts to set a ceiling on, even a roll back of, the forces of supranationalism as they can be seen as crossing a new threshold on the route towards a European transnational polity.'[33] Schmitter's interpretation of the Maastricht outcome goes even further to suggest that '[a] confirmed neo-realist could read it with joy and conviction since it literary reeks "statism", especially in its frequent mention of the role of the Council of Ministers and repeated (but not exclusive) insistence on unanimity voting.'[34] To be sure, the reform package agreed at Maastricht, including no less than seventeen Protocols and thirty-three declarations, came into being more as a result of partial reconciliations among sovereignty-conscious governments, than by pressures generated by 'the birth of a transcendental European entity'.[35] Hence, the key to its viability rests on the striking of a new balancing act between the functional need for joint management structures (along the traditional path of state-controlled incrementalism) and the political claim for appropriate territorial safeguards (for fear of impairing the integrity of the subunits), or between interdependence and autonomy, as two interconnected dynamics of equal weight. Thus the TEU opened the way 'for the institutionalization of diversity'.[36]

Turning to the Union's lack of an international legal personality, and following Ress's analysis through the lens of public international law, '[the EU] must be considered a new *international organisation sui generis*'.[37] If by the term 'international organization' we mean 'a formal, continuous structure established by agreement between members . . . from two or more sovereign states with the aim of pursuing the common interests of membership',[38] then challenging this view is no easy task. On the other hand, however, an international legal personality should not be seen as a prerequisite either for successful EU polity-building or even for meaningful regional federalization, defined here as an ensemble of processes sustaining a union of polities. Such a personality is, after all, a property of statehood (usually coupled with claims to nationhood and self-determination) that the Union is most unlikely to acquire, at least in terms of transforming itself into a conventional state 'of the organizational form that governs bounded territories'.[39] On the contrary, the novelty of the European polity, as epitomized by Schmitter, 'lies in the growing dissociation between territorial constituencies, functional *compétences* and collective identities . . . What seems to be asserting, and even consolidating, itself is a plurality of polities at different levels of aggregation . . . that overlap in a multitude of domains.'[40] As Taylor puts it, 'It is truly a departure from the world offered by traditionalists and federalists, but is more consciously addressed to fundamentally altering the society of existing states, than to creating a new transcendent state.'[41] Or, as Forsyth writes, although the Union is not a (federal) state, 'this does not prevent it from being a federal union, that is to say a permanent linking together of states to form a corporate entity with a distinct boundary *vis-à-vis* the outside world, and possessed of two coexisting structures of government . . . '.[42] Let us simply add to the above that the confusion over the constitutional nature of the TEU suggests that the questions of what kind of union the EU 'really' is, and what one should call it, remain largely unanswered.

What is also striking in the central arrangements brought about by the TEU is the insistence of states on protecting their own cultural, political and constitutional features. Article F (1) TEU sharpens this point: 'The Union shall respect the national identities of the Member States, whose systems of government are founded on the principles of democracy.' Embodied in this is the need to sustain a pluralistic form of society at the regional level, implying that any challenge to constituent identities would be both legally and politically unacceptable. Increasing the level of European authority, in other words, should not be at the expense of cultural distinctiveness and its underlying value-systems. The legal and political consensus among both homogeneous and heterogeneous states – Denmark, Ireland and Greece on the one hand; Spain, Belgium and the United Kingdom on the other – is that, whatever 'the calculus of cultural costs' may be,[43] national governments have now an obligation to preserve the pluriformity of the European polity and with it the distinctive cultural spheres of the constituent units. Transcending territoriality; minimizing transaction costs; facilitating the four freedoms of movement; combating cultural (among other forms of) discrimination; respecting linguistic equality; institutionalizing multiple citizenship; creating avenues for subnational representation at the central level; respecting minority rights – all the above are not merely part of the Union's *vie politique*, sustained by a presumption of tolerance between the member states and demoi, but are also essential components of its emerging *acquis constitutionnel*. It appears, then, that the federalist-inspired principle of 'unity in diversity' epitomizes the preferred pattern of interaction between transnational and domestic cultural spheres.

These points substantiate the view that the TEU gave birth to a sensibly arranged 'union of diversities' based on a unique system of inter-institutional power-sharing, whilst offering an advanced conception of political co-determination. The latter practice became evident at both interstate and Union–state relations: horizontally, by producing a sense of symbiosis within the community of states; vertically, through the application of a consociationalist logic, according to which national authorities remained concerned about their capacity for self-governance without obstructing extensive working within regional arrangements, provided that 'the principle of sovereignty and equality of states in the common system should be respected'.[44] The intensity of the ties fostered between central and state levels was operationalized through the application of a mixed system of consensus and majority government, close to what Forsyth calls 'unanimity at the base, majority voting in the superstructure'.[45] By the mid-1990s, a view began to emerge that the TEU could shed light on the form of the end-situation since state and regional organization found themselves bound in a symbiotic relationship and this was 'a recognition of the inherent duality of the Community's arrangements . . . '.[46] In both treaty reforms, in the mid-1980s and early 1990s, although one could conceivably predict an increase in centralized management and authority, in reality, 'reserved powers were retained by states, and many Community competences were shared by them in central mechanisms'.[47] Although the theoretical implications of this argument are further explored in Chapter 5, together with the principles of subsidiarity and proportionality, a point made by Majone on the limits of European competences is worth quoting at some length:

> The TEU also throws new light on the limits of previous grants of powers by means of Article 235 of the Rome Treaty, which enables the Council to take appropriate measures in cases where action by the Community is found to be necessary to attain an objective of the treaty and there is no specific power available for that purpose. In the past, the Council has made liberal use of Article 235 to expand Community competences or to broaden the reach of EC legislation in such areas as economic and monetary union, social and regional policy, energy and environment, and co-operation agreements with third countries. Post-Maastricht, however, Article 235 makes sense only if the reference to the attainment of a Community objective is in the course of the operation of the common market. This means that subsidiary powers would be created under this article only for matters directly connected with the policies that lie at the very core of the EU . . . [48]

The political 'fragility' of the TEU became clearly manifested not only during the negotiations leading up to its signing in February 1992, but also during its arduous course of ratification – most notably, due to the negative result of the first Danish referendum on 2 June 1992, but also because of France's *petit oui* on 20 September later that year – and the subsequent 'opt-outs' secured by the more sceptical members as a *quid pro quo* for consenting to the new treaty. Against the background of an ever-more cynical electorate questioning the social legitimacy of the European polity, any residual touch of optimism from the mid-1980s seemed to have evaporated by the conclusion of the ratification process. Although the TEU finally managed to survive the tides of euroscepticism, a new 'democratic disjunction' became manifest between the wishes of national leaders and popular political sentiments.[49] As in past treaty revisions, the TEU reflected in a most tenacious way the continuing tussle between those defending the prerogatives of states and those projecting an independent legitimacy for the larger polity. In Neunreither's words, 'It is a text for insiders, not only in being difficult to read and to digest, but even more because of its paternalistic approach – everything is done *for* the people, not very much *by* the people.'[50] Or, as Lister comments, 'Anyone who has ventured to read and digest the 253-page treaty realizes that a very complex political entity is in the process of formation.'[51] But the strongest line of criticism came from Hoffmann who wrote that 'the somewhat Byzantine setup of the Union . . . is a compromise between the inadequate [a strictly inter-governmental operation] and the impossible [a leap to a federal system].'[52] As for the most colourful statement, finally, it cannot but be attributed to Schmitter:

> It is as if 'Europe' – having been previously invited by its nation states to sit down to a light snack of regional cooperation and by its supranational civil servants to a copious *prix fixe* dinner of centralized governance – suddenly found itself before a *repas à la carte* prepared by several cooks and tempting the invitees with diverse, but unequally appealing, arrangements for managing their common affairs.[53]

Whether it is a clear guide to imagining one out of many possible integration outcomes, the above depiction is a perfect illustration of the fact that the configuration of authority that is currently emerging in the European polity confirms that 'reality is richer than fantasy'!

Overall, the end-product of the Maastricht process revealed that, without a substantive consensus at the highest political level, there could be no viable treaty reform. This accords with what most students of European integration had implicitly assumed: over the past decade, the weight of evidence is that the relationship between the scope and level of the regional arrangements – best captured by the term 'spill-around'[54] – has exploited a crucial property of consensual politics: the capacity to reconcile the challenges of institutional innovation with the need for operational continuity so as to arrive at a mutual but stable form of governance. But let us now turn to some important theoretical insights developed in the 1990s fuelling a heated debate between the two general strands of contemporary EU studies: state-centrism *v.* multi-level governance.

State-centrism *v.* multi-level governance

The appearance of Moravcsik's powerful critique of the resurgence of neofunctionalist theorizing post-SEA aimed at restoring the superiority of state-centric approaches to the explanation of how European integration proceeds. The thesis he advanced was that the SEA represented the outcome of preference convergence around the neoliberalist-inspired single market programme between the United Kingdom, France, and West Germany.[55] In arguing the case for state primacy, Moravcsik developed a few years later a liberal intergovernmentalist approach that, compared to his earlier analysis, attributed a higher value to international institutions 'as facilitators of positive sum governing'.[56] This approach arguably widened the spectrum of scholarly debate about the evolution of the

Community system, its internal decision-making arrangements and, more crucially, the relationship between domestic politics (and interests) and international cooperation.[57] Liberal intergovernmentalism purports to explain, on the one hand, the interaction between states and international organization and, on the other, the relationship between national preference formation, coalitional behaviour and interstate bargaining. What effectively distinguishes this approach from earlier state-centric accounts of European integration is that it enlarges the range of intellectual opportunities for going beyond 'unicausal theorizing' by integrating three important subfields of general international relations theory: regime analysis, negotiation theory and intergovernmentalism. The wider theoretical concern in Moravcsik's perspective revolves around the development of causal understandings between a liberal interpretation of how national preferences are formed (a concern it shares with neoliberal international theory which links external and domestic politics processes), the rationality of actors pursuing their interests at the central level and the distinct nature of interstate bargaining within the Community system (what essentially accounts for the conduct of regime politics). A welcoming aspect in Moravcsik's state-centrism is that it puts forward a series of causal connections between the domestic political orders and economic agendas of the component states and modes of collective decision-making and coalition-formation in the intergovernmental Council.

Moravcsik argues that Community institutions strengthen the power of national governments in two important respects: by increasing 'the efficiency of interstate bargaining' and by strengthening 'the autonomy of national political leaders *vis-à-vis* particularistic societal groups within their domestic polity'.[58] State executives, the theory goes, mediate between domestic interests and Community action: integration outcomes are determined by the relative bargaining power of national governments themselves – in this hypothesis, larger states exert greater influence on rule-making and policy outcomes – and by the distribution of preferences amongst them. By using Putnam's analogy of the two-level games – i.e. state executives are involved concomitantly in coalition-building with domestic groups in the national arena and in (strategic) bargaining with other states at the international level[59] – Moravcsik establishes a link between domestic and regional politics. This liberal-pluralist emphasis accounts, in Rosamond's analysis, for one of the theory's key advantages in linking intergovernmental theory with the domestic sources of legitimacy.[60] In the words of Moravcsik, 'An understanding of domestic politics is a precondition for, not a supplement to, the analysis of strategic interaction among states.'[61] The gist of Moravcsik's thesis lies in the assumption that the Community regime 'has developed through a series of celebrated intergovernmental bargains, each of which set the agenda for an intervening period of consolidation'.[62] Community institutions are taken as highly reactive agents – operating within a 'passive structure' – that serve the interests of states, which in turn decide to delegate powers to supranational authorities in response to growing pressures generated by regional and international interdependence, as well as to augment their respective autonomy in relation to domestic groups in certain domains of policy action. Moravcsik's 'new' intergovernmentalism has been criticized on the grounds of effectively denying supranational institutions (especially the Commission and the ECJ) and transnational actors and processes (interest associations and policy networks, among other agents in the development of transnational society) a decisive role in provoking integrative growth (as in the field of functional task expansion), having an impact on the political behaviour of states (through norm-setting, rule-making and the supply of regulatory legislation) and determining integrative outcomes. Another important line of criticism has been of Moravcsik's working assumptions about state rationality and his tendency to downplay the impact of actual decision rules and institutional preferences.[63]

According to Moravcsik, the Community's transaction cost-reducing function (as in the crucial areas of information and negotiation), its highly institutionalized and innovative policy coordination environment, and the way in which the process of institutional delegation or 'pooling' of state sovereignty takes place at the larger level of aggregation – i.e. in the Council, mainly through majority rule – are important factors towards a viable negotiating order: 'a successful intergovernmental regime designed to manage economic interdependence through negotiated policy co-ordination'.[64] In general terms, liberal intergovernmentalism, in a manner not dissimilar to Hoffmann's earlier critique of the formative process theories of integration, represents an attempt to bridge the gap between neofunctionalist pre-theorizing and 'substantive' theorizing, by proposing a state-centric research agenda that emphasizes the primacy of intergovernmental bargaining in determining the pace and depth of European integration.

In stark contrast to the above is the 'multi-level governance' approach, which aims to inform our understanding of the emerging configuration of authority in a polity that is characterized by overlapping competences among different levels of governance. Although the term 'governance' has been criticized for its vagueness, research analysis has seen in it 'a particular value in examining the pattern of rule in the EU'.[65] Being critical of both realist state-centric and supranationalist accounts of the regional process, Marks, Hooghe and Blank have put forward an alternative approach, focusing on the polity-creating process that integration has brought about. The general assessment is that integration is leading to a situation where 'authority and policy-making influence are shared across multiple levels of government', and where national governments 'have lost some of their former authoritative control over individuals in their respective territories'.[66] Accordingly, 'the locus of political control has changed' since member state executives no longer monopolize decision-making competences, while state sovereignty has become ever-more diluted in the regional polity, not only through collective decision-making in the Council, but also through the increased levels of autonomy and independent influence that supranational institutions have come to enjoy.[67]

Underlying the 'new governance' turn in EU studies is the belief that there exist considerable limits to both individual and collective (state) executive control within the increasingly pluralistic context of European polity-formation. Such limits stem, *inter alia*, from increased majoritarianism (or alternative voting procedures) in the Council and the regression of its (once dominant) 'veto culture' – the argument here being that '[m]ajority rule lowers the costs of co-operation that stem from the danger of non-decision';[68] the mistrust characterizing central state executives; informational asymmetries between national and supranational authorities; unintended consequences of institutional change; new competitive pressures generated in liberal democratic polities; the role of interest group organizations and transnational actors in EU policy processes; the intensified interconnection of different political arenas (with supranational actors not being nested exclusively within national arenas); the increased complexities and specialization of collective public policy-making (requiring detailed regulation); the introduction and extension of the scope of parliamentary co-decision (with the Council now becoming part of a complex inter-institutional system); the agenda-setting role of the Commission, together with its substantive informational capacity, 'discretion to interpret legislation and issue administrative regulations',[69] and policy implementation influence; the political dynamics of the ECJ's legal activism; domestic party political competition; increased subnational mobilization; and national constitutional constraints on formal treaty change.

In this view, European policy-making 'is characterised by mutual dependence, complementary functions and overlapping competences',[70] with supranational authorities having an independent influence in generating and shaping policy outcomes. Although it is not claimed that supranational institutions will eventually supersede the member state executives, or that national governance arenas will be rendered obsolete by a process of 'transnational interest mobilization', Hooghe makes the point that multi-level governance 'amounts to a multi-layered polity, where there is no centre of accumulated authority, but where changing combinations of supranational, national and subnational governments engage in collaboration'.[71] This view accords with Wallace's classification of the European policy process as 'post-sovereign' on the grounds that '[i]t spills across state boundaries, penetrating deep into previously domestic aspects of national politics and administration'.[72] The Union is thus conceived of as a multi-level system of governance composed of interlocked arenas for political contest, where direct links are established among actors in diverse political spaces and policy domains, where political control is diffuse (often leading to 'second-best' policy outcomes) and where states 'no longer serve as the exclusive nexus between domestic politics and international relations [or intergovernmental bargaining]'.[73] An important difference, therefore, between liberal intergovernmentalism and multi-level governance is that, in the former, the activities of domestic interests are modelled in the context of a two-level game (with domestic actors influencing EU policy developments indirectly by pressing their governments to bargain their interests in state-dominated arenas), while the latter recognizes and attempts to explain 'the mobilization of domestic actors directly in the European arena . . . [through] a set of overarching, multi-level policy networks'.[74] Another crucial difference between the two is that, from a governance perspective, the role of the state 'has changed from authoritative allocation and regulation "from above" to the role of partner and mediator' or simply 'from actor to arena', thus encouraging networking,[75] while 'intergovernmental bargaining is not a constant or immovable feature that floats above politics'.[76]

Theorists of multi-level governance advance the notion of 'a Europe *with* [rather than *of*] the Regions', referring to 'the demand on the part of regional governments for influence alongside, rather than in place of, state executives . . . '.[77] Instead of regions, therefore, competing with central political executives for control over territorial interest aggregation, thus finding themselves in a relationship of 'contested hierarchy', substate authorities become additional, non-hierarchical channels for subnational mobilization in the European polity.[78] Hooghe explains: 'Subnational mobilization does not erode, but complements the aggregating role of member states . . . Actors are linked through networks, which span several levels and in which each actor brings in valuable resources.'[79] As Marks et al. remind us, a major incentive for subnational governments to mobilize their energies at the larger level of aggregation and, hence, to lead their claims directly to supranational institutions of governance is that, while in the domestic political arena they may be pitched against a national majority, in the transnational arena they represent one out of many competing subnational groups, none of which is dominant (although much depends on available financial resources for regions to 'lobby Brussels' more effectively and, hence, institutionalize their position at the central political level).[80]

At the policy level, the approach developed by Peterson in the mid-1990s merits our attention, for it entails some serious methodological implications for the study of the European policy process. Peterson argues the case for a 'middle-range theory' based on a tripartite level of analysis: the super-systemic, the systemic and the meso-level.[81] Each level is best explained through the employment of different theoretical perspectives: the super-systemic level, which focuses on the conditions of change in the wider political and economic environment, including treaty reform among other instances of interstate bargaining, is analysed through the logic of 'macrotheoretical' devices such as those derived from intergovernmentalist and neofunctionalist analysis; the systemic level, which calls attention to the question of institutional change in Community policy-setting, is best understood by employing the conceptual and analytic lenses of new institutionalist theory (see below); and the meso-level, whose decisive variable takes the form of 'resource dependencies', is best captured by reference to policy network analysis, emphasizing the informal, day-to-day operative character of policy interaction among a cluster of actors representing multiple organizations. Such networks can facilitate the exchange and sharing of information and resources among the involved actors and are capable of producing positive-sum games, by facilitating 'reconciliation, settlement or compromise between different interests which have a stake in outcomes in a particular policy sector'.[82] Although the model advanced by policy network analysis has been subjected to serious criticism for downplaying the importance of formal institutional politics at EU level and for finding it difficult to justify its claims in the empirical world by measuring the actual influence of policy networks on EU decision-making – something that can be said of Richardson's actor-based model on the role and impact of epistemic and policy communities at the regional level[83] – it occupies a central position in the recent 'governance turn' by purporting 'to offer a theory of the everyday politics of the EU'.[84]

Multi-level governance carries at least two important meanings in relation to national sovereignty, a central tenet of state-centric thinking. First, there is a notion of a single, albeit pluralistic and asymmetrically structured – both vertically and horizontally[85] – regional polity within which sovereignty is dispersed (and even fragmented) among competing political actors that interact with the central institutions, thus bypassing their central national authorities. From this '(dis)ordering framework', to borrow Rosamond's term,[86] an 'autonomous voice' is born at the larger level of aggregation. From a systemic point of view, the European polity transcends the traditional bond between territory, function and, increasingly, identity, and becomes a new venue for the resolution of conflicts, the articulation of territorial interests and the representation of claims stemming from 'smaller', diverse, but politically organized units. The role and nature of the component nation-states in this depiction of the European polity could be linked (if not reduced) to the notion of a 'penetrated political system', a conceptual scheme developed by Rosenau in the mid-1960s. Within such a system, actors that are not formally part of the domestic society – in our case, the national political arenas – participate both directly and authoritatively through joint actions in the allocation of values and the mobilization of systemic support.[87] The resulting political entity is a 'composite of subnational, national and supranational elements',[88] capable of projecting domestic roles at the larger level. This perspective, which in many respects leads to a postmodern approximation to political reality, stresses the limits of state sovereignty in advanced processes of union and the penetration of national social and political settings. Doubtless, both of these themes form a central part of the radical and, as compared to realist state-centric writings, conceptually refined vocabulary of multi-level governance theorists. Not surprisingly, the latter find it analytically useful to conceptualize European polity-formation as a dynamic exercise based on the practice of 'co-constitution' and, hence, to replace the rather more conventional conceptions of regional cooperation and collective policy coordination.[89]

A second meaning of the term denotes a new type of collective action that recognizes the constitutional foundations of sovereignty as resting on the member state polities, but challenges the (functional) autonomy of states – what has been referred to as 'the second vernacular meaning of sovereignty'[90] – to respond to pressing socio-economic realities. In this sense, subnational mobilization and the forging of direct links among actors in diverse settings become additional vehicles for the reallocation of authoritative problem-solving capacity to constitutive entities within a polity that remains dependent in critical ways on the national subsystems, but which also allows for new structures of political opportunity to emerge. This implies a more dynamic understanding of governance, not so much as the political capacity to steer, but mainly as a practical means for subnational units to influence complex policy-making by 'hit[ting] several points of access immediately', resulting from 'the extraordinarily frag-mented character of decision-making'.[91] To summarize the two conceptions of sovereignty: in the first case, there is an explicit acknowledgement of the structural transformation of the nation-state which is now part of a new multi-level polity of diffused public authority, with state sovereignty being diluted in the transnational arena by collective governance arrangements. This conception bears a close resemblance to Deudney's account of the Philadelphian political system that, contrary to the hierarchical order of the Westphalian sovereignty regime, contains the idea of 'central-state incapacity' as a positive element in a compound polity of diffused governance functions.[92] In the second case, the West European state retains *de jure* sovereignty but in effect loses its autonomy – its capacity to control events, rather than its authority to do so – in performing its task as the principal political actor for the articulation of domestic territorial interests, as well as in projecting its political domination of large-scale institution-building and collective problem-solving.

For state-centrists, on the other hand, the dominant model of regional politics is one in which states are the dominant agents of European governance, collective decision-making and regional constitution-building. This is primarily reflected in the capacity of state executives to shape and influence integration outcomes. State power is safeguarded and even strengthened through negotiated policy coordination within a manage-ment system based on the pooling of individual sovereignties for specific purposes (especially in areas where there is strong functional reason for collective policy action). It would be wrong, however, to equate Moravcsik's liberal intergovernmentalism, Milward's thesis about the 'European rescue of the nation-state' (where integration is essential for the survival of states and the preservation of their executive capacity at the domestic level),[93] Bulmer's domestic politics model (emphasizing the interaction of national preference formation and the relationship between domestic policy styles and EC policy-making),[94] Wessel's fusion thesis (accepting the centrality of governmental elites in determining integration outcomes),[95] Scharpf's joint decision-trap hypothesis (in that joint decisions lead to sub-optimal policy outcomes),[96] Kirchner's cooperative federalism analogy to European intergovernmentalism,[97] and Taylor's modified intergovernmentalism in the form of consociationalism (see Chapter 5), with the conventional realist billiard-ball image of international politics, where states are 'hard-shelled, highly polished units without bonding surfaces, propelled only by their internal dynamics, and doomed to a life of perpetual collision'.[98] For states are not, in Leibniz's words, 'windowless monads'.[99] Rather, state-centred scholarship perceives sovereignty as an integral part of the logic of statehood itself: it attributes a normative content to sovereignty, which distinguishes it from the praxis of institutionalized shared rule (as in the setting of collective norms and joint-decision rules). The latter, it is claimed, results from rising levels of complex (mainly economic) interdependence, the satisfaction of felt needs in the domestic social and political arenas of states, and the search for more effective and cost-reducing means of organizing, structuring and executing collective policy programmes that nevertheless remain crucial for the political viability of the constituent units.

It is worth mentioning, however, that what both state-centric perspectives and the multi-level governance approach have in common is that the Union is not conceptualized in terms of being firmly, let alone necessarily, situated in the *terra incognita* between a conventional international organization (or system of states) and a supranational political community (or federal state). Instead, scholars representative of these schools have more often than not expressed clear views about the political physiognomy of the larger entity: for state-centrists, the regional system is constituted by the sovereign statehood of the component polities. It represents an expression of a highly interactive and densely institution-alized system of 'open states',[100] with the Union taking the form of a complex negotiation system, a regional regime, a symbiotic consociation, a system of horizontal *Kooperativer Staaten*, a joint-decision system, and so on. As Smith puts it, 'the EU is a "safe" form of pluralism, effectively tolerated by state authorities in return for the preservation of their privileges'.[101] For multi-level governance theorists, on the other hand, the Union represents a transcendence of the Westphalian nation-state system, constituting a polity whose governance structures account for the extension of political spaces, civic arenas and public spheres across, below and beyond the traditional state. It thus challenges the authority of sovereign statehood and the presumed centrality of state executives in the evolving 'EU order'. Whether this depiction approximates to a 'neo-medieval' arena with highly dispersed and localized sources of public and private influence,[102] the point is made that the era of an easily identifiable power structure in Europe is long gone.

By way of conclusion, let us note that it is essentially what distinguishes these opposing strands in integration thinking that adds to the intellectual pluralism of this largely 'undisciplined' field: the challenging question for EU scholarship is whether the process of theorizing about the social science and respective ontologies of distinct approaches to European integration will be capable of drawing analytical insights from the exploration of both state and non-state variables so as to arrive at more balanced accounts for evaluating contemporary events. At least, this is one plausible way of avoiding, or even transcending, the pitfalls of argumentative circularity, theoretical parsimony and methodological individualism.[103] At most, it is a means of bridging the gap between the constitutive elements of state-centric rationalism based on the explanatory power of interstate bargaining and the new patterns of institutionalized governance and multi-level shared rule. It also offers, to borrow from Cox, a solid basis for arguing that 'state power ceases to be the sole explanatory factor and becomes part of what is to be explained'.[104] In any case, and irrespective of the particular intellectual preferences and orientations that may arise in EU theory development, this is an analytically rewarding path to test the strengths (and limits) of a new type of interdisciplinary synthesis, whilst allowing for higher levels of theoretical reflexivity or metatheoretical investigations (see Chapter 6); namely, the art of navigating through the *a priori*, foundational or underlying assumptions – also known as 'first principles' – that are embedded in distinct theoretically informed and empirically grounded routes to understanding contemporary social reality.

Institutionalism strikes back

'There are strange ironies in the annals of research', writes Tarrow, and explains: 'Over thirty years ago, the modernists in political science rejected what has been called the "legal/institutionalist" approach . . . [and] joined a behavioural revolution, carrying out systematic studies of voters, parties, and legislators.'[105] He then makes an equally valid observation: 'In the study of European integration, there has been a recent re-embrace of institutions. In part for descriptive purposes, and in part to find a venue for the previously-institutionless abstractions of formal theory, both area specialists and formal modelers have avidly turned to study the institutions of Europe.'[106] What follows offers a comprehensive summary of the arguments mounted in support of this theoretical trend.[107]

First, supranational institutions have an impact on the behaviour of national governing elites and domestic policy actors, while at the same time becoming important venues for the resolution of conflicts. Second, the Union offers the most advanced and well-developed form of regional institutionalization and, to borrow from Tarrow again, 'nothing pleases students of comparative politics and international relations like the "new"'.[108] Third, the post-SEA era is marked by renewed institutional dynamism, prompting contemporary scholarship to cast doubt on realist state-centric claims for viewing institutions as 'passive, transaction-cost reducing sets of rules' designed to facilitate intergovernmental bargains.[109] Fourth, supranational institutions can play a meaningful autonomous role in the European policy process, albeit periodically, in furthering the scope of the common functional arrangements and imposing constraints on rule-based state behaviour. Fifth, European integration has often led to 'unintended consequences' regarding the growth, influence and competence acquisition of supranational agencies, largely at the expense of national executives which can no longer act as gatekeepers. Sixth, it is not only through the study of the so-called 'grand episodes' or 'history-making' decisions of the European Council – after formal interstate negotiations and subsequent treaty reforms – that one may hope to explain the evolution of European integration as a whole, let alone capture the profound complexity embedded in its governance structures. Finally, supranational institutions like the Commission and to a lesser extent the EP possess agenda-setting powers that limit the capacity of states to exercise formal political control, collectively or individually, over integration outcomes. This is supported by the wider claims of EU policy analysts that the formation of a European policy-making arena increasingly relies on a distinctive set of collective policy norms and everyday regulatory practices, posing 'a permanent challenge to national political systems because they are confronted with the need to adapt to a normative and strategic environment that escapes total control'.[110]

Focusing on the impact of the major Community institutions, Bulmer analyses the transformation of European governance from a comparative public policy perspective.[111] This new institutionalist account aims to go beyond purely descriptive empiricism and reductionist perspectives – i.e. 'to explain how political institutions work by means of non-political actors'[112] – and place institutions 'in a context which allows differentiation between formal political institutions, informal conventions and the norms and beliefs embedded within those institutions'.[113] The underlying assumption here is that 'institutions matter' since 'political struggles are mediated by prevailing institutional arrangements'.[114] New institutional theory treats institutions as instruments capable of producing determinate policy and of shaping 'the pattern of political behaviour', thus going 'beyond the formal organs of government' to include 'standard operating procedures, so-called soft-law, norms and conventions of behaviour'.[115] Both the SEA and the TEU, writes Bulmer, can be understood from an historical institutionalist perspective (see below) for they created and extended the competences of the general system and have generated important changes in the conventions and norms embedded in supranational institutions.[116] Bulmer's new institutionalism does not point either to a holistic or to a unifocal approach to the Union's institutional system, nor does it proclaim a kind of 'unifying heuristic' for the study of European integration as a whole. Rather, it complements other approaches to theorizing European governance in the 1990s.

Despite the methodological sophistication of new institutionalist political science, a large number of its explanations of policy outputs and social outcomes are based on a relatively straightforward assumption: that institutions make a difference in the process of organizing public life. Rosamond explains: 'Rather than being simple and passive vessels within which politics occurs, institutions provide contexts [or venues] where actors can conduct a relatively higher proportion of positive sum bargains ... They act as intervening variables between actor preferences and policy outputs.'[117] While new institutionalism should not be interpreted or for that matter treated as a single and/or coherent body of thought, let alone a comprehensive research agenda, the above depiction reveals a fundamental principle underlying the rationale of contemporary institutional analysis: institutions, whether formal or informal in character, are not merely epiphenomena; rather, they form a constitutive part and contribute substantively to the development of a fuller and more profound understanding of social reality itself.

The revival of institutional theory in political science is partly to do with the emergence of challenging questions about the changing relationship between the institutions of the liberal constitutional polity and actual processes of social and economic governance – civic governance still being a relatively unexplored theme – and partly to do with an attempt to explain the causal impact different institutions of governance have on particular policy outcomes by shaping the political behaviour of actors and influencing (in terms of systematizing, structuring, constraining etc.) the formation of their preferences and the pursuit (be it tactical, strategic or other) of their interests. But the renewed interest in institutional accounts of human governance has also explored the particular impact institutions have on those working within their structures. As Olsen and Peters tellingly put it, 'Institutions contain some sort of governmental DNA and tend to transmit that genetic code to the individuals who take up roles within them.'[118] To this, another layer of theorizing is added, focusing on the emergence of norms and rules that impinge upon various domains of collective policy action and joint problem-solving.

The point here is that institutions facilitate the exchange of information among actors, provide the possibility of informal contacts, assist the internalization of norms, enhance the quality of communicative action, promote patterns of cooperative behaviour (and even consensus) and act as real testing grounds for trust-building. But perhaps one of the most crucial services institutions perform as non-neutral arenas of governance is that they offer alternative ways of mapping the expectations of actors on issues of social and political change. In Olsen's words: 'Institutions, then, are seen as having the potential to form and transform actors, their mentality and identity and change logics of actions, e.g. from expected utility calculation to identity based rule-oriented behaviour.'[119] He adds: 'Institutions authorise and enable, as well as constrain, change. Therefore, there is a need for understanding how institutions may transform, modify, redirect and integrate, and not only aggregate, the demands, interests, and powers of societal actors and forces.'[120] Irrespective of the extent to which scholars perceive institutions as purposive agents of systemic change, or indeed of the level of autonomy attributed to them in the political process, they play an increasingly crucial role in structuring 'the access of political forces to the political process',[121] whilst offering a peaceful means of changing the rules of the game through a politics of deliberation.

The new institutionalist literature can be divided into three important theoretical strands: historical, rational choice, and sociological institutionalism. Rosamond has recently performed a valuable task in capturing the diversity embedded in these variants:

> Historical institutionalism grew out of critiques of conventional group theories of politics, while rational choice institutionalism reflects the successful support of the axioms of microeconomics into political science. At the same time, sociologists became interested in the capacity of cultural and organizational practices (institutions) to mould the preferences, interests and identities of actors in the social world (hence 'sociological institutionalism').[122]

Historical institutionalism treats institutions as instances of both formal and informal interaction and as 'systems of norms', including 'conventions, codes of behaviour and standard constraints upon behaviour'; rational choice institutionalism 'tends to define institutions as formal legalistic entities and sets of decision rules that impose obligations upon self-interested actors'; sociological institutionalism emphasizes the cognitive properties of institutions, that is, the way in which institutions influence behaviour, whilst stressing the mutual constitution of institutions and actors: 'Institutions . . . become the mechanisms through which the world is rendered meaningful to social actors.'[123] The differences between the latter two categories are substantive in relation to collective behaviour. Whereas rational choice institutionalism subscribes to a 'thin' definition of institutions (as rules in the sense of institutionalized norms that are taken as choice options), sociological institutionalism is informed by a 'thick' interpretation of institutions (as organizations, behaviour patterns, interests and belief-systems).[124] In the former case, institutions are but one important aspect of collective behaviour; the other being the rules that direct interaction among the participants. In the latter case, collective behaviour is primarily structured by institutions themselves or by institutionalization, as 'the process through which rules or norms are implemented in the sense that they meet with acceptance and that violations toward them are met with sanctions, in one form or another, that are considered legitimate by the group concerned'.[125] More specifically:

Whereas a rational choice institutionalist looks upon collective behaviour as framed by institutions as rules, the sociological institutionalist regards institutions as collective behaviour including all its aspects . . . The difference between [them] . . . becomes most critical in their entirely different opinions about the nature of interests or preferences in collective behaviour . . . To the rational choice institutionalist, collective behaviour is the outcome of the interaction of individual choice participants' preferences, framed by means of the rules of the game. To the sociological institutionalist, collective behaviour establishes institutions as organizations which have interests of their own, such as the promotion of the institution or its survival . . . the interests of institutions as organizations reflect historical legacies, national interests and community needs. Parliaments, governments and courts promote interests that reflect their images of themselves and what they can contribute to society. Thus, institutions become actors, which is impossible in rational choice institutionalism.[126]

'Not surprisingly', writes Rosamond, 'the different institutionalisms have alternative accounts of how institutions actually matter.'[127] This in fact brings us to a central problem confronting new institutionalist analysis. Namely, how to apply empirically tested models to the much-acclaimed importance of institutions in relation to major social and political outcomes, as well as to other forces or factors that are equally capable of contributing to determinate results. In the words of Lane and Ersson:

Thus, one may wish to know more about which specific institutions are critical for which identifiable outcomes as well as what the relative contribution of rules is in relation to, for example, structural or cultural forces . . . There is a real danger that new institutionalism will become just another fad, if we cannot replace the vague statement [that institutions are important] with more specific ones modelling for which outcomes institutions are important.[128]

But what is really 'new' about new institutionalism? Bulmer offers the following answer:

One is a wider interpretation of what constitutes institutions. Thus, there is a shift away from formal constitutional-legal approaches to government, with their tendency to be configurative. It is possible to take into account some of the less formalised arenas of politics. A new institutionalist concern, therefore, encompasses these broader aspects of governance: a wider remit than the formal institutions of state governance . . . A second distinction [stemming from March and Olsen's analysis] is a concern with the 'beliefs, paradigms, codes, cultures and knowledge' embedded within the institutions . . . This concern with institutional values is important, for the machinery of government is steeped in norms and codes of conduct and it is difficult to isolate formal institutional rules from the normative context . . . New institutionalism places the analytical focus on the polity. We can understand politics as comprising three separate components: politics, polity and policy. The presumption is that the polity structures the input of social, economic and political forces and has a consequential impact on policy outcome.[129]

Among recent applications of new institutionalism, Armstrong and Bulmer's study of the governance of the Single European market, Pierson's account of the relationship between institutional design and unintended consequences, Pollack's examination of the strengths and weaknesses of the institutionalist approach itself, and Wincott's analysis of EU judicial politics, have all contributed to the emergence of an interdisciplinary route to the study of European governance and its functionally structured regimes.[130]

On the credit side, new institutionalism raises challenging, if not fascinating, research questions about the institutional dynamics of macro-political order-building; the consequences of institutional form; the impact of constitutive norms on policy and performance; the ways and means institutions structure the interaction between different actors, shape their choices and influence their behaviour; the relationship between institutional continuity and change; the interplay between institutional affirmation and transformation; the intrinsic and extrinsic importance of institutional settings, and so on. Yet, it is imperative that the central institutionalist tenet – that institutions matter – be further qualified. As Lane and Ersson succinctly put it, 'The crucial question in relation to the new institutionalism is: important – yes, but for what?'[131] Their comparative research also raises serious questions about (regime) performance and (institutional) causality:

> The new institutionalism, in its search for institutional effects, must remain aware of the problem of spurious correlations as well as the difficulty in separating cause from effect. All that we can arrive at are probability connections between institutions, on the one hand, and outputs and outcomes, on the other, where one cannot jump to any conclusions about causality. First, factors other than institutions may be at work. Policy outputs and outcomes tend to depend upon party preferences, people's cultures and social forces . . . Second, outcomes may cause institutions, meaning that we face the difficult problem of causal interpretation, when two entities go together in constant conjunction, which one is the cause and which one is the effect.[132]

In relation, finally, to European polity-formation, and before we move on to the comparativist turn in EU studies, Olsen's architectural analogy is worth quoting at length:

> Building European institutions of governance may be compared to building San Pietro in Vatican – Saint Peter's Basilica. Some trace its history nearly two thousand years back, and even the current (new) Basilica took generations to build. There have been many builders, popes and architects, as well as artists and workers. Plans have been made, modified and rejected. There have been conflicts over designs and over the use of resources. There have been shifting economic and political conditions and changing cultural norms, including religious beliefs and fashions of architecture. Such factors have affected both the motivation and ability to develop the Basilica. Yet, as parts have been

added, modified and even demolished, the project has had a dynamic of its own, constraining both the physical development, the use of, and meaning of, the Basilica.[133]

Capturing the comparativist turn

What light might a comparative investigation throw on the emerging European polity? This question has sparked the imagination of comparative political scientists post-SEA in evaluating the structural transformation in the workings and political orientation of the regional system from market-making to polity-building. The resulting 'comparativist turn' in EU studies reflected the outcome of a conscious scholarly effort to reassert the importance of comparative theorizing by extending the logic and method of comparative political analysis to a field that remained heavily dependent on international relations theory. But what is the methodological justification for comparative political science?

To start with, comparative political analysis is as old as the study of politics itself. For example, Aristotle studied the political constitution of the Greek city-states, while Herodotus compared the Greek to the (then known) non-Greek world. Despite, however, being the subject of intellectual curiosity for centuries now, the study of comparative politics has only recently started to attract serious attention.[134] Today, comparison is considered by many as the 'principal method' in political science for testing theoretical arguments (and hypotheses), despite the fact that setting the boundaries of comparison is in itself problematic. This raises the question of what we mean by comparative political research. According to Rose's working definition, the comparative method involves the presentation of 'empirical evidence of some kind in an attempt to compare systematically and explicitly political phenomena'.[135] *Grosso modo*, comparative analysis claims to bestow a greater degree of specificity on political science research, to avoid the framing of ill-founded or arbitrary hypotheses about the 'exceptionalism' of the case study, and to clarify the principal causes responsible for the way in which a particular system, be it a single country or a group of countries, operates in relation to others, or performs the tasks assigned to it by making evident both similarities and differences. But since no single comparative method, however specific or panoramic its focus may be, is perfect, one is rather inclined to speak of different strategies, interpretations, research designs and forms of comparative analysis such as statistical, qualitative, empirical, normative, narrative, descriptive and so on. It thus follows that the range of possibilities employed by comparativist researchers for the conduct of their respective investigations is undoubtedly wide.

Blalock, among others, has argued that one of the fundamental problems of the social sciences is the failure to dismiss theories that do not adequately explain.[136] Indeed, most comparativists tend to treat theories as tools to frame and explain empirical puzzles. Yet, at one end of the methodological spectrum, are those inspired by a variety of reflexivist claims in the post-positivist tradition, doubting the value of causal explanations altogether and thus of conventional comparative theorizing. At the other extreme, are those who claim that all social actors, including those operating within the political space, are first and foremost rational utility-maximizers. It is in between these two poles that most comparativists rest, pursuing theoretically informed empirical analysis through diverse conceptual lenses and by means of utilizing a variety of data, qualitative or quantitative (with some scholars being driven by a firm commitment to causal generalizations).[137]

According to Mackie and Marsh, there exist three types of comparative analysis: case studies, systematic comparisons of a limited number of cases and global statistical analysis.[138] Peters, however, offers a more comprehensive approach by identifying five types of studies. They include: single country description of politics; analysis of similar processes and institutions in a limited number of countries; studies developing typologies or other forms of classification schemes for countries or subnational units; statistical or descriptive analysis of data from a subset of countries testing some hypothesis about the relationship of variables within that 'sample'; and statistical analysis of all countries attempting to develop patterns and/or test relationships across the entire range of political systems.[139] Despite their differences, all the above types constitute viable components of comparative analysis. Moreover, it is important to note that the comparability of political phenomena, whether strictly confined within national boundaries (intra-systemic) or extending beyond or even alongside traditional state structures (cross-systemic), becomes a crucial organizing principle for any reliable, 'focused' and 'structured' comparative investigation[140] – by 'focused' is meant that the research in question deals selectively with certain aspects of the case study, employing general questions to guide analysis.[141]

In developing the comparativist argument, former US President Wilson wrote that 'our own institutions can be understood and appreciated only by those who know other systems of government . . . By the use of a thorough comparative and historical method . . . a general clarification of views may be obtained.'[142] Although in the context of comparative politics Wilson's definition meant almost entirely descriptive institutional analysis, the study of political institutions and processes may well be comparative-historical, emphasizing both the 'path dependency' of political life and the impact of institutions on social and political developments. It is also widely acknowledged in the literature that any comparative analysis is dependent on the selection of the case studies which, in turn, rely on the justificatory logic of the research design itself. Out of several methods and possibilities of selection, there are mainly two research designs which maximize the uses of comparison: the 'most different' and the 'most similar' systems designs. International experience shows that the majority of comparativists have opted for the latter when selecting on the *explanandum* or the 'dependent variable' – i.e. what is to be explained – as well as on the lessons to be drawn (and learned) from the comparative exercise. But what is equally crucial for the 'quality' of the research product is that the choice of designs and, hence, of the case studies themselves, should not be based on the principle of convenience, but rather should reflect the outcome of a well-thought-out process of selection in relation to the nature of the type of comparative results to be sought.[143] All in all, comparative research focuses on analytical relations among variables. Although such a focus is subject to modification by differences in the observation and measurement of these variables, once the value of the comparison is established, it is the researcher's responsibility to avoid pitfalls in the formulation of 'laws', 'tendencies' or 'predictions'.

Comparative politics has been traditionally confined to the study of political systems or regimes – taken, in the broadest sense of the terms, as forms of government – that were either fully invested with the constitutional properties of statehood or were in the process of acquiring them; as, for instance, in comparative research on political movements aspiring to the formal attributes of stateness or in the comparative study of stateless nations. The general focus has been, mainly but not exclusively, on what might be called the formal institutions of (again mainly) territorial government, as well as on the lessons to be learnt and insights to be drawn from the comparative exposition of structural, functional and behavioural properties embedded in the political processes and policy arenas of national polities. Put differently, the bulk of comparative political research has been on the limits and possibilities of establishing patterns or lines of correspondence among different systems or models of domestic (intrastate) governance.

There is no doubt that a shift in emphasis from the domestic arena to transnational units could not but confront comparative political analysts with a new set of challenges. Of which, one of the most intriguing is to conceptualize the Union in political systemic terms and, hence, to challenge the continued dominance of international theory in the study of European integration. Signs of such a disciplinary precedence have been invariably, even triumphantly, epitomized for years by the likes of (neo)functionalism and (neo)realism, to mention but two alternative modes of theorizing the European experience. It never looked, however, as if the days of international relations approaches were numbered, for the Union, a multi-state entity itself,[144] is almost by default a system of polities – a sympolity – within which the international dimension of politics, both as a condition and as a process for organizing, structuring and ordering public life, will remain an essential and, as many relevant paradigms confidently assert, an integral part of its systemic properties.

On top of this, there are still fundamental questions about the appropriate role and 'operational capabilities' of the Union in world politics and economics, especially following the seismic changes in the international system since the late 1980s. Such changes have brought about the collapse of the bipolar 'overlay', the remaking of world orders, the pluralization of sovereign statehood, the mushrooming of semi-sovereign peoples, and last but not least the disintegration (or de-federation) of multi-ethnic states like the former Soviet Union and Yugoslavia. Likewise, there are still important issues to be raised by integration theorists, who draw their insights from the conceptual apparatus and methodological arsenal of international political analysis, concerning the relationship between the pursuit of national (domestic) interests and their accommodation in mutually acceptable compromises or negotiated package-deals; the role of international bureaucracies in furthering the scope and level of collective governance; the problem-solving and crisis-management capacities of international institutions; the dynamics of large-scale community-formation in relation to new norms of transnational governance; the ever-pertinent issue of domestic compliance to international regulations and so on. Although this list could be indefinitely extended, the point is made about the explanatory potential of international relations theory, both as a generic analytical framework and as a specific intellectual venue for studying the behaviour and patterns of interaction among states, between states and non-state actors, and among a fast-growing number of institutionalized bodies within an ever-globalizing, if not already globalized, civil society.

But it would be no less myopic authoritatively to proclaim international relations as the natural 'disciplinary homeland', to use Rosamond's words, of EU studies. For the recent comparativist contribution to EU theorizing – taking the European polity both as a multi-level system of formal/institutionalized rule and an arena of informal/functionalist-driven policy interactions – has been a much-welcomed development. All the more so, if one takes into account that such theorizing has been instrumental in enriching an already impressive methodological laboratory so that a more profound understanding of present-day European governance arrangements can be reached. Writers like Sbragia, Watts, Wessels, Bulmer, Kirshner, Forsyth, Elazar and Lister, among others, have furthered our insights into the Union's political properties and constitutional design in comparison to other federal and confederal polities. Terms like cooperative federalism, inverse federalism, *Politikverflechtung*, *Kooperativer Staaten*, *Staatenverbund*, confederence, segmented federalism, compound or composite polity and the rest, all have in common a view of the Union as a pluralist political formation, whose emerging and increasingly overlapping structures of governance rest on complex and multi-level policy interactions through formal and *ad hoc* negotiations among state and non-state, local and transnational actors.

From these comparative investigations, we have learnt a lot about the nature of constitutive autonomy within federal political orders; the relationship between central and constituent governments; the formulation of policies with varying effects on the subunits; the allocation of competences among competing decision-making centres; the strategies employed by interest associations in joint lobbying activities at the central (federal) level; the operation of different democratic procedures among parliamentary and executive institutions; the legitimation of political authority in multi-level (and multi-ethnic) polities; the nature of compound – territorial and non-territorial – representation; different forms for the protection of minority rights and consensual outcomes and so on. In general, what is highly instructive about comparative federalism as applied to contemporary EU studies is that it helps us to grasp how to reconcile the concurrent demands for unity and diversity within the evolving process of a union based on majoritarian and unit-veto arrangements.

Comparative federalism is not interested in transplanting a particular form of government from the experience of contemporary federal states to the Union, but rather focuses on the insights that can be drawn from the systematic examination of comparable exercises in institution-building, territorial and non-territorial interest representation, joint decision-making (and its potential traps), multiple identity-holding and, more recently, demos-formation. In this context, too, the point has been clearly made by comparative analysts that, however unique the Union appears to be as a multi-level political system of a more or less (con)federalist orientation, the study of political integration in contemporary Europe should not be left outside the wider concerns of the kind of pluralist political science that is sympathetic to the principle of interdisciplinarity. Hence Sbragia's remark that 'the study of the Community could both be incorporated into and contribute to the study of comparative politics rather than be isolated from the general conceptual and theoretical concerns of political scientists interested in comparing political systems'.[145]

In defence of the comparative method, Hix has prompted comparativists 'to take up their pens and challenge the dominance of the international approaches', by arguing that there is no reason why EU 'politics' should not be seen as 'inherently different to the study practice of government in any democratic system', and that there is no need to develop a general theory of the 'internal' politics of the Union, as we do not have an overarching theory of German, American, Italian or any other country-specific politics.[146] Rather, captured in conventional political systemic terms, the Union becomes yet another polity 'dominated by questions of representation and participation, the distribution and allocation of resources, and political and administrative efficiency'.[147] This way, its study becomes open to the comparative scrutiny of political scientists on such mainstream areas of comparative research as legislative behaviour, party-political alignments, cleavage-formation, informal exchanges, distributional conflicts, interest intermediation and articulation, competence allocation, constitution-making, market regulation and so on.

Writing on the credit side of the comparativist turn, Rosamond points out that:

the discussion between comparative policy analysis and EU studies is likely to generate a mutually beneficial intellectual conversation . . . [This way] scholars of the EU . . . will avoid two fundamental caricatures of the EU: the focus on singular moments of change or crisis and the tendency to portray the dynamics of integration as centering on an opposition between the poles of nation-state and 'superstate'.[148]

It logically follows that any 'either/or' way of thinking about the process of European 'integration' or 'polity-formation' – as international and comparative approaches would respectively have it – should be dismissed from the outset on the grounds that the evolving EU reality deviates both from the Westphalian 'system of states' model and the traditional paradigm of the liberal constitutional state. Instead, present-day EU politics is as much about the daily running of regulatory policy-making – so clearly exemplified by Majone's writings[149] – as it is about the rather more startling but also more sporadic instances of 'high' politics in the form of 'history-making' episodes and/or 'grand constitutional' moments. In addition to this, there is a more general case to be made against the separation of 'high' and 'low' politics issues. Risse-Kappen explains:

> Comparative foreign policy analysis shows . . . that the distinction between 'low' and 'high' politics is flawed. On the one hand, executive control over foreign policy depends to a large degree on the nature of the political institutions and domestic structures in general . . . On the other hand, 'high' politics issues such as foreign policy might well become politicized in the domestic sphere similarly to 'low' politics.[150]

It is rather ironic that the very antagonism between these two dominant paradigms renders them as complementary intellectual tools to the search for adequate explanations, conceptual categories and analytical propositions in the study of European integration. In the end, the lesson to be drawn from this discussion is that neither of the two approaches is *a priori* intellectually privileged over the other. For they both raise equally legitimate questions about the ontology and epistemology of the same complex phenomenon that remains, after half a century of systematic theorizing, essentially contested. As Puchala might have put it, they both capture different parts of the 'elephant'. In both fields, attempts to generate theoretically relevant scholarship may have more of either a macro- or a micro-focus: international relations and comparative politics theories range from the systemic to the individual level, although, post-1989, one could argue that contemporary events are moving us to macro-level theory-building and towards a new kind of area studies that, according to Katzenstein, connect comparative and international research.[151]

Focusing on European integration as a distinct form of regionalism cutting across societal, state and disciplinary boundaries, to explain and understand the emerging European polity requires the bridging of comparative and international analysis. All too often, for instance, international scholarship calls for a blurring of the distinctions between political economy, security and, increasingly, culture.[152] The same can be said of the renewed interest in transnational relations and international institutions by international relations scholarship, embracing the impact of both domestic and international structures and actors and interests in determining outcomes.[153] Likewise, there has been a revival of comparative policy analysis of vertical and horizontal, symmetrical and asymmetrical interactions, the result of which has been a reconceptualization of European policy-making away from the Weberian model of the hierarchical state – characterized by rational bureaucracies, centralized authority and clearly defined spheres of territorial jurisdiction[154] – and closer to a polycentric and multi-logical pattern of governance based on formal and informal practices, private and public actors, and intermediating policy structures. Comparative studies of the Europeanization of domestic policy arenas are a good case in point. But the linkage between international relations and comparative politics is also justified by the growing importance of the global marketplace and the view that governments can no longer govern in ways they have been accustomed to in the past.[155] Here, although the logic of comparison does not *stricto sensu* fit Peters's general typology which mainly concerns country-specific or cross-country studies, it does add to the spectrum of comparative theorizing, by virtue of involving, if not requiring, the analysis of both domestic politics and international relations. As Gourevitch succinctly put it, 'The international system is not only a consequence of domestic politics and structures, but a cause of them . . . International relations and domestic politics are therefore so interrelated that they should be analyzed simultaneously, as wholes.'[156]

The case is thus made for an open and constructive discourse on the uses of international and comparative theory in the domain of EU studies. The links between the two should be kept and strengthened, and so should the pluralism within the discipline as a whole. Otherwise, its very liveliness will be greatly impaired and with it the prospects for developing new and better ways of thinking about Europe's integrative journey. This last observation leads us on to the next chapter which, in the hope of contributing to the transcendence of the 'international-comparativist' divide, explores the insights that can be drawn from consociational theory for the study of the Union, and the implications of the Amsterdam reforms for the relationship between the collectivity and the segments.

Notes and references

1 See particularly D. Mutimer, '1992 and the Political Integration of Europe: Neofunctionalism Reconsidered', *Journal of European Integration*, 13, no. 1, 1989, pp. 75–101; and J. Tranholm-Mikkelsen, 'Neo-functionalism: Obstinate or Obsolete? A Reappraisal in the Light of the New Dynamism of the EC', *Millennium*, 20, no. 1, 1991, pp. 1–22.

2 See R. O. Keohane and S. Hoffmann, 'Institutional Change in Europe in the 1980s', in R. O. Keohane and S. Hoffmann (eds), *The New European Community: Decisionmaking and Institutional Change*, Boulder, CO: Westview Press, 1991, pp. 1–39; and W. Sandholtz and J. Zysman, '1992: Recasting the European Bargain', *World Politics*, 42, no. 1, 1989, pp. 95–128.

3 M. Forsyth, 'Federalism and Confederalism', in C. Brown (ed.), *Political Restructuring in Europe: Ethical Perspectives*, London and New York: Routledge, 1994, pp. 54–5.

4 P. Taylor, *The European Union in the 1990s*, Oxford: Oxford University Press, 1996, p. 178.

5 R. Dehousse, 'Constitutional Reform in the European Community: Are There Alternatives to the Majority Rules?, in J. Hayward (ed.), *The Crisis of Representation in Europe*, London: Frank Cass, 1995, p. 118.

6 P. C. Schmitter, 'Imagining the Future of the Euro-polity with the Help of New Concepts', in G. Marks et al. (eds), *Governance in the European Union*, London: Sage, 1996, p. 150.

7 P. Taylor, *International Organization in the Modern World: The Regional and the Global Process*, London: Pinter, 1993, p. 94.

8 Leo Tindemans' Report to the European Council, *Bulletin of the European Communities*, supplement 1–1976.

9 M. Forsyth, 'The Political Theory of Federalism: The Relevance of Classical Approaches', in J. J. Hesse and V. Wright (eds), *Federalizing Europe? The Costs, Benefits, and Preconditions of Federal Political Systems*, Oxford: Oxford University Press, 1996, p. 28.

10 S. Hix, 'The Study of the European Community: The Challenge to Comparative Politics', *West European Politics*, no. 17, no. 4, 1994, pp. 1–30.

11 B. Rosamond, *Theories of European Integration*, Basingstoke: Macmillan, 2000, p. 2.

12 B. Laffan et al., *Europe's Experimental Union: Rethinking Integration*, London and New York: Routledge, 1999, p. 74.

13 Ibid., p. 98.

14 Ibid.

15 M. Newman, *Democracy, Sovereignty and the European Union*, New York: St Martin's Press, 1996, pp. 19–22.

16 S. Hix, 'The Study of the European Union II: The "New Governance" Agenda and its Rival', *Journal of European Public Policy*, 5, no. 1, 1998, pp. 38–65; J. Caporaso, 'Regional Integration Theory: Understanding our Past and Anticipating our Future', *Journal of European Public Policy*, 5, no. 1, 1998 pp. 1–16. For an overview, see also L. Cram, *Policy-making in the European Union: Conceptual Lenses and the Integration Process*, London and New York: Routledge, 1997.

17 D. J. Elazar, *Constitutionalizing Globalization: The Postmodern Revival of Confederal Arrangements*, Lanham: Rowman and Littlefield, 1998, p. 55.
18 J. Caporaso, 'The European Union and Forms of State: Westphalian, Regulatory or Post-modern?', *Journal of Common Market Studies*, 34, no. 1, 1996, p. 30. On the latter interpretation, see J. Rosenau, 'Governance, Order and Change in World Order', in J. Rosenau (ed.), *Governance without Government: Order and Change in World Politics*, Cambridge: Cambridge University Press, 1992, pp. 1–29.
19 Forsyth, 'Political Theory of Federalism', p. 41.
20 R. A. Wessel, 'The International Legal Status of the European Union', *European Foreign Affairs*, 2, 1997, p. 114.
21 Taylor, *International Organization*, p. 99.
22 Taylor, *European Union in the 1990s*, p. 181.
23 Ibid., p. 182.
24 European Community, 'Report of the Council of Ministers on the Functioning of the Treaty on European Union', April 1995, Annex IV; quoted in Laffan et al., *Europe's Experimental Union*, p. 83.
25 This formulation draws on S. D. Krasner, 'Structural Causes and Regime Consequences: Regimes as Intervening Variables', in S. D. Krasner (ed.), *International Regimes*, Ithaca, NY: Cornell University Press, 1983, p. 2.
26 S. Bulmer and A. Scott, 'Introduction', in S. Bulmer and A. Scott (eds), *Economic and Political Integration in Europe: Internal Dynamics and Global Context*, Oxford: Blackwell, 1994, p. 8.
27 Laffan et al., *Europe's Experimental Union*, p. 78.
28 See D. N. Chryssochoou, *Democracy in the European Union*, London and New York: I. B. Tauris, 1998.
29 P. Demaret, 'The Treaty Framework', in D. O'Keeffe and P. M. Twomey (eds), *Legal Issues of the Maastricht Treaty*, London: Wiley Chancery Law, 1994, p. 6.
30 Forsyth, 'Political Theory of Federalism', p. 37.
31 Ibid., pp. 37–8.
32 R. Pryce, 'The Maastricht Treaty and the New Europe', in A. Duff et al. (eds), *Maastricht and Beyond: Building the European Union*, London: Routledge, 1994, p. 3.
33 H. Wallace, 'European Governance in Turbulent Times', *Journal of Common Market Studies*, 31, no. 3, 1993, p. 294.
34 Schmitter, 'Imagining the Future', p. 122.
35 P. Taylor, *The Limits of European Integration*, New York: Columbia University Press, 1983, p. 114.
36 Schmitter, 'Imagining the Future', p. 127.
37 G. Ress, 'Democratic Decision-making in the European Union and the Role of the European Parliament', in D. Curtin and T. Heukels (eds), *Institutional Dynamics of European Integration: Essays in Honour of Henry G. Schermers*, Vol. II, Dortrecht: Martinus Nijhoff, 1994, p. 156.
38 C. Archer, *International Organizations*, 2nd edn, London: Routledge, 1992, p. 37.
39 Rosamond, *Theories of European Integration*, p. 30.
40 P. C. Schmitter, 'Federalism and the Euro-polity', *Journal of Democracy*, 11, no. 1, 2000, p. 45.
41 Taylor, *European Union in the 1990s*, p. 7.
42 Forsyth, 'Political Theory of Federalism', p. 40.

43 P. M. Leslie, 'The Cultural Dimension', in Hesse and Wright (eds), *Federalizing Europe?*, pp. 121–65.

44 Taylor, *European Union in the 1990s*, p. 190.

45 M. Forsyth, 'Towards a New Concept of Confederation', in *The Modern Concept of Confederation*, European Commission for Democracy through Law, Council of Europe, Conference Proceedings, 1995, p. 66.

46 Taylor, *European Union in the 1990s*, p. 75.

47 Ibid., p. 180.

48 G. Majone, 'The Regulatory State and its Legitimacy Problems', *West European Politics*, 22, no. 1, 1999, pp. 18–19.

49 For details, see S. Stavridis, 'Democracy in Europe: West and East', in *People's Rights and European Structures*, Manresa: Centre Unesco de Catalunya, Conference Proceedings, September 1993, p. 130.

50 K. Neunreither, 'The Syndrome of Democratic Deficit in the European Community', in G. Parry (ed.), *Politics in an Interdependent World: Essays Presented to Ghita Ionescu*, London: Edward Elgar, 1994, p. 96.

51 F. K. Lister, *The European Union, the United Nations and the Revival of Confederal Governance*, Westport, CT: Greenwood Press, 1996, p. 73.

52 Quoted in ibid., p. 75.

53 Schmitter, 'Imagining the Future', p. 130.

54 P. C. Schmitter, 'A Revised Theory of Regional Integration', in L. N. Lindberg and S. A Scheingold (eds), *Regional Integration: Theory and Research*, Cambridge, MA: Harvard University Press, 1971, p. 242.

55 A. Moravcsik, 'Negotiating the Single Act', in Keohane and Hoffmann (eds), *The New European Community*, pp. 41–84.

56 Rosamond, *Theories of European Integration*, p. 143.

57 A. Moravcsik, 'Preferences and Power in the European Community: A Liberal Intergovernmentalist Approach', *Journal of Common Market Studies*, 31, no. 4, 1993, pp. 473–524.

58 Ibid., p. 507.

59 R. D. Putnam, 'Diplomacy and Domestic Politics: The Logic of Two-level Games', *International Organization*, 42, no. 3, 1988, pp. 427–60.

60 Rosamond, *Theories of European Integration*, p. 136.

61 Moravcsik, 'Preferences and Power', p. 481.

62 Ibid., p. 473.

63 Rosamond, *Theories of European Integration*, pp. 144–7. See also G. Garrett and G. Tsembelis, 'An Institutionalist Critique of Intergovernmentalism', *International Organization*, 46, no. 2, 1996, pp. 269–73; and D. Wincott, 'Institutional Interaction and European Integration: Towards an Everyday Critique of Liberal Intergovernmentalism', *Journal of Common Market Studies*, 33, no. 4, 1995, pp. 597–609.

64 Moravcsik, 'Preferences and Power', p. 408.

65 S. Bulmer, 'New Institutionalism, the Single Market and EU Governance', ARENA Working Papers, no. WP 97/25, 1997, p. 2. Cf. R. A. W. Rhodes, 'The New Governance: Governing without Government', *Political Studies*, 44, no. 5, 1996, pp. 652–67.

66 G. Marks et al., 'European Integration from the 1980s: State-centric *v.* Multi-level Governance', *Journal of Common Market Studies*, 34, no. 3, 1996, p. 342.

67 Ibid., pp. 342–3.

68 B. Kohler-Koch, 'Catching Up with Change: The Transformation of

Governance in the European Union', *Journal of European Public Policy*, 3, no. 3, 1996, p. 363. On the effectiveness of the Luxembourg veto, see A. Teasdale, 'The Life and Death of the Luxembourg Compromise', *Journal of Common Market Studies*, 31, no. 4, 1993, pp. 567–79.

69 Marks et al., 'European Integration from the 1980s', p. 367.

70 Ibid., p. 372.

71 L. Hooghe, 'Subnational Mobilisation in the European Union', in J. Hayward (ed.), *The Crisis of Representation in Europe*, London: Frank Cass, 1995, p. 176.

72 W. Wallace, 'Collective Governance', in H. Wallace and W. Wallace (eds), *Policy-making in the European Union*, 4th edn, Oxford: Oxford University Press, 2000, p. 532.

73 Marks et al., 'European Integration from the 1980s', p. 372.

74 G. Marks et al., 'Competencies, Cracks and Conflicts: Regional Mobilization in the European Union', in Marks et al. (eds), *Governance in the European Union*, p. 41.

75 Kohler-Koch, 'Catching Up with Change', p. 371.

76 Marks et al., 'Competencies, Cracks and Conflicts', p. 63.

77 Hooghe, 'Substantial Mobilisation', p. 178. For the second quotation, see ibid, p. 61.

78 Ibid., p. 177.

79 Ibid., p. 178.

80 Marks et al., 'Competencies, Cracks and Conflicts', p. 62.

81 J. Peterson, 'Decision-making in the European Union: Towards a Framework of Analysis', *Journal of European Public Policy*, 2, no. 1, 1995, pp. 69–93. Likewise, Sandholtz notes that in attempting to answer the evolution of the EU system from an interstate agreement to a multi-level polity, 'it is probably pointless to seek a single theory of European integration . . . Rather, we should probably admit that different kinds of theories are appropriate for different pieces of the EU puzzle'; see W. Sandholtz, 'Membership Matters: Limits of the Functional Approach to European Institutions', *Journal of Common Market Studies*, 34, no. 3, 1996, p. 405. On the merits of middle-range theories, see R. K. Merton, *Social Theory and Social Structure*, New York: Free Press, 1957, pp. 3–16.

82 J. Peterson, 'Policy Networks and European Union Policy Making: A Reply to Kassim', *West European Politics*, 18, no. 2, 1995, p. 391; quoted in Rosamond, *Theories of European Integration*, p. 123.

83 J. Richardson, 'Policy-making in the EU: Interests, Ideas and Garbage Cans of Primeval Soup', in J. Richardson (ed.), *European Union: Power and Policy-making*, London and New York: Routledge, 1996.

84 Rosamond, *Theories of European Integration*, p. 125. For a recent critique and revision of Peterson's model, see A. Warleigh, 'History Repeating? Framework Theory and Europe's Multi-level Confederation', *Journal of European Integration*, 22, no. 2, 2000, pp. 173–200.

85 T. Christiansen, 'Reconstructing European Space: From Territorial Politics to Multilevel Governance', in K-E. Jørgensen (ed.), *Reflective Approaches to European Governance*, Basingstoke: Macmillan, 1997, p. 65.

86 Rosamond, *Theories of European Integration*, p. 111.

87 J. N. Rosenau, 'Pre-theories and Theories of Foreign Policy', in R. B. Farrell (ed.), *Approaches to Comparative and International Politics*, Evaston, IL: Northwestern University Press 1966, pp. 65; quoted in C. Pentland,

International Theory and European Integration, London: Faber and Faber, 1973, p. 222.

88 Ibid., pp. 63–4; quoted in Pentland, *International Theory*, p. 222.

89 K. E. Jørgensen, 'Studying European Integration in the 1990s', *Journal of European Public Policy*, 3, no. 3, 1997, p. 487.

90 J. Joffe, 'Rethinking the Nation-state: The Many Meanings of Sovereignty', *Foreign Affairs*, 78, no. 6, 1999, p. 122.

91 Marks et al., 'Competencies, Cracks and Conflicts', p. 45. Cf. M. Grodzins, 'American Political Parties and the American System', in A. Wildavsky (ed.), *American Federalism in Perspective*, Boston: Little Brown, 1967, pp. 127–46.

92 D. Deudney, 'Binding Sovereigns: Authorities, Structures, and Geopolitics in Philadelphian Systems', in T. Biersteker and C. Weber (eds), State Sovereignty as Social Construct, Cambridge: Cambridge University Press, 1996, p. 229. This point is drawn from R. Prokhovnik, 'The State of Liberal Sovereignty', *British Journal of Politics and International Relations*, 1, no. 1, 1999, p. 75.

93 A. S. Milward, *The European Rescue of the Nation State*, London: Routledge, 1992.

94 S. Bulmer, 'Domestic Politics and European Community Policy-making', *Journal of Common Market Studies*, 21, no. 4, 1983, pp. 349–63.

95 W. Wessels, 'An Ever Closer Fusion? A Dynamic Macropolitical View on Integration Processes', *Journal of Common Market Studies*, 35, no. 2, 1997, pp. 267–99.

96 F. W. Scharpf, 'The Joint-decision Trap: Lessons from German Federalism and European Integration', *Public Administration*, 66, no. 3, 1988, pp. 239–78.

97 E. Kirchner, *Decision Making in the European Community: The Council Presidency and European Integration*, Manchester: Manchester University Press, 1992. On the impact of European integration on the German federal system, see K. H. Goetz, 'National Governance and European Integration: Intergovernmental Relations in Germany', *Journal of Common Market Studies*, 33, no. 1, 1995, pp. 91–116.

98 Joffe, 'Re-thinking the Nation-state', p. 123.

99 Quoted in ibid.

100 W. Wessels, 'The EC Council: The Community's Decisionmaking Centre', in Keohane and Hoffmann (eds), *The New European Community*, p. 153.

101 M. Smith, 'The European Union and a Changing Europe: Establishing the Boundaries of Order', *Journal of Common Market Studies*, 34, no. 1, 1996, p. 9.

102 On this point, see M. Jachtenfuchs, 'Theoretical Perspectives on European Governance', *European Law Journal*, 1, no. 2, 1994, pp. 115–33.

103 Rosamond, *Theories of European Integration*, p. 152–3.

104 R. Cox, 'Social Forces, States and World Orders', in R. O. Keohane (ed.), *Neorealism and its Critics*, New York: Columbia University Press, 1986, p. 223; quoted in Smith, 'European Union', p. 13.

105 S. Tarrow, 'Building a Composite Polity: Popular Contention in the European Union', Institute for European Studies Working Paper, no. 98/3, Cornell University, 1998, p. 14.

106 Ibid.

107 For a good introduction on new institutionalism, see B. G. Peters, *Institutional Theory in Political Science: The 'New Institutionalism'*, London and New York: Pinter, 1999.

108 Tarrow, 'Building a Composite Polity', p. 15.
109 A. Moravcsik, 'Preferences and Power in the European Community: A Liberal Intergovernmentalist Approach', *Journal of Common Market Studies*, 31, no. 4, 1993, p. 508. See also A. Moravcsik, *The Choice for Europe: Social Purposes and State Power from Messina to Maastricht*, Ithaca, NY: Cornell University Press, 1998, pp. 60–7.
110 Laffan et al., *Europe's Experimental Union*, p. 84.
111 S. Bulmer, 'The Governance of the European Union: A New Institutionalist Approach', *Journal of Public Policy*, 13, no. 4, 1993, pp. 351–80.
112 J-E. Lane and S. Ersson, *The New Institutional Politics: Performance and Outcomes*, London and New York: Routledge, 2000, p. 27. Cf. J. March and J. Olsen, *Rediscovering Institutions: The Organizational Basis of Politics*, New York: Free Press, 1989.
113 Bulmer, 'The Governance of the European Union', p. 353.
114 Ibid., p. 355.
115 Ibid.
116 Ibid., p. 370.
117 Rosamond, *Theories of European Integration*, p. 114.
118 J. P. Olsen and B. G. Peters, 'Learning from Experience', ARENA Reprints, no. 96/5, 1996, p. 28.
119 J. P. Olsen, 'Organising European Institutions of Governance: A Prelude to an Institutional Account of Political Integration', ARENA Working Papers, no. WP 00/2, 2000, p. 10.
120 Ibid., p. 14.
121 Bulmer, 'New Institutionalism', p. 7.
122 Rosamond, *Theories of European Integration*, p. 114. See also P. Hall and R. Taylor, 'Political Science and the Three Institutionalisms', *Political Studies*, 44, no. 5, 1996, pp. 936–57; V. Lowndes, 'Varieties of New Institutionalism: A Critical Appraisal', *Public Administration*, 74, no. 2, 1996, pp. 181–97; and J. March and J. Olsen, 'Institutional Perspectives on Political Institutions', *Governance*, 9, no. 3, 1984, pp. 247–64.
123 Ibid., pp. 115, 119.
124 Lane and Ersson, *New Institutional Politics*, p. 4.
125 Ibid., p. 3.
126 Ibid., p. 8.
127 Rosamond, *Theories of European Integration*, p. 116.
128 Lane and Ersson, *New Institutional Politics*, p. 9.
129 Bulmer, 'New Institutionalism', pp. 6–7. Cf. March and Olsen, *Rediscovering Institutions*, p. 26.
130 See, respectively, K. Armstrong and S. Bulmer, *The Governance of the Single European Market*, Manchester: Manchester University Press, 1998; P. Pierson, 'The Path to European Integration: A Historical Institutionalist Analysis', *Comparative Political Studies*, 29, no. 2, 1996, pp. 123–63; and M. A. Pollack, 'The New Institutionalism and EC Governance: The Promise and Limits of Institutional Analysis', *Governance*, 9, no. 4, 1996, pp. 429–58; and D. Wincott, 'The Role of the Law or the Rule of the Court of Justice? An 'Institutional' Account of Judicial Politics in the European Community', *Journal of European Public Policy*, 2, no. 4, 1995, pp. 583–602.
131 Lane and Ersson, *New Institutional Politics*, p. 20.
132 Ibid., p. 14.

133 Olsen, 'Organising European Institutions', pp. 20–1.
134 M. Kamrava, *Understanding Comparative Politics: A Framework for Analysis*, London and New York: Routledge, 1996, p. 7.
135 R. Rose, 'Comparing Forms of Comparative Analysis', *Political Studies*, 39, no. 3, 1991, p. 439.
136 H. Blalock, *Basic Dilemmas in the Social Sciences*, Beverly Hills, CA: Sage, 1984.
137 For more on the competing theoretical debates and why should the 'centre' hold, see A. Kohli, P. Evans, P. J. Katzenstein, A. Przeworski, S. Hoeber, J. C. Scott and T. Skocpol, 'The Role of Theory in Comparative Politics: A Symposium', *World Politics*, 48, no. 1, 1996, pp. 1–49.
138 T. Mackie and D. Marsh, 'The Comparative Method', in D. Marsh and G. Stoker (eds), *Theory and Methods in Political Science*, London: Macmillan, 1995, pp. 173–88.
139 B. G. Peters, *Comparative Politics: Theory and Methods*, London, Macmillan, 1998, p. 10.
140 R. Hague, M. Harrop and S. Breslin, *Comparative Government and Politics: An Introduction*, Basingstoke, Macmillan, 1992, pp. 39–40.
141 A. L. George, 'Case Studies and Theory Development: The Method of Structured, Focused Comparison', in P. G. Lauren (ed.), *Diplomacy: New Approaches in History, Theory and Policy*, New York: The Free Press, 1979, pp. 43–68.
142 W. Wilson, *The State: Elements of Historical and Practical Politics*, London: Isbister, 1899, p. xxxiv; quoted in R. A. W. Rhodes, 'The Institutional Approach', in D. Marsh and G. Stoker (eds), *Theory and Methods in Political Science*, London: Macmillan, 1995, p. 45. Cf. F. F. Ridley, *The Study of Politics: Political Science and Public Administration*, Oxford: Martin Robertson, 1975, pp. 7, 102.
143 Peters, *Comparative Politics*, p. 56;
144 Rosamond, *Theories of European Integration*, p. 153.
145 A. M. Sbragia, 'Thinking about the European Future: The Uses of Comparison', in A. M. Sbragia (ed.), *Euro-politics: Institutions and Policy-making in the 'New' European Community*, Washington, DC: The Brookings Institution, 1992, p. 267–8; quoted in Rosamond, *Theories of European Integration*, p. 105.
146 Hix, 'Study of the European Community', pp. 24, p. 1.
147 Ibid.
148 Rosamond, *Theories of European Integration*, p. 106.
149 See particularly G. Majone (ed.), *Regulating Europe*, London and New York: Routledge, 1996.
150 T. Risse-Kappen, Exploring the Nature of the Beast: International Relations Theory and Comparative Policy Analysis Meet the European Union', *Journal of Common Market Studies*, 34, no. 1, 1996, p. 57.
151 P. J. Katzenstein, 'Regionalism in Comparative Perspective', ARENA Working Papers, no. 1, 1996.
152 See P. J. Katzenstein (ed.), *The Culture of National Security: Norms and Identity in World Politics*, New York: Columbia University Press, 1996.
153 For a detailed account of this literature, see Risse-Kappen, 'Nature of the Beast', pp. 57–9.
154 Caporaso, 'European Union and Forms of State', p. 34. On the question of 'asymmetrical governance' in the EU, see M. O'Neill, 'Theorising the

European Union: Towards a Post-foundational Discourse', *Current Politics and Economics of Europe*, 9, no. 2, 1999, p. 125.

155 See, *inter alia*, S. Strange, *The Retreat of the State: The Diffusion of Power in the World Economy*, Cambridge: Cambridge University Press, 1996; W. Greider, *One World, Ready or Not: The Manic Logic of Global Capitalism*, New York: Simon and Schuster, 1997; and D. Held et al., *Global Transformations*, Cambridge: Polity Press, 1999.

156 P. Gourevitch, 'The Second Image Reversed: The International Sources of Domestic Politics', *International Organization*, 32, no. 4, 1978, p. 911.

5

Theorizing the European Consociation

Introduction

The themes examined in this chapter touch upon some of the issues that have been at the heart of integration scholarship for some time now: the changing conditions of sovereign statehood in contemporary Europe, the role of consensual and majoritarian modes of decision-making in determining integration outcomes, and the relationship between popular fragmentation and stable governance. Exploring these issues reflects a concern with consociational theory and its validity in portraying the Union as a system of consensus elite government within which the development of patterns of political co-determination among the member state executives has preserved, and even augmented, the sovereignty of their respective polities; albeit, often at the expense of mainstream democratic practices. Before examining in greater detail what this theory contains for the study of European integration today, let us trace its historical and conceptual evolution from Althusius's political philosophy to the contemporary comparative politics literature.

A preface to consociational theory

'Consociation' derives from the Latin *consociatio*, which means 'the action or fact of associating together' or 'union in fellowship'.[1] The term appears as early as 1603 in Althusius's *Politica Methodice Digesta*, partly as an attempt to analyse the process of new polity creation in the early seventeenth-century Low Countries, 'without either a strong governmental apparatus or an articulate national identity',[2] and partly as a response to Bodin's *Les six livres de la république* of 1576 and his novel conception of sovereignty.[3] Althusius, a major proponent of associational principles in the organization of public life, takes consociation to denote some kind of *contractus societatis* in which 'the constitutive parts of the state . . . retain not only the right to resist the ruler who broke the contract . . . but also the right to secede from one state and to make a contract with another'.[4] Consociation thus appears as a compound association of collectivities, and in Elazar's words 'a *universitas* composed of *collegia*',[5] which lacks genuine sovereignty of its own, with central political authority being evenly divided among the subunits so as to avoid the danger of segmental subordination. In this 'network' of multiple authorities, equal partnership, as opposed to segmental dominance or any other form of hegemonic control, emanates as a common defining property of consociational political systems.

For Althusius, politics denotes the art of associating people for the establishment and preservation of social life *qua* symbiosis. In the words of Carney: 'Symbiotic association involves something more than mere existence together . . . Wherever there is symbiosis there is also communication, or the sharing of things, services, right.'[6] Or, as Elazar puts it, 'Althusius' *Politica* . . . represented a theory of polity-building based on a polity as a compound political association established by its citizens through their primary associations on the basis of consent rather than a reified state imposed by a ruler or an elite.'[7] It thus follows that the application of Althusian principles to composite polities – 'developed out of a series of building blocks or self-governing cells . . . each of which is internally organized and linked to the others by some form of consensual relationship'[8] – is a means of enabling the peoples of diverse communities, republics, commonwealths and the like 'to live together on more than a Hobbesian basis'.[9]

The first modern exponent of consociationalism was Apter who, in his study of bureaucratic nationalism, defined this form of political organization as '*a joining together of constituent units which do not lose their identity when merging in some form of union*'.[10] According to Apter, the main elements of a consociation include: a pyramidal authority (with power being dispersed and shared between the parts and the whole); multiple loyalties (operating within a multi-level system of allegiances); the necessity for compromise (with policy being a commonly accepted minimal programme); pluralism (characterized by diverse and competing forces in society); and ideological diffuseness (as a means of cementing what would otherwise be simply a set of alliances).[11] He adds:

Consociational forms may range from a relatively loose confederation of groups and states to federal arrangements with a recognized structure. A characteristic feature of the consociational system is that its consensus derives from an acceptance of a common denominator or a shared set of interests by which groups are willing to interrelate. It is essentially a system of compromise and accommodation.[12]

But it was Lijphart who first stressed its stabilizing effects in plural societies characterized, in Sartori's words, by 'cumulative, reinforcing, and, specifically, "isolative" cleavages'.[13] Thereafter, consociationalism, comparable types of which are Lorwin's notion of 'segmented pluralism', Lehmbruch's models of *Proporzdemokratie* and *Konkordanzdemokratie*, and Bluhm's theory of 'contractarianism',[14] has tried to answer the question of how democratic forms of governance can survive in composite polities lacking commonly shared values, characterized instead by a fragmented social base. Stevenson explains: 'in such countries the population is segmented in subgroups, each represented by political elites who are trusted to bargain with other elites on behalf of the group's interests.'[15] Thus, the consociational model aims to strike a balance (or a meaningful correspondence) between 'positive-sum' and 'zero-sum' governing by means of replacing majoritarian modes of decision-making with 'joint consensual rule'. The emphasis here is on informal institutions of governance that structure elite behaviour.[16]

Reflecting on the 'paradoxical' nature of the Dutch polity, in combining political stability, religious differences and social fragmentation, Lijphart offered 'a refinement of pluralist theory'.[17] The thesis he put forward was that it is possible to achieve conditions of democratic political stability in 'plural', 'vertically segmented', 'communally divided' or 'fractionalized' societies if there is overarching cooperation among the segment elites based on a set of unwritten rules of the game.[18] By inducing from the rather restricted Dutch case, however, Lijphart developed a general model, if not indeed a grand theory, of 'consociational democracy', departing from classical pluralist theory in so far as the latter required 'criss-crossing conflicts and multiple loyalties to produce stability'.[19] Lijphart's theoretical system constitutes a major contribution to the comparative study of democratic regimes, not least because the mainstream pluralist approaches to the democratic process were not equipped to explain the preservation of democracy in conflict-laden polities. (Conversely, one of the questions raised within the pluralist camp was why some advanced countries that relied on democratic institutions have experienced conditions of political instability, such as the Weimar Republic, the Third and Fourth French Republics, as well as postwar Italy and Finland.)[20] Notably, consociational theory 'is not interested in the reasons for segmentation (the content of cleavages) but in their empirical existence'.[21] It focuses on elite-driven ways of transcending the immobilism caused by divisive and mutually reinforcing cleavages in society. Lijphart's general model, which is largely to do with political stability *per se*, rather than with democratic decision-making, consists of the following four defining properties: grand coalition, mutual veto, proportionality and segmental autonomy.[22] The combined effect of these distinctive political features, notes Boulle, 'give[s] rise to a system of power-sharing at the national level . . . and group autonomy at the subnational level'.[23]

Grand coalition refers to a 'summit diplomacy forum', a 'coalescent style of leadership', a 'coalition cabinet' or a 'grand council', where bargains are struck by what Dahrendorf called 'a cartel of elites'.[24] Although this arrangement allows for considerable variation in institutional terms, all societal segments should be proportionally represented in its structures. But its efficiency, i.e. its capacity to deliver consensual outcomes on divisive issues through elite accommodation, rests on a second structural require-ment: the existence of a mutual veto or 'negative minority rule', a practice that is synonymous with Calhoun's model of 'concurrent majorities'.[25] Lijphart made the case for a mutual veto on the following grounds: 'Although the grand coalition rule gives each segment a share of power at the central political level, this does not constitute a guarantee that it will not be outvoted by a majority when its vital interests are at stake.'[26] At the other extreme, Powell argues that mutual vetoes may be used by recalcitrant groups to block decisions 'to the great advantage of the supporters of the status quo and the disadvantage of the have-nots'.[27] As for the principle of proportionality, it ensures that all segments influence decisions in proportion to their numerical strength, in contrast to the 'winner-takes-all' outcomes that characterize the operation of majoritarian systems. The *locus classicus* in the latter case is the Westminster model based on strong executive dominance and adversarial politics among the major (party) political players, producing 'single-party simple majority govern-ments'.[28] Weiler et al. make the point well: 'Consociationalism rejects the democratic legitimacy of permanent minorityship which is possible, even likely, for a fragmented polity operating a pluralist, majoritarian election and voting system . . . [it] seems, thus, to enhance legitimacy in its inclusiveness and the broadening of ultimate consent to government.'[29] In a word, the tyranny of the minority is preferred to the dictatorship of the majority. Segmental autonomy completes the overall picture by allowing 'autonomous rule-making and rule application by each of them without interference from the others, or the joint authorities'.[30] A rather moderate interpretation of this condition is that consociational arrangements institute, if not guarantee, 'a framework within which dissenting minorities can be allowed eventually a measure of autonomy'.[31] Applied *in extremis*, however, the claim to self-governance may reinforce segmental cleavages through the institutionalization of a form of 'personal jurisdiction', whereby 'each . . . segment is enabled to take decisions on matters of exclusive concern to it'.[32]

These, then, are the defining properties of consociational democracy, whose successful operation 'presupposes not only a willingness on the part of elites to cooperate but also a capacity to solve the political problems of their countries'.[33] Apart therefore from the 'cooperative efforts' of rival group elites in the bargaining process, what is also required is the deployment of accommodationist techniques in the form of 'continuing procedural guarantees' to maintain overall systemic stability and, in Lijphart's words, 'counteract the centrifugal tendencies of cultural fragmentation'.[34] As Lane and Ersson have recently summarized the consociationalist predicament:

> These agreements or pacts need not be institutionally sanctioned or explicitly translated into institutions, as long as all important players are brought on board. What matters is the actual elite behaviour, consisting of all kinds of behaviour from participation in oversized governments or grand coalitions to the making of formal or informal pacts outside of government, which promote a mutual understanding of politics and policies, accommodating differences.[35]

Consociationalism, both as a process of consensual decision-making and as a pattern of elite behaviour, can be seen as a strategy of cooperative conflict resolution (and even of conflict prevention), whereby the elites transcend intergroup fragmentation through negotiated agreements or settlements based on a politics of accommodation. Thus, elite accommodation constitutes the main determinant of systemic stability, with politics itself becoming, in Hallowell's words, 'the institutionalized art of compromise'.[36] But where does the above leave us in terms of representative and responsible government? Should the striking of a political compromise be welcomed even when reached outside the realm of citizen participation in the affairs of the polity? Does public engagement in the democratic process practically constitute a hindrance to consociational outcomes? Do elite-driven political ends justify less democratic means of institutional accommodation?

First, consociational arrangements are not concerned with the development of a *Gemeinschaft* at the popular level and 'its structural concomitant, namely . . . "cross-cutting cleavages"'.[37] They require neither a 'sense of community', nor a popular affirmation of shared values, much less the existence of a single and undifferentiated demos united by the overarching power of a higher civic 'we-ness'. In fact, consociational regimes are defined by the very absence of the above conditions since there exist two or more distinct demoi and a positive aggregation of segmental interests hardly ever exists as such. Holden explains: 'Due to the fundamental nature of the sectional divisions and conflicts, demands cannot simply be aggregated or synthesised.'[38] Accordingly, consociationalism often 'ceases to be a theory about the nature of democratic decision making and becomes instead a theory about how much decision making remains possible in the face of grave difficulties'.[39] The development of attitudes and values among the 'decision-receivers' is of lesser importance compared with developments at the level of the 'decision-makers'. And even there, trust-building among the elites may not be comparable to that found in polities with relatively congruent public spaces. Equally, the process of 'macro-level loyalty building' should not be associated with the integration or amalgamation of the component publics into a common political form that overrides citizens' 'fixed primary loyalties'.[40] What is absolutely essential to the functionality and policy responsiveness of the plural polity is *a priori* acceptance of the need for cooperative shared rule among the group leaders. From this view, the praxis of politics rests on the realization that 'economic and political interests are best advanced by staying together in a sensibly arranged political union'.[41] As Taylor rightly observes, the irony of the situation lies in 'the need to generate enthusiasm for stability precisely because of the continuing threat of fragmentation'.[42] It is important to note here that the range, quality and consistency of such cooperative interplay among the elites – i.e. the extent to which the members of the elite cartel are prepared to commit themselves credibly to the working principles of mutual governance and the preservation of the integrity and cohesion of the general system – will in the end determine the effectiveness of the common institutions to accommodate the particular interests of the segments.

Moreover, conflict-regulating practices are employed by the participants in the grand coalition as 'closed', highlighting the elitist character of the regime and rendering the relationship between elites and the public highly problematic: overall demos control over elite activities is the exception rather than the rule of the political game, in contrast to Almond's 'Anglo-American' type of democracies where the existence of 'overlapping and crosscutting memberships' and a 'homogeneous political culture' make systems of collective accountability (or indirect demos control) easier to apply.[43] Instead, the underlying pattern in consociational polities is that each section of the fragmented citizen body exercises controlling functions over the dominant segment elites through its own procedures. Still, though, one cannot exclude the possibility that, by claiming that societal mobilization around sensitive or controversial issues will be detrimental to the interests of systemic stability itself, the members of the elite cartel may successfully exclude themselves from extensive public scrutiny through the institutions of *ex post* ruler accountability. In this context, 'the faith of democracy' lies more in a 'belief in the principle of compromise itself'[44] than in the principles of open and responsible government. This is especially the case if one subscribes to the view that 'consociational politics typically favour the social status quo and, while mediating the problems of deeply fragmented societies, also are instrumental in maintaining those very fragments'.[45]

At times, however, a compromise based on reciprocal concessions among the elites can become an almost self-sufficient condition for the articulation of divergent interests, without resort to exclusionary practices: where majority rule is unacceptable to so-called 'cleavage minorities', the consociational model provides a reasonably balanced structure for keeping all sections of the population under a common political roof, usually in the form of a composite state. Notwithstanding Sartori's empirical observation that 'in all democracies most decisions are not majoritarian',[46] the capacity of consociational democracy to produce conditions of political stability rests on the ability of the elites to arrive at unanimous, and at times near-unanimous, decisional outcomes. Interestingly, consociationalism has long passed its high point of development at the national level of governance, only to manifest itself at a higher level of political organization, whose *modus operandi* is best captured by the term 'consensus elite government' – in systems of common management and joint decision-making operating within a multi-level political order as currently represented by the Union. It is to the latter that we now turn.

Politics in a consociation of states

Although most would agree that the Union virtually defies any authoritative definition, it may still be conceived as a 'managed *Gesellschaft*', a term coined by Taylor during the consensual phase of European integration (see Chapter 3) to describe 'a decentralized, though co-ordinated, system in which participating actors . . . have a high level of interdependence with each other, but, nevertheless, preserve and even augment their autonomy'.[47] Taylor's description not only remains relevant to the Union's confederal properties – i.e. its treaty-based nature, the fact that its component polities are distinct historically constituted national states, the absence (or at best inchoateness) of a sovereign European demos, the reality of mutual vetoes in the Council, the unanimity requirement for treaty reform and so on – but also to the logic of consociational governance itself. This is especially true after the coming into force of the TEU and the creation of the pillar system presided over by the European Council, courtesy of Article D TEU, as the EU's top political organ that is equivalent to a grand coalition in a consociational regime.

As part of this theoretical trend, the present writer has tried to build on Taylor's initial application of consociational theory to the Community political system in the early 1990s,[48] by introducing the model of confederal consociation. According to the latter, the Union is defined along the lines of a compound polity whose distinct culturally defined and politically organized units are bound together in a consensual form of union, without either losing their sense of forming collective national identities or resigning their individual sovereignty to a higher central authority. To borrow from Furnivall, the regional entity takes the shape of a complex and composite political formation whose separate national demoi often 'mix but do not combine'.[49] The basic premise underlying this depiction of the Union is that, although a series of mutual concessions were taken by the national governing elites to meet the challenges of joint decision-making in matters of common concern, they did not lose sight of the quest for autonomous action within their domestic arenas. Thus emerged the new dialectic between the extension of the common functional arrangements and the concomitant rise of pressures encouraging self-rule.

Indeed, the TEU's unique blend of procedural and substantive mechanisms for accommodating varying degrees of cultural distinctiveness and subsystem autonomy has furthered the joining together of diverse political entities within a single institutional system that nevertheless respects their integrities. In doing so, it has preserved those state qualities that make the subunits survive as distinct constitutionally organized polities. It follows that the political edifice created by the TEU – and effectively preserved by the AMT (see below) – challenges the organic (or compact) theory of the polity, without relying on the properties of 'segmented differentiation': although the Union does not threaten the separate existence of the component polities, it does allow for a less rigid understanding of sovereign statehood and national self-determination (not necessarily in that order). This is made practically possible through the operation of a 'mixed' system of shared governance comprising both consensus and majority rule and designed to bridge the tensions arising from a strict interpretation of the principle of (legal) state sovereignty as complete, irreducible and unchallengeable decision-making power in the domestic sphere. Rather, sovereignty in the European consociation may take several forms, ranging from 'ultimate responsibility' (most explicitly, in the case of a potential conflict of norms for the protection of fundamental liberties), to powers reserved to the states, and even to an inclusive 'unit of participation' within which states are called commonly to determine issues of mutual interest. In short, the condition of sovereignty is no longer to be equated with the exclusive right to self-rule in the tradition of a full-blown conception of internal sovereignty,[50] or for that matter with an 'expression of separateness' in the performance of functional tasks. 'But this end-situation', Taylor notes, 'also involved a paradox: that the Community did not challenge the identity of the member states, but rather enhanced that identity. The states became stronger through strengthening the collectivity.'[51]

The Union thus offers an advanced conception of the practice of political co-determination that seeks to accommodate the divergent expectations of the segments, whilst allowing them to enjoy what Lijphart has defined as 'a high degree of secure autonomy in organizing their own affairs'.[52] Clearly, this corresponds to the principle of segmental autonomy as a feature *par excellence* of consociational governance. *Ceteris paribus*, all remaining properties of consociation can be found in the political system of the Union: its domination by an elite cartel that takes the form of a management coalition of sovereign states; a proportional representation of the segments to the central decision-making institutions; and a qualified right of mutual veto (within a non-coercive decision system) for the protection of minority interests. But what qualifies the present Union as a confederal consociation, as opposed to a federal polity, is that it is composed of equally sovereign demoi, each with its own distinctive national identity, political tradition, social structure and civic culture. The point being made here is that the segments composing the transnational society consist of separate national electorates, each represented by a sovereign and politically legitimate government. They are not parts of a single pluralist state, whether of a centralized or decentralized nature. Herein lies the importance of segmental autonomy and grand coalition to the viability of the Union's political constitution: 'decision-making authority is delegated to the separate segments as much as possible', while 'on all issues of common interest, the decisions are made jointly by the segments' leaders, but on all other issues, decision-making is left to the segments'.[53]

Having said this, it is important to note that the Union's confederal character is a key to understanding its consociational nature. Confederal and consociational elements do not merely co-exist in the European polity, but rather complement each other and, to a considerable extent, overlap. In particular, the Union remains a 'contractual union of states', that is, a treaty-constituted body politic and not the unilateral act of an aspiring demos, let alone a fully fledged one. Second, the Union does not derive its political authority directly from the European citizen body – let us immediately note that Union citizenship is conditional upon national citizenship (see Chapter 6) – but rather from the legitimate governments of the states, each representing a historically constituted demos (although the degree of homogeneity of the respective demoi varies considerably from one to another). Third, the Union 'falls short of a complete fusion or incorporation in which one or all the members lose their identity as states'.[54] Fourth, the states voluntarily decide to band together by way of mutual agreement and the decision to dissociate themselves from the Union rests solely with them (who would possibly imagine a European 'civil war' on the grounds of any member breaking away from the Union?).[55] Fifth, both the constitutional identity and international legal personality of the Union are dependent on the component states in critical ways, rather than on a constituted federal authority. Sixth, control over the legislative extension of Community competences remains vested in the executive branches of the constituent units. Finally, the Union is still composed of self-determining collectivities and does not challenge, at least in any fundamental way, their constitutional capacity to determine the fate of their respective polities, although it does represent an unprecedented exercise in collective governance with profound implications for our understanding of large-scale institutionalization and cooperative power-sharing.

Lejeune makes a similar point: 'The states remain fully sovereign but have created an integrated interstate area for which they have adopted new uniform rules and principles for the harmonisation of their national legislation.'[56] Not without good reason, therefore, did the German Constitutional Court in its ruling of 12 October 1993 describe the Union as a *Staatenverbund* (confederation of states), whose legitimacy derives directly from the *Staatsvölker*, i.e. the member state demoi.[57] All the above confirm a notion of European political order which, far from relying on an outdated sovereignty paradigm, suggests that sovereignty in general, and the constitutional attributes of statehood in particular, still rest firmly with the participating entities, rather than with a superordinate central authority. At the same time, this view does not reject the idea that policy functions, administrative roles and legislative competences are distributed among several governing bodies within a compound, multi-layered polity. Nor does it challenge the idea that the common institutions of governance are not empowered to deal directly with issues that affect the daily lives of European citizens both closely and importantly. It does question, however, the assumption (and often contention) that the emerging political structure is conducive to the development of a state-like European centre characterized by the accumulation of supranational authority that greatly impinges upon the constitutional conditions of state sovereignty. The state, put bluntly, is not left as a residual category for the management of second-order functions. Instead, its central executive branches retain a key role in collective regional management, although the creation of new functional arrangements may enhance the centripetal dynamics of the general system and release pressures towards greater decision-making centralization. But such processes do not lead to a structural fusion of the component polities into a new regional centre, nor do they account for their qualitative transformation into a federal state or some form of multi-level European republic. The (West) European state system and the fundamental norms of governance embedded in the states are 'refashioned but not fundamentally altered'.[58]

Furthermore, in matters of common concern, there is a continuous search by the segment elites for accommodationist outcomes in collective decision-making; a tendency which, supported by the reality of Council vetoes, replaces the logic of mutual antagonism or exclusion with that of mutual reconciliation. In operational terms, the latter takes the form of 'reversible dissensus' practices in joint decision-making, reflecting the Union's *modus decidendi* or what has been termed by Taylor 'confined dissent'.[59] The point here is that the higher the level of integration – i.e. the ways in which the various functional arenas are managed – and the higher the stakes involved in central decision-making, the higher the propensity of European leaders to produce consensual outcomes. 'It is not surprising, therefore', Majone notes, 'that the European institutional architecture includes so many non-majoritarian features . . . [that] are best understood as mechanisms of cleavage management.'[60] This is particularly the case in formal treaty changes through a state-controlled process of agenda-setting and negotiation among executive-centred elites. Finally, the principle of proportionality serves both as the basic standard for the allocation of votes when qualified majorities are formally required by the treaties and as the working method for central administrative appointments, especially in the case of the Commission. Overall, the component states get a fair share of their representative quota in the Union's major decision-making institutions, or at least one that is subjected to further interstate bargaining and treaty amendments. For instance, such is the case when proportionality is or appears to be under threat from prospective enlargements.

Consociationalism highlights the determination of the segment elites to exercise managerial control over the integration process, preserve the collective power of their respective executives and make progress towards 'ever closer union' dependent on the convergence of state preferences (often at the expense of reaching agreement on the basis of the lowest common denominator). It also allows the states to resist the forging of horizontal links among their respective demoi, something that would in principle facilitate the making of a transnational civic identity but weaken the domestic power base of the segment elites. Hence, the latter tend to promote vertical integration in order to retain ultimate authority and control within their domestic structures and even enhance their influence over domestic opposition elites. More important, perhaps, vertical integration enhances the status of the elite cartel in the larger management system as the principal site for the promotion of collective segmental interests, while strengthening the individual capacity of its members to influence the definition and articulation of such interests. It is in this light that state-centred scholarship has reached the conclusion that the integration process 'tends to reinforce rather than weaken the nation-state'.[61] As put by Moravcsik:

> the EC does not diffuse the domestic influence of the executive; it centralizes it. Rather than 'domesticating' the international system, the EC 'internationalizes' domestic politics. While cooperation may limit the *external* ability of executives, it simultaneously confers greater domestic influence . . . In this sense, the EC strengthens the state.[62]

What happens, however, when elite and popular interests do not coincide, or even clearly diverge? From a consociationalist perspective, it is only the segment elites that are formally empowered to steer the central political system, even in directions that may not be particularly reflective of popular political sentiments. An additional danger here is that log-rolling practices and 'pork-barrel' solutions that characterize consensual interstate bargaining are not easily understood and, hence, legitimized by the citizen body, not least because they tend to operate clandestinely.[63] Barry provides the hypothesis: 'the nearer a system comes to requiring unanimity for decisions, the more prevalent we may expect to find the "pork barrel" phenomenon'.[64] As a result, positive citizen identification with the central institutions and their respective decisional outcomes is more difficult to achieve, weakening the social legitimacy of the compound polity. Related to this, albeit indirectly, is the point that the mere proliferation of transnational actors – interest associations, civic organizations, pressure groups and the like – does not in itself guarantee the social legitimation of the general system. But, for the latter to occur, it is imperative that a European 'civic space' be established with the view to upgrading the participative potential of the constituent demoi in integration processes. Although no miracle-producing recipes exist to that end, the view taken in this study (see Chapter 6) is that this is best achieved through the institutionalization of European 'civic competence' so that the members of the transnational political society are empowered actively to engage themselves, individually or collectively, in the governance of the larger polity.

Consociationalism also enables national elites to 'mediate between the conflicting dynamics of cooperative confederalism and entrenched territorialism'.[65] The operational code adopted by the Council of Ministers and the European Council points to a mode of political accommodation similar to that depicted by Taylor as 'government by alliance'.[66] Such rules of the transnational political game refer to a coalescent style of leadership that emphasizes the conditions under which states decide to do certain things in common (especially when there are strong functional reasons to do so). At the same time, they set the limits of acceptable behaviour within the regional consocation. In the context of this innovative attempt at 'group government', the Union may thus be paralleled, as Chapter 4 hinted *in passu*, with a system of horizontal *Kooperativer Staaten*, largely inspired by the contemporary political properties of the German federal system. In it, the formulation of common – and in the German case, national – policies rests on the existence or not of prior agreement between state and central (or federal) agents, while their implementation relies almost exclusively on the administrative capacity of the component state systems.

Far from relying on a federalism founded upon hierarchical authority structures, as federal systems often do, the Union offers an alternative political arrangement to the old centre–periphery model, by institutionalizing member state participation in the joint exercise of power. At the same time, Sbragia comments, it raises the possibilities for 'a federal type organisation to operate without a centre traditionally conceptualized . . . constructed by member governments without its being detached from the collectivity of constituent units'.[67] Within this polycentric arrangement, the defence of the collective interests of distinct segments often coincides with the need to strike a deal (through issue-linkage, side-payments and the like) in the context of a positive-sum game. Hix explains:

> In international organizations, national governments negotiate as if outcomes are zero-sum (about dividing-the-pie), and can always exit the organization if the costs of defeat are too great. In the EU, in contrast, there is a high level of mutual interest amongst the elites of the national groups, who consequently perceive the policy process as a positive-sum exercise (about increasing the size of the EU pie). Moreover, exit from the consensual pattern of decision-making has a high price for all national groups, as they would be unable to maintain the same level of social and economic development outside the EU.[68]

The resulting pattern of rule might best be defined as one of 'inverse federalism', whereby political authority tends to be decentralized as much as possible to the executive branches of the constituent polities, rather than to the central institutions of governance. In brief, territorial politics in the Union is becoming stronger rather than weaker as the scope of joint decision-making is being extended, bringing the *locus decidendi* of the larger system closer to the domain of state agents. This view conflicts with the early projections of neofunctionalist writers about the parallel extension of the scope and level of European integration (in so far as these were taken as mutual reinforcements) and the incremental centralization of supranational political authority. It also deviates, albeit to a lesser extent, from the idea of an 'emerging European territoriality' that strengthens considerably the salience of 'a collective Union space' and places significant constraints on the capacity of states for collective action.[69] A 'new territoriality' may well be on its way, especially given the recent growth of subnational mobilization, but that does not immediately or necessarily translate into a diminution of state capabilities themselves.

This point relates also to the idea of 'controlled pluralism', which highlights even further the elite-dominated character of the European consociation in two important respects: first, the member state governments retain exclusive political control over the process of reforming the 'constitution' of the central arrangements, i.e. the treaties; and, second, they are induced to adopt the working principles of 'joint consensual rule', especially in conflict-prone areas. The result is the nurturing of an interstate cooperative dynamic that supports the emergence over time of a transnational political culture among the relevant governing elites. One could add here the decisive impact of the Council Presidency since the mid-1970s for sustaining the symbiotic process in reconciling state and Union interests, and for acting as a crucial link between national and European dynamics: a point where two different incentives of politics and governance are brought together within a highly institutionalized framework of interactions. Taylor explains:

> the administrations of the states that had the Presidency were fully aware that they also needed to relate to the Community and they became a part of the transnational Community political system. They had been socialized within the system to the extent of seeking values within it which reflected the interests of the collectivity, and they promoted the idea that the interests of the collectivity and the states had to be compatible and symbiotic.[70]

Of such dynamic accommodation, Almond's famous dictum that 'politics is not a game' provides both the underlying normative justification for the members of the elite cartel to reach substantive compromises and the main operational tool towards their achievement.

Consociational theory implies that the extension of European competences – i.e. what the Union is legally empowered to do – is compatible not only with the very idea of statehood (states do not cease to be states simply by joining the larger association), but also with processes of national state-building, multiple identity-holding and overlapping political memberships. It also contains a suggestion of the non-conflictual character of power-sharing among different institutional agents, and the practical means through which the separateness of states accords with the joint exercise of sovereignty. In this dynamic interplay between coordinated interdependencies and diffused political authority – but not 'mixed sovereignty' in the republican tradition – the interests of the 'territorial state' co-exist with those of the collectivity in so far as they are products of consensually predetermined objectives, convergent national prefer-ences and 'exchanged concessions' among the different action arenas. This pragmatic approach to integration, in a manner similar to Puchala's concordance system (see Chapter 3), classifies confederal consociation as a regional pluralist system driven by an informal culture of consensus-building at the highest political level. To borrow from Puchala, the model represents what is 'coming into being "out there" in the empirical world', offering an alternative interpretation to those who perceive European integration as a linear process towards a clearly discernible federal end. Overall, confederal consociation suggests that 'the burden of proof' lies more on federalism, rather than intergovernmentalism (or modified schemes of state-centrism) both as a condition and a method for promoting European integration. But where does the current state of the Union, following the Amsterdam reforms, fit in the above theoretical discussion? Before turning to this question, let us examine first whether the inclusion of the principles of subsidiarity and proportionality into the treaty framework supports the theory of consociationalism and with it our previous claims about the continued centrality of states in the regional system.

Perspectives on competence allocation

Former Commission President Delors once remarked that 'you can't fall in love with a single market; you need something else . . . '.[71] Yet, it could be safely argued that, even for *aficionados* of EU politics, 'subsidiarity' did not do the trick either! Since the principle is closely linked in both conceptual and operational terms to a wider discussion about competence allocation in multi-level polities, some general observations are in order. To start with, a feature common to all multi-layered political systems, whether formally federal or highly decentralized, has been the allocation of competences among different 'levels' or 'orders' of government. Such polities perform functions that are either shared among two or more levels of decision-making or are assigned to particular governmental settings that are seen as being either more legitimate or more efficient structures for the performance of the given tasks. Hardly surprising, tensions are more likely than not to arise between these two criteria for the allocation of authoritative decision-making power; namely, legitimacy (usually in the form of decisional closeness to the demos) and efficiency (focusing on policy outputs). After all, the polities within which competence allocation applies are compound states, based as much on elements of shared rule, including informal arrangements and *ad hoc* procedures, as on internal political pressures for self-governance. Thus, the search for appropriate forms and means of a division of responsibilities is at the heart of the political viability of composite systems that aim to reconcile what arguably constitutes the cornerstone of all systems of dispersed authority: 'unity in diversity' and, at the level of joint decision-making, 'consensus in pluriformity'.

From a comparative federalist perspective, Watts's excellent account of the political dynamics underlying the distribution of authority is worth quoting at length:

> Where the process of [federal] establishment has involved the aggregation of previously distinct units giving up some of their sovereignty to establish a new federal government, the emphasis has usually been upon specifying a limited set of exclusive and concurrent federal powers with the residual (usually unspecified) powers remaining with the constituent units [e.g. The United States, Switzerland, and Australia, with Austria and Germany following this pattern] . . . Where the creation of a federation has involved a process of devolution from a formerly unitary state, the reverse has been the case: the powers of regional units have been specified and the residual authority has remained with the federal government [e.g. Belgium and Spain] . . . Some federations like Canada, India and Malaysia have involved a combination of these processes of aggregation and devolution, and they have listed exclusive federal, exclusive provincial, and concurrent powers with the residual authority, in Canada and India . . . but not in the Malaysian Federation, assigned to the federal government.[72]

Following Watts's analysis, the Anglo-Saxon tradition favours the assignment of executive and legislative responsibilities to the constituent governments in the same fields, for such an arrangement reinforces the autonomy of legislative institutions and 'assures to each government the authority to implement its own legislation which might otherwise prove meaningless'; in the European (continental) tradition, on the other hand, administrative and legislative competences do not generally coincide: the former is usually assigned by the constitution itself to the unit governments, for 'the federal legislature to lay down considerable uniform legislation, while leaving this to be applied by regional governments in ways that take account of varying regional circumstances'.[73]

A voluminous literature already exists on the study of formal, informal and quasi-formal constitutional and procedural mechanisms through which political system-builders attempt to transcend real or perceived divisions among the subunits over what might be termed as 'capacity for governance'. In this context, the distribution of formal legislative and executive authority, the form and range of such distribution, as well as the various possibilities for exclusive, concurrent or residual competences, are of central concern. What is more, in contemporary liberal polities there is a strong predisposition towards the essential features of democratic governance, such as meaningful representation, political legitimacy, public accountability and policy responsiveness. The immediate implication stemming from this is that the tensions between two or more levels of political authority are often exacerbated by reference to their acclaimed 'democrativeness' in comparison to that of their respective competitors. Such problems are compounded further by the extent to which the polity in question is characterized by centralized or decentralized tendencies, symmetrical or asymmetrical relationships among the subunits, centri-petal or centrifugal political and societal dynamics, and constitutionally entrenched or less formalized guarantees for the protection of constituent autonomy and, crucially, segmental identity. When the founding act of the polity, as in non-statist entities like the Union, is not a formal constitution accompanied by a supreme court, a system of rule based on Montesquieu's *trias politica*, and a *Kompetenzkatalog* for the demarcation of legislative, executive and administrative responsibilities, but instead rests on a consti-tutive act, pact, contract, convention or treaty, then the level of systemic ambiguity about who should be rendered ultimately responsible for which decision(s) may increase dramatically.

To all intents and purposes, the European polity represents an excellent case for studying questions of multi-level competence allocation, not least due to the pluralism and variability inherent in its governance structures. In this context, the inclusion into the formal treaty framework of the federally inspired principle of subsidiarity is a good point of departure. Enshrined in the TEU as a basic but poorly thought-out guideline for the (vertical) division of (shared) responsibilities between the Union and the states, subsidiarity has arguably opened the way for two separate lines of development: the protection of national autonomy against excessive institutional centralization, and the extension of the Union's legislative competences. Whereas the former, and more widely accepted view, supports the thesis of confederal consociation, perceiving subsidiarity as an effective restraint in both legal and political terms on European law-making powers, the latter points in the direction of a more federally definable structure of shared rule. In fact, much depended on the preferred interpretation of Article 3b EC, which reads:

> The Community shall act within the limits of the powers conferred upon it by this Treaty and of the objectives assigned to it therein. In areas which do not fall within its exclusive competence, the Community shall take action, in accordance with the principle of subsidiarity, only if and in so far as the objectives of the proposed action cannot be sufficiently achieved by the

Member States and can therefore, by reason of the scale and effects of the proposed action, be better achieved by the Community.

Prima facie, subsidiarity seems to create both a 'sufficiency' and an 'effectiveness' criterion concerning the appropriate arena for action: the first suggests that Community institutions must demonstrate that state action is not sufficient, while the second implies that Community action must be better able to achieve the objective at hand.[74] From this view, the question of competence comes down to the 'comparative efficiency' of the means that are at the disposal of the Community and the states. Here, Lenaerts notes, 'a necessary condition for Community action is that at least one Member State has inadequate means at its disposal for achieving the objectives of the proposed action.'[75] But there also exists a third criterion which, albeit indirectly related to the principle itself, links the previous two criteria with a central tenet of contemporary democratic governance: that decisions should be taken 'as closely as possible to the citizen'.[76]

Subsidiarity chimes well with a consociationalist understanding of EU politics, for it justifies a potential flow of decision-making powers to nation-state authorities, thus offering a 'partial offset' to the quest for legislative autonomy by the component polities. This line of reasoning confirms Taylor's argument that the principle resembles a kind of 'reserved powers' to the constituent governments, implying that the states have effectively managed to countervail any potential federalizing tendencies by means of balancing 'the loss of power in one realm against the gain of or retention of powers in another'.[77] A similar point is made by Lenaerts on the principle's political significance:

> For the Member States, the principle of subsidiarity then constitutes a mechanism – and presumably a judicially enforceable one – of self-defence against what they perceive as a risk that the Community will make excessive use of its non-exclusive powers, and thus preempt their residual powers. In this respect, the principle of subsidiarity serves as a substitute for the wavering of 'political safeguards of federalism'.[78]

From this analytical prism, it is difficult to overlook signs of an inverse type of federalism limiting the concentration of legislative competences to the central institutions, while favouring their diffusion down to national tiers of governance. As de Búrca puts it:

> [Article 3b EC] does not reflect the philosophy of allowing smaller units to define and achieve their own ends, and refers only to two levels of authority: that of the nation state and that of the Community . . . and the only criterion given for determining which level is appropriate is one of outcome or effect [concerning the capacity of the two levels to meet the end in view], rather than process [referring to the democratic nature of the decision-making process].[79]

In so far as these signs articulate a presumption of competence to national political units, consociationalism remains a useful instrument for analysing competence allocation in the Union. Procedurally, this means that the 'burden of proof' lies with the Community institutions (mainly the Commission) that now have to justify – through a public reason argument – the compatibility of the proposed legislation with the principle of subsidiarity.

Subsidiarity is far from being a new term in the vocabulary of EU politics. The principle appeared in the 1975 Tindemans Report as a means of extending the scope of Community competences; in the 1977 McDougal Report as a 'bottom-up' approach to fiscal federalism; in the 1984 Draft Treaty on European Union prepared by the EP, linking subsidiarity with cross-frontier dimension effects; in the SEA, albeit not *expressis verbi*, in Article 130r (4) EC, concerning environmental issues; in the 1987 Padoa-Scioppa Report in relation to economic intervention by the Community; in the 1989 Delors Report on EMU with reference to macro-economic policy; and in the 1990 Martin Report stressing the tasks that are essential to the viability of the Union.[80] Unlike, however, the Tindemans Report and the Draft Treaty, the Union envisaged by Maastricht is not 'an entirely new creation'; nor is there any provision in the text determining the precise allocation of competences between the collectivity and the segments; nor, finally, is there any distinction between different types of competences such as exclusive, concurrent (or non-exclusive) and potential (areas which might in the future come under European competence but which initially remain with the states).[81]

Given 'the open-textured nature of the provision',[82] it is hardly coincidental that most legal experts have resented its inclusion in the treaty from the outset. Lord MacKenzie-Stuart went as far as to describe it as 'gobbledygook' on the grounds that questions of 'effectiveness' will be incapable of judicial resolution.[83] Scharpf concurs:

> Given the heterogeneity of conditions and capacities among the member states, it is hardly conceivable that a court could strike down any European measure that was in fact supported by a qualified majority in the Council of Ministers . . . Thus, it is probably more realistic to see the clause primarily as a political appeal for self-restraint directed at the Council of Ministers itself.[84]

The difficulty lies in the 'objectivity' of the legal grounds on which the ECJ would rule that a given task is better achieved at the Community level without being accused of being 'politically' biased against lower-level authorities. Or, as an independent report has asserted, 'there is a risk that, in straying into very obviously political territory, the Court may jeopardise its hard-won credibility.'[85] All the above amount to 'the problem of competence': the absence of an explicit formal mechanism for allocating responsibilities within the Union, outside the areas that are considered as belonging to its exclusive sphere of activity such as commercial policy, the protection of the sea and, according to the Commission, the four freedoms of movement and the policies that are a corollary to them. It follows that these areas falling within the internal market sphere are not subject to the principle of subsidiarity, but are determined by the pre-emption doctrine: 'once the Community legislates in a field, it occupies that field, thereby precluding Member State action.'[86] Thus, subsidiarity can be used as a rule for competence allocation only in cases of concurrence, when decision-making power is shared between the Union and the states, or when the Community has for the first time passed legislation on a new policy area. In matters unaffected by Community law it is presumed that the states retain exclusive competence. It is in relation to this last observation that a number of controversies arise.

More specifically, Toth claims that the distinction between 'exclusive' and 'concurrent' competences is unknown to Community law in so far as one understands the idea of concurrent competence as 'a situation in which two different bodies can act with equal authority at the same time'.[87] For the powers that have been conferred upon the Community are in principle exclusive and, hence, there is no room for any powers shared with the states. This contention seems to create more legal problems than it actually solves. One reason for this is that in Toth's thesis – i.e. 'where Community competence begins that of the states ends'[88] – subsidiarity becomes irrelevant, as the polity's legal basis now stands. In his words: '[Article 3b EC] cannot *create* or *confer* competences on the Community. It can only be used to allocate the *exercise* of competences which have already been created by other provisions of the Treaty.'[89] If, on the other hand, Toth's formulation is invalid, then subsidiarity is the decisive, if not formally the sole, criterion for the delineation of disputed legislative boundaries. Arguably, the legal ambiguity and political uncertainty surrounding the application of subsidiarity are compounded further by the fact that the treaty itself does not attempt to articulate in any precise manner

> what the scope of the Community's conferred competence is, whether there are areas over which the Community has sole competence to the exclusion of Member States action, what the areas are in which it shares competence with the Member States, nor whether there are areas in which it simply lacks competence.[90]

There is a case to be made, therefore, for the powers specifically entrusted to the 'centre' to be enlisted in the treaty, as for instance the Australian Constitution does (Article 51 stipulates 39 areas which fall within the jurisdiction of the Federal Parliament); or that a clear mechanism to delegate specific competences to the 'centre' be provided, as in the case of the German *Grundgesetz* (Article 72 II enlisting the conditions under which the *Bund* has the right to legislate), or even that a 'residual clause' be included in a manner similar to the US Constitution (the Tenth Amendment of 1791 that creates a sense of 'constitutive autonomy' on the part of the states). But an ensemble *sui generis* formula of some of the above possibilities should not be excluded either. Reflecting, however, on the federalist experience, the case for the allocation of competences to the 'centre' has to be proved. Otherwise, power rests with the constituent units. This has been justified on the grounds that the latter, in the form of previously independent polities, preceded the creation of the federation. This approach, by favouring the diffusion of powers to lower-level units, falls within the logic of 'bottom-up' subsidiarity derived from the theoretical foundations of European Catholic thought on the relationship between the individual, the state and society, as well as on a federalist division of political authority on a vertical axis. In Streeck's words:

> In Catholic social doctrine where the concept originated, subsidiarity implied a duty on the part of higher levels of governance to enable smaller units at lower levels to conduct their affairs in responsible 'social autonomy'. Part of this duty was to see to it, if necessary by active intervention, that more 'organic' units like firms or parochial charities were able to resolve problems themselves that otherwise might have become problems for the society as a whole.[91]

Subsidiarity is accompanied in Article 3b EC by the principle of proportionality – already an element of Community case law – according to which 'Any action by the Community shall not go beyond what is necessary to achieve the objectives of this Treaty.' This principle does not alter the attribution of competence, but rather concerns the way in which Community power should be exercised once the Community level of governance has been authorized as the most appropriate level to take action. The rationale behind this principle is that Community action should not exceed what is necessary to meet the end in view: such action has to be *intra vires*. In this logic, the principle 'seeks to ensure that the nature and intensity of the proposed action are in proportion with what is necessary to achieve the objectives of that action'.[92] According to Lenaerts, a broader interpretation of the principle that links it with that of subsidiarity leads to the view that:

> proportionality suggests that the Community should take action only in so far as such action is required in order to compensate for the Member States' inability to achieve sufficiently the objectives of the action proposed. The value that this expression of the proportionality principle means to protect is very clear, namely the sovereignty of the Member States and their subnational authorities. Under this view, the residual powers of the States should not be impaired any more than is necessary in order for the Community and the Member States, each acting in a spirit of loyal cooperation, to attain the objectives of the proposed action.[93]

Following de Búrca's analysis, the proportionality principle seems to apply across the policy domains of Community action and, therefore, does not appear to be restricted by the idea of non-exclusive competence.[94] She then makes the point that:

Although the proportionality question purports to deal with the *means* by which an objective is pursued, and the second part ('subsidiarity proper') with whether the *objective* is best pursued by Community action or by Member State action in the first place, it would often be difficult to answer the second question without knowing what *kind* of action is envisaged. That is to say, the objective of an action and the means to achieve that action cannot readily be separated.[95]

Overall, and given the vagueness characterizing the treaty provisions on the objectives to be pursued by the Community, proportionality arguably adds to the existing legal maze.

Attempts to clarify further the conditions for the application of subsidiarity, not least as a result of the negative Danish vote on the TEU in June 1992, were taken at the Edinburgh European Council later that year. The Commission was asked to prepare a report for the Edinburgh Summit, in which it explicitly asserted the primacy of states:

[the] conferment of powers is a matter for the writers of our constitution, that is to say of the treaty. A consequence of this is that the powers conferred on the Community, in contrast to those reserved to the states, cannot be assumed . . . national powers are the rule and the Community's the exception.[96]

According to Taylor, the report 'recognized that the powers of the states were superior, that they were the conferring agency, and that they could de-confer: in other words it asserted the continuing sovereignty of the states'.[97] In the end, the following criteria for Community action were set out as 'guidelines' on subsidiarity: whether the issue at hand has transnational effects that cannot be satisfactorily regulated by state action; whether state action alone or lack of Community action would conflict with the requirements of the Treaty or significantly damage states' interests; whether the Council must be satisfied that Community action would produce clear benefits of scale or effects. These guidelines were incorporated into the 1993 Inter-institutional Agreement on the implementation of the principle, and four years later found their way into a detailed protocol as a result of the Amsterdam reforms (see below).

By way of conclusion, let us note that what remains of crucial importance is for a balance to be struck between state and Union competences on the question of what level of aggregation should act on which types of issue. As Taylor has rightly suggested: 'the optimum distribution would be to have national control in areas that are adjacent to areas of community control. This might be called the principle of *balanced competences* which should be set alongside *subsidiarity* as a key principle for the governance of the European Union.'[98] At the moment, however, subsidiarity appears to be too nebulous a concept to address, let alone resolve, the problem of competence allocation within the European polity. The mere fact that EU scholarship has delivered such diverse verdicts on the principle as 'the word that saves Maastricht', 'an effective barrier "against the enterprises of ambition", 'a meaningless or even misleading term in English', or even 'an ugly word but a useful concept', is a clear enough indication to justify a rather cautious approach to what Cass has described as 'a still-maturing principle' of Community law.[99]

The Amsterdam reforms

During the small hours of 18 June 1997 agreement was finally reached among the Fifteen on a new treaty. The latter was signed on 2 October later that year and came into force on 1 May 1999, four months after the introduction of the single currency, following a rather uncontroversial ratification process, at least compared with that of the TEU. But the initial joy of perceiving the Amsterdam treaty-amending process as a success story soon started to fade among scholars and practitioners alike. Given the moderate nature of the reforms embedded in the final draft (controversial issues on enlargement and voting adjustments were simply deferred to a future review conference), it is fair to suggest that the European construction had been 'stirred' rather than 'shaken'. As Moravcsik and Nikolaïdis put it: 'Given its lack of a single, clear substantive focus, it is no surprise that Amsterdam, more than any Treaty of Rome revision since 1957, became a melting pot of disparate measures lacking coherent vision of either substantive co-operation in a particular area or the future institutional structure of Europe.'[100] Underlying the largely incomplete outcome of the Amsterdam process has been a preference for a managerial type of reform to improve effectiveness in policy output, whereas the deepening of integration was referred *ad calendas Graecas*. Put simply, the AMT reflected the outcome of a state-controlled process of limited treaty reforms subject to the *liberum veto* of the member states, rather than a profound redesign of the Union's political constitution. In Schmitter's words, the Amsterdam experience 'demonstrates that no committee of the whole will be given a mandate for minor reforms and come back with a wholesale refounding of the institutional order'.[101] Devuyst is thus right to point out that, '[r]ather than focusing on pre-emptive institutional spillover in preparation for enlargement, the Amsterdam negotiation was characterized by a "maintaining national control trend"'.[102] Or, as *The Economist* colourfully put it: the Amsterdam Summit 'produced more of a mouse than a mountain'.[103]

Hailed by some as a 'reasonable step', while criticized by others as 'lacking ambition', it is fair to consider the AMT 'as one more step, smaller than expected, but sure to be followed by others'.[104] It is equally fair to argue that the AMT consolidated state competences by preserving the Union's three-pillar structure and with it its two separate legal mechanisms (see Chapter 4). Perhaps the most important development was the partial communitarization of immigration, asylum and visa policies (as well as judicial cooperation on issues with cross-border effects), previously falling into the third pillar, which now reads 'Police and Judicial Cooperation in Criminal Matters'. The progressive transfer (within five years) of these sensitive areas of (previously nationally determined) policy to the Community pillar means that they 'will be subject to the normal EC procedures for regulation and control – both judicial and non-judicial'.[105] Yet, judicial review was not institutionalized in crucial areas affecting the citizen such as those associated with the operations of Europol (still not a Community agency), while the Schengen *acquis*, which previously constituted an agreement *inter se*, became fully incorporated into the treaty framework (with the United Kingdom and Ireland having secured an opt out).

In the CFSP pillar, the AMT set out the basic guiding principles of the Union's foreign and security policy, while reaffirming the central role of the European Council in steering the international politics of the Union. More specifically, it provided for a limited extension of QMV in the Council on detailed policy implementation or joint actions, putting into practice common strategies already agreed by the European Council on the basis of unanimity; the appointment of a 'high representative' to give a human face to the Union's external political relations, direct the action decided by the Council and work closely with representatives of the Council Presidency and the Commission; the creation of a new agency under the title 'Policy Planning and Early Warning Unit' to centralize and analyse information provided by the member states, the Commission and the Western European Union; and the possibility of 'constructive abstention' under the condition that the members wishing to abstain do not account for more than one-third of the vote.[106]

It was also agreed that at the first enlargement the big states would lose their second Commissioner provided that they were compensated through a reweighting of votes in the Council or a system of dual majority including a certain proportion of the population, thus instituting a mixed system of state and popular votes. This clearly pointed to an accommodationist-type arrangement between small and large states, although a final decision was deferred until a review conference was convened, at least one year before Union membership exceeds twenty. It is expected that an enlarged Union of, say, twenty-five or so members will upset further an already delicate balance of voting rights in the Council. Hence, a new decision-making formula should be so devised as to ensure that the smaller states would not be alienated in the new structure. In this light, and given the current asymmetries in the Council's voting rules, the introduction of a system of 'double concurrent majorities' may in the end prove capable of establishing a more equitable system of state/popular representation, according to which 'a two thirds majority would require two thirds of the number of states accounting for two thirds of the population'.[107] Whether or not such a system will be practically realized with the view to bridging the existing gap between democracy and demography in EU decision-making, it is certain that for some members the emphasis will be on the possibilities of forming an effective minority veto in the Council, while for others on the introduction of procedural means for overcoming a small minority of dissenting states.

Moving on to the question of the hierarchy of Community Acts – an issue also raised during the 1990/91 IGCs but rejected on the grounds that it would produce a *de facto* classification of levels of governance and a *de jure* classification of institutions 'top-down' – it is useful to recall that the Italian government and the EP formed an alliance during the Maastricht negotiations, suggesting the following types of Community Acts: Constitutional Acts (treaty-amending process); Organic Laws (functioning of EU institutions); Regular Laws (formal EU decision-making procedures); and Regulations (policy implementation). Differences between these types reflect mainly the differences in the actual decision-taking mode for each category as the required majorities get lower if one moves down from Constitutional Acts to Organic Laws. There was to be a slight modification of this proposal in the August 1995 Interim Report of the Reflection Group, in merging Regular Laws and Regulations. State representatives in the Group did not discuss this issue in any detail, preferring instead to refer the matter to the IGC, which failed however to reach consensus, thus missing an opportunity to clarify further the relationship between the Community legal architecture and the state legal orders (as well as looking at the full range of questions determining the practical consequences and effect of Community legislation). The need for such clarifications is all the more pressing now that the proliferation of novel governance practices in the Union involve 'more direct forms of societal steering such as soft law (recommendations, action plans)'.[108] In short, the Amsterdam experience clearly revealed that differences among the member state governments were more or less reproducing those of the previous IGCs.

Under the new treaty rules, the use of QMV has been extended in the fields of emergency immigration measures, employment (guidelines and incentive measures), customs cooperation, countering fraud, social exclusion, equality of opportunity and treatment of men and women, public health, transparency (general principles), fundamental rights sanctions, outermost regions and statistics (data protection).[109] The now simplified co-decision procedure applies also to citizens' rights, social security for migrant workers, rights of self-employed, cultural measures and, after five years of the treaty coming into force, to visa procedures and conditions, as well as visa uniformity rules.[110] The legislative procedures involving the EP are now reduced to co-decision, consultation and assent (the cooperation procedure survives only in some areas concerning the EMU). But the AMT failed to extend equally the scope of QMV and parliamentary co-decision, as well as the EP's right of assent to legislation in third-pillar issues – where it still largely remains an institution *non grata* – in decisions over the Community's financial 'own resources' and, more importantly, in treaty amendments themselves (constitutional competence).[111] Likewise, it fell short of tackling the comitology phenomenon, according to which the Commission 'has the authority to adopt a large number of implementing acts on the basis of a delegation conferred on it by the Council', thus excluding the EP altogether.[112] On the credit side, the EP was given the right to approve the nomination of the Commission President, who now has a formal say over the nomination of the other Commissioners (previously the President was merely consulted on the issue). Moreover, it was decided that EP representatives should not exceed 700, irrespective of the Union's next waves of enlargement, and that the EP can put forward suggestions concerning the performance of its members' duties (conditional though upon a unanimous Council vote).

A new protocol was enshrined in the AMT so as to define more precisely the criteria for applying the principles of subsidiarity and proportionality. It states: 'In exercising the powers conferred on it, each institution shall ensure that the principle of subsidiarity is complied with', and 'any action of the Community shall not go beyond any action necessary for the attainment of the objectives of the Treaty.' These principles shall respect the *acquis communautaire* and the institutional balance, while taking into account that 'the Union shall provide itself with the means necessary to attain its objectives and carry through its policies'. But it is still the Community that has to justify the compliance of proposed legislation to the above principles. This is a clear enough indication that competence allocation within the EU system effectively remains the prerogative of states. Moreover, as in the TEU, there is no mention of subnational levels of government, while the wording of the new provisions clearly 'privileges efficiency over all other criteria for assessing the appropriateness of particular levels of decision-making'.[113] *Ceteris paribus*, directives should be preferred to regulations and so should framework directives to detailed measures, leaving as much scope for national decisions as possible. This is fully in accord with a state-centric reading of subsidiarity and proportionality, according to which these principles become effective means of protecting the states' constituent autonomy in the legislative sphere against excessive decision-making centralization.

Although flexibility or *coopération renforcée* was finally included in the AMT, it precludes the creation of a *Europe à la carte* by introducing stringent conditions for its application, to the extent that Wessels has argued that '[t]he provisions might work as a negative, to encourage reluctant members states to resort to the Union's normal provisions'.[114] In particular, flexibility should further the objectives and interests of the Union; respect the principles of the treaties and the single institutional framework; be used only as a last resort mechanism; concern at least a majority of states; respect the *acquis communautaire*; not affect the competences, rights, obligations and interests of those members that do not wish to participate therein; and remain open to all states. The new 'flexible' arrangements will be governed by the same decision-making rules as in the TEU, adjusted accordingly for membership. But the AMT precludes EU members from initiating such practices in areas falling within the Community's exclusive competences (especially those related to the functioning of the single market); affect Community policies, actions or programmes; concern Union citizenship or discriminate between member state nationals; fall outside the limits of the powers conferred upon the Community by the treaty; and constitute discrimination or restrict trade and/or distort competition between member states. Authorization for such 'flexible' schemes 'shall be granted by the Council, acting by a qualified majority', but any objection by a state on the grounds of 'important and stated reasons of national policy' results in the whole matter being referred to the European Council for a decision by unanimity. This is a classical example of sovereignty-conscious states wishing to retain ultimate political control in a sensitive area, given that, without a normative and substantive consensus around the nature of political solidarity, the idea of flexible, multi-speed or other forms of differentiated integration is treated with considerable suspicion in some national capitals, as well as by some aspiring members. The main fear in this respect is that flexibility may open the way for a politics of institutionalized exclusion. As Edwards and Wiessala have observed:

> if the purpose is to maintain a momentum or create a new dynamic through closer co-operation, it inevitably creates pressures on those whose initial preferences might have been to remain outside to conform – if they can. Anxiety about exclusion, of the danger of missing the bus, may often be a last minute realization but it can, nonetheless, be a potent motivation, without necessarily making those jumping on enthusiastic passengers . . . [115]

A series of exciting research questions arises in relation to the flexibility principle, most notably its potential transformation from one out of many organizational logics of European governance to a constitutional principle *per se*, thus shaping the future political format of the European polity. At a more practical level, it raises the question whether the institutionalization of flexible practices or 'variable geometry' schemes become the basic guiding norm of European policy-making and, if so, whether that would exacerbate further existing asymmetries between states in the application of the Union's shared body of laws. Also, embedded in the principle is the possibility of what Shaw and Wiener call 'complex overlapping systems of authority',[116] thus adding to the systemic complexity of an already messy institutional structure that is badly in need of both organizational and decisional clarity, at least from the perspective of enhancing the legitimacy of the central institutions and facilitating citizen identification with integrative outcomes. Finally comes the question of overall polity cohesion *vis-à-vis* the Union's constitutional properties: the incorporation of a flexibility clause into the treaty framework, *prima facie* at least, seems to legitimize the view that wants the political constitution of the Union to be an exercise in asymmetrical institutional pluralism, policy differentiation and actor variability, rather than to form a coherent set of quasi-constitutional norms and rules that may, in time, become part of a formal constitutional settlement. The one thing that remains certain is that the new challenges these questions generate for the future of theorizing the European condition, and particularly the relationship between normative and empirical research on possible integration outcomes, will not escape the analytical scrutiny of EU scholarship.

In overall terms, and to borrow again from Devuyst: 'On controversial issues, the negotiators proved able to arrive at a unanimous compromise formula only as long as the reluctant governments were confident that they would be able to maintain control over the decision-making process in the policy areas in question . . . '.[117] In fact, for the first time in European treaty reform, there is evidence to suggest that 'the French interpretation of the Luxembourg compromise was formally recognised in the Treaty . . . '.[118] In the same vein, those who linked the end-product of the revision process with the making of a 'constitutive polity' based on mutually reinforcing legitimation structures have no real grounds for celebration. In the end, political pragmatism seems to have had its way, for the changes introduced failed to deliver the much-needed clarification of the properties of the system. Instead, the AMT relates to the well-known saying *plus ça change, plus c'est la même chose*, and it is likely to go down in history as the 'uncourageous Treaty'. Contrary to previous treaty reforms, Amsterdam is characterized by a lack of vision about the making of a more democratic union, offering instead a series of 'partial offsets' to the Union's democratic pathology, by focusing on its institutional rather than sociopsychological aspects. To open a small parenthesis here, the latter aspects relate to the normative qualities embodying the construction of a European 'civic space' where citizens share among themselves a sense of public sphere (as a civic virtue element that serves as a valuable resource for the polity) and a regard for 'good governance' (as a training ground for civic learning). Both elements are crucial since, as J. S. Mill rightly reminds us, '[p]olitical machinery does not act of itself'.[119] Rather, it has to be constantly worked and reworked by the citizens themselves. This civic conception of the European polity, arguably a long way from its current configuration, contributes significantly to the making of a regional democratic order steered by an active society of sovereign citizens, rather than merely by the dominant governing elites (see Chapter 6).

From early on, the 1996/7 IGC was greeted with mixed feelings: some states showed extreme caution towards substantive reforms, others thought it was too early for another revision after the recent coming into force of the TEU, and others were hesitant to disturb whatever institutional and power balance was created by the latter. The IGC itself was part of a 'pre-reform process',[120] consisting of no less than forty meetings of the representatives of Foreign Affairs Ministers (Reflection Group), sixteen meetings of the Ministers themselves, and five Summits of the Heads of State and Government. Although this *prima facie* implies that important issues were at stake during the IGC, it is somewhat ironic that what was not explicitly discussed in its context proved more significant for the future of the Union. Issues concerning the granting to European citizens of effective 'civic competence' to engage themselves in the actual governance of the Union is a good case in point. The idea here is not so much of the crystallization of liberal democratic norms in the political constitution of the Union, but rather of the continuing search for a transnational civic space within which citizens can mobilize their democratic energies in the pursuit of a new civic order. Underlying this normative assertion is the belief that democratic reform is not really the cause, but rather the consequence, of popular aspirations to democratic shared rule; namely, a desire on the part of the civic body to participate fully in a socially legitimized political environment. Similarly, European treaty reform should not be seen as an end in itself, but rather as a means of building upon existing policies and institutions with a view to improving the democratic quality of integration and, hence, the ways in which citizens can identify with the deliberative outcomes of the larger polity. For one thing, democratization presupposes the existence or at least the development of a self-conscious political unit within which large-scale institutional reform can actually take place. Put differently, it requires a collective civic consciousness that has to emerge from the composite citizen body itself.

With the benefit of *a posteriori* knowledge, three (political) options for European constitutional change were feasible during the Amsterdam process. The initial dilemma was between a pragmatic and a normative approach, although at the final stage of the negotiations a 'mixed' approach effectively prevailed – itself an ensemble *sui generis* of the previous two. According to the first option, the Union remains a 'contractual union of states' – a *Staatenverbundsystem* – that fails to develop an independent basis from which a genuine European sovereignty and a system-wide constitutional hierarchy might emerge. The second option portrays a federalizing regional order embodying a civic conception of non-hierarchical forms of shared governance. The third option implies that the Union remains *in limbo* between a regional regime of coordinated interdependencies and the breaking of a new, transnational polity. Table 5.1 summarizes the alternatives.

The implications stemming from the prevalence of a 'mixed' approach to the Amsterdam reforms are relevant to the confusion surrounding the political nature of the Union, currently representing a sensibly arranged mix of *Gesellschaft* and *Gemeinschaft* elements, along the lines of a confederal consociation. Put differently, changes in the workings of the general system by the late 1990s did not affect its essential character of being closer to 'a many turned into one without ceasing to be many'.[121] Although a hindrance to formal federation-building, such an approach managed to preserve a balance between state and international organization by producing a sophisticated system of mutual governance based on the practice of political co-determination. These concepts are a key to understanding the changing conditions of sovereignty, which may now be interpreted as the right to be involved in the joint exercise of competences, to play full part in the

TABLE 5.1 *Typology of European treaty reform*

Properties	Approaches		
	Pragmatic	Normative	Mixed
Form of polity	Confederation (Union of states)	Federation (Union of peoples)	Confederal consociation (Compound polity)
Modus operandi	Flexibility/efficiency (Rationalization)	Demos-formation (Social legitimation)	Controlled pluralism (Accommodation)
Locus of sovereignty	State rule (Treaty-constituted)	Civic rule (Demos-oriented)	Consensus elite government (Elite-driven)
Central arrangement	Constitutions (State autonomy)	Constitution (New sovereignty)	Constitutional engineering (Co-determination)

transnational community and 'to represent there the interests of the state'.[122] In a nutshell: 'sovereignty was now a condition, even a form, of participation, in the larger entity.'[123] Moreover, the quasi-governmental structure of the Union, when disconnected from a Weberian understanding of hierarchically structured forms of polity, 'has no classic aspiration of its own . . . [it] is too complex and too amorphous to be presented as emerging from a new abstract constituent power'.[124] Instead, responsibility for the making of such a non-state/non-unitary polity, but with an increasingly state-like agenda, rests – as in any confederal system – with the component state governments. And so does the consolidation of the Union's legitimizing self: the right to publicly binding decisions.

As in the case of Maastricht, so in Amsterdam, '[t]he system rests on the member states but works on the basis of embedding the national in the European [and vice versa]'.[125] The point here is that the Union, on the one hand, breaks down 'the boundedness of national polities' by embedding them in a wider (multi-level) arena of politics and policy-making, while on the other it is still crafted on to national polities.[126] From a more state-centric perspective, however, European treaty reform in the early and late 1990s made it clear that preserving the constitutive autonomy of states both as *Herren der Verträge* and as the central actors in EU constitutional engineering is part of the system's *acquis conferencielle*.[127] Sovereign statehood thus acquired through intense formal and informal interactions a new cooperative dynamic of its own within a highly institutionalized framework: it no longer refers to 'a private world into which the outside world was not permitted to enter',[128] nor is it subsumed by 'a new "hierarchy", in which the dominant form of regulation is authoritative rule'.[129] This is not to imply that the Union is only concerned with meeting the functional requirements of a transnational policy space merely based on a system of 'network governance'.[130] Rather, it has greatly impinged upon the way in which sovereignty relations are to be understood within a pluralistic arena that is neither hierarchical nor anarchical, but rather subject to 'positive-sum governing': competences exercised on behalf of citizens by the common institutions are necessary to preserve the symbiotic nature of integration itself. As Taylor defines this new dialectical quality in sovereignty: 'Having the right to participate in the management of common arrangements with other states was a much more important consideration in sovereignty than the traditional right to exclusive management . . . .'[131]

Conclusion

In general terms, the AMT forms part of a wider political, but less federal, evolution towards a multi-level, pluralist structure of institutionalized governance between relatively autonomous, yet interrelated, tiers of political decision-making. But it can also be argued that the new treaty brings the Union into yet another transition phase best captured by the term 'nascent *Gemeinschaft*'. Although at present the role of affective/identitive politics, as opposed to the more rationalist/utilitarian motives underlying the behaviour of states, is yet to become part of the Union's systemic properties, increased awareness about the importance of questions of polity, the search for greater democratic legitimacy of integration outcomes and various attempts to bring the Union closer to its citizens have all sparked an interest in establishing a more purposeful relationship between domestic and European political spaces. At least, it is now clear that the challenge ahead for the regional polity is to find ways of connecting civic statehood with transnational processes so as to alleviate the tensions arising from the tactical consolidation of state prerogatives and the continued efforts of supranational institutions to acquire an autonomous presence in the general system. Whatever the winds of further treaty reform may hold for the future, and whether domestic and common institutions of governance will be able to rediscover through new and creative synergies a sense of purpose in relation to the European citizen, democracy is likely to remain at the top of the Union's political agenda.

To put the matter in its historical perspective, just as Hallstein's 'First Europe' (1958–66) (characterized by functional federalism and institutional centralization) was succeeded by Dahrendorf's 'Second Europe' (1969–74) (based on a creative version of intergovernmentalism) and that by Taylor's 'Third Europe' (1974–97) (consolidating a politics of symbiosis between the collectivity and the segments), so the latter might be said to be gradually giving way to a 'Fourth Europe' based on the praxis of political co-determination and the institutionalization of the joint exercise of sovereignty, with the view to establishing stronger links among the members of the European political society. It is through this prism that, over the past decade, EU polity-building can be seen as part of an increasingly politicized process – a constituent process – which remains relevant to the making of a more democratic process of union and a politically organized European *Gemeinschaft*. In this light, the prospects for a 'Fourth Europe' chime well with Lijphart's normative understanding of consociationalism as a transition stage on the road to greater unity, which may in time lead to a more congruent and majoritarian European polity.[132]

Notwithstanding the normative implications of EU polity-building, it is equally fair to suggest that the moderate nature of European treaty reform in the 1990s seems to reinforce the thesis of the reversal of the Mitranian logic to international integration since the structural properties of the larger management system are to a considerable extent responsible for both the quality and proliferation of joint integrative schemes. Put differently, it is the practice of political co-determination within the multi-arena system that, together with the development of cooperative norms of governance characteristic of consociational polities, set the bases for mutually rewarding integration outcomes. Thus, systemic growth is not so much the result of functionalist-driven dynamics leading to a multi-sector fusion (or merger), as it is the product of complex and often protracted intergovernmental negotiations through which states control the level of the regional process. This is the opposite of what neofunctionalists had hoped to achieve: instead of politicization (or increased controversiality, linking the management of EU affairs with the daily lives of European citizens) becoming an additional weapon in the hands of pro-integrationist forces, it is increasingly used by the more sceptical actors, making it difficult to mobilize the constituent demoi toward a European *Gemeinschaft* and closer to a 'complete equilibrium' among different levels of governance. Such a development, by contesting any federalist determinism in Europe's integrative journey – i.e. the teleological transformation of a multi-state polity into a federal state – may bring the Union closer to a system of 'multiple flexible equilibria' based on 'variation in both the territorial and the functional constituencies',[133] or indeed closer to Haas's conception of 'asymmetrical authority overlap', whereby '[political] authority is not proportionally or symmetrically vested in a [dominant] central authority' (see Chapter 1).[134] But it also rejects the view that the implied benefits of commonly performed functions at the larger level, even when they formally require resort to majority rule, would somehow overcome any potentially disturbing tensions that may arise as European integration proceeds.

Another insight drawn from the Amsterdam process is that, unlike the Maastricht reforms, treaty negotiators have cautiously attempted to exclude from the agenda issues that might trigger unpleasant domestic debates about the macro-political implications of economic and monetary integration and, by extension, about the prospects for a more equitable redistribution of costs and benefits from the single currency. This is of crucial importance for the development and internal cohesion of the Union, not least because it confirmed a hidden political consensus among state executives that issues of structural socio-economic adjustment and, by extension, the uncertain future of the West European welfare state system would be dealt with on a rather *ad hoc* basis in subsequent Council meetings, rather than being formally linked to a comprehensive reform process subject to public scrutiny, debate and criticism. More important, perhaps, no systematic attempt was made during the Amsterdam discussions to deepen the citizens' socio-economic rights (especially those relating to social welfare, working conditions and non-corporatist management participation schemes), with the view to democratizing Europe's extensive liberalization project. With the exception of the issue of unemployment, which formed a central element in the Amsterdam talks (leading to the inclusion of a new Employment Title as a job-creation mechanism, but without challenging national competences), the governments' preferred anti-inflationary, stability-oriented macroeconomic and monetary policies (and corollary fiscal adjustments in their public finances) were not challenged by questions of social and economic cohesion.[135] As Moravcsik and Nikolaïdis observe:

> In comparison with previous treaty reforms, nearly all of which were driven by an overriding substantive, generally economical goal . . . the Amsterdam Treaty was preceded by a near total lack of concrete substantive proposals for policies that could be pursued under new institutional provisions . . . In short, there has been much debate about who belongs in the 'core' of Europe and much less about what the core is.[136]

The preceding reflections on the current political shape of the Union bring to the fore yet another striking paradox: although politicization necessitates the democratization of the European polity, especially in terms of strengthening its social legitimacy, this very process remains under the control of the segment elites who, in the interests of decisional efficiency, compromise the principles of ruler accountability and responsible governance. It is highly plausible, then, that any proposed changes to the functioning of the central system that may disrupt the existing equilibrium of forces and interests within the elite cartel – i.e. what essentially makes for the Union's *modus consociandi* – be considered a distant possibility. A recurrent theme here concerns the search for appropriate institutional (formalized rules, voting mechanisms, routinized procedures, norm-setting practices) and extra-institutional (novel forms of collective social engineering) means for the Union to break away from the politics of executive elite dominance and open up its social and political spaces to civic engagement. On that front, the debate will continue to excite the interest of both policy-oriented and normative-driven analyses, at least for the foreseeable future. As for now, it seems fair to conclude that European integration is not about the subordination of the component states to a higher central authority, let alone a new regional state, but rather it is about the preservation of those state qualities that allow the subunits to survive as distinct collectivities, while engaging themselves in mutually rewarding interactions.

Thus survives the spirit of consensus elite government in the political management of the larger consociation.

Notes and references

1 B. Barry, 'Political Accommodation and Consociational Democracy', *British Journal of Political Science*, 5, no. 4, 1975, p. 478.
2 H. Daalder, 'On Building Consociational Nations: The Cases of The Netherlands and Switzerland', *International Social Science Journal*, 23, no. 3, 1971, p. 358.
3 J. Bodin, *On Sovereignty: Four Chapters from the Six Books of the Commonwealth*, ed. and trans. J. H. Franklin, Cambridge: Cambridge University Press, 1992 [1576]. See also J. Althusius, *Politica*, ed. and trans. F. S. Carney, Indianapolis: Liberty Fund, 1995 [1603].
4 V. Vasovic, 'Polyarchical or Consociational Democracy?', in T. Vanhanen (ed.), *Strategies of Democratization*, Washington: Crane Russak, 1992, p. 91.
5 D. J. Elazar, 'Althusius' Grand Design for a Federal Commonwealth', in Althusius, *Politica*, p. xli.
6 F. S. Carney, 'Translator's Introduction', in Althusius, *Politica*, p. xv.
7 Elazar, 'Althusius' Grand Design', p. xxxv.
8 Ibid., p. xxxviii.
9 D. J. Elazar, *Constitutionalizing Globalization: The Postmodern Revival of Confederal Arrangements*, Lanham: Rowman and Littlefield, 1998, p. 202.
10 D. Apter, *The Political Kingdom in Uganda: A Study in Bureaucratic Nationalism*, Princeton, NJ: Princeton University Press, 1966, p. 24.
11 Ibid., pp. 24-5.
12 Ibid., p. 24.
13 G. Sartori, *Theory of Democracy Revisited*, Chatham, NJ: Chatham House, 1987, p. 238.
14 See V. R. Lorwin, 'Segmented Pluralism: Ideological Cleavages and Political Cohesion in Small European Democracies', *Comparative Politics*, 3, no. 2, 1971, pp. 141-75; G. Lehmbruch, 'Consociational Democracy in the International System', *European Journal of Political Research*, 3, 1975, pp. 377-91; and W. T. Bluhm, 'Nation-building: The Case of Austria', *Polity*, 1, 1968, pp. 149-77.
15 G. Stevenson, *Unfulfilled Union: Canadian Federalism and National Unity*, rev. edn, Toronto: Gage, 1982, p. 37.
16 A. Lijphart, 'Consociation and Federation: Conceptual and Empirical Links', *Canadian Journal of Political Science*, 12, no. 3, 1979, p. 500.
17 L. J. Boulle, *Constitutional Reform and the Apartheid State: Legitimacy, Consociationalism and Control in South Africa*, New York: St Martin's Press, 1984, p. 46. See particularly A. Lijphart, *The Politics of Accommodation: Pluralism and Democracy in The Netherlands*, Berkeley, CA: University of

California Press, 1968; and A. Lijphart, 'Typologies of Democratic Systems', Comparative *Political Studies*, 1, no. 1, 1968, pp. 3–44.

18 I. Lustick, 'Stability in Deeply Divided Societies: Consociationalism versus Control', *World Politics*, 30, no. 3, 1979, pp. 325–44.

19 Ibid., p. 327.

20 For more on this, see J-E. Lane and S. Ersson, *The New Institutional Politics: Performance and Outcomes*, London and New York: Routledge, 2000, p. 208.

21 J. H. H. Weiler et al., 'European Democracy and its Critique', in J. Hayward (ed.), *The Crisis of Representation in Europe*, London: Frank Cass, 1995, p. 29.

22 A. Lijphart, *Democracy in Plural Societies: A Comparative Exploration*, New Haven, CT: Yale University Press, 1977, pp. 25–52.

23 Boulle, *Constitutional Reform*, p. 47; Cf. H. Daalder, 'The Consociational Democracy Theme', *World Politics*, 26, no. 4, 1974, pp. 604–21.

24 R. Dahrendorf, *Society and Democracy in Germany*, London: Weidenfeld and Nicolson, 1967, p. 269; Boulle, *Constitutional Reform*, pp. 46–7; and B. G. Powell, Jr, *Contemporary Democracies: Participation, Stability, and Violence*, Cambridge, MA: Harvard University Press, 1982, p. 214.

25 Sartori, *Theory of Democracy Revisited*, p. 239. See J. A. Calhoun, *A Disquisition on Government*, New York: Peter Smith, 1943 [1853].

26 Lijphart, 'Consociation and Federation', p. 501.

27 Powell, *Contemporary Democracies*, p. 214.

28 Boulle, *Constitutional Reform*, p. 49; Lane and Ersson, *New Institutional Politics*, p. 212. See also J. Steiner, 'The Principles of Majority and Proportionality', *British Journal of Political Science*, 1, no. 1, 1971, pp. 63–70.

29 Weiler et al., 'European Democracy', pp. 30–1.

30 Boulle, *Constitutional Reform*, p. 51.

31 P. Taylor, 'Federation and Consociation as Approaches to International Integration', in A. J. R. Groom and P. Taylor (eds), *Frameworks for International Co-operation*, London: Pinter, 1990, p. 173.

32 Boulle, *Constitutional Reform*, p. 51

33 A. Lijphart, 'Consociational Democracy', *World Politics*, 21, no. 2, 1969, p. 218. See also S. M. Halpern, 'The Disorderly Universe of Consociational Democracy', *West European Politics*, 9, no. 2, 1986, pp. 181–97.

34 A. Lijphart, 'Cultural Diversity and Theories of Political Integration', *Canadian Journal of Political Science*, 4, no. 1, 1971, p. 9.

35 Lane and Ersson, *New Institutional Politics*, p. 209.

36 J. H. Hallowell, *The Moral Foundation of Democracy*, Chicago: University of Chicago Press, 1954, p. 29.

37 Taylor, 'Federation and Consociation', p. 173.

38 B. Holden, *Understanding Liberal Democracy*, 2nd edn, London: Harvester Wheatsheaf, 1993, p. 112.

39 Ibid.

40 J. Lodge, 'Loyalty and the EEC: The Limits of the Functionalist Approach', *Political Studies*, 26, no. 2, 1978, p. 234.

41 Boulle, *Constitutional Reform*, p. 31.

42 Taylor, 'Federation and Consociation', p. 174.

43 See G. A. Almond, 'Comparative Political Systems', *Journal of Politics*, 18, no. 3, 1956, pp. 398–9.

44 Hallowell, *Moral Foundation of Democracy*, p. 45

45 Weiler et al., 'European Democracy', p. 31.

46 Sartori, *Theory of Democracy Revisited*, p. 239

47   P. Taylor, 'Confederalism: The Case of the European Communities', in P. Taylor and A. J. R. Groom (eds), *International Organization: A Conceptual Approach*, London: Pinter, 1978, p. 317.

48   P. Taylor, 'The European Community and the State: Assumptions, Theories and Propositions', *Review of International Studies*, 17, no. 2, 1991, pp. 109–25.

49   J. S. Furnivall, *Colonial Policy and Practice: A Comparative Study of Burma and Netherlands India*, Cambridge: Cambridge University Press, 1948, p. 304; quoted in Lijphart, *Democracy in Plural Societies*, p. 17.

50   The literature on sovereignty, in both legal scholarship and political philosophy, is voluminous. For a comprehensive treatment of the subject in relation to the Community legal system, see P. Eleftheriadis, 'Begging the Constitutional Question', *Journal of Common Market Studies*, 36, no. 2, 1998, pp. 255–72.

51   P. Taylor, *The European Union in the 1990s*, Oxford: Oxford University Press, 1996, p. 97.

52   Lijphart, 'Consociation and Federation', p. 506.

53   Ibid., p. 500.

54   M. Forsyth, *Unions of States: The Theory and Practice of Confederation*, Leicester: Leicester University Press, 1981, p. 1.

55   R. Bellamy and A. Warleigh, 'From an Ethics of Integration to an Ethics of Participation: Citizenship and the Future of the European Union', *Millennium*, 27, no. 3, 1998, p. 452.

56   Y. Lejeune, 'Contemporary Concept of Confederation in Europe – Lessons Drawn from the Experience of the European Union', in *The Modern Concept of Confederation*, European Commission for Democracy through Law, Council of Europe, Conference Proceedings, 1995, p. 140.

57   See *Bundesverfassungsgerichts*, cases 2BvR 2134/92 and 2BvR 2159/92. For an extensive analysis of this ruling, see M. Herdegen, 'Maastricht and the German Constitutional Court: Constitutional Restraints for an "Ever Closer Union"', *Common Market Law Review*, 31, no. 2, 1994, pp. 235–49; U. Everling, 'The Maastricht Judgement of the German Federal Constitutional Court and its Significance for the Development of the European Union', *Yearbook of European Law*, 14, 1994, pp. 1–19; and J. H. H. Weiler, 'Does Europe Need a Constitution? Demos, Telos and the German Maastricht Decision', *European Law Journal*, 1, no. 3, 1995, pp. 219–58.

58   P. Taylor, 'A Conceptual Typology of International Organization', in Groom and Taylor (eds), *Frameworks for International Co-operation*, p. 21.

59   P. Taylor, *International Organization in the Modern World: The Regional and the Global Process*, London: Pinter, 1993, p. 88.

60   G. Majone, 'The Regulatory State and its Legitimacy Problems', *West European Politics*, 22, no. 1, 1999, p. 19.

61   Taylor, 'Federation and Consociation', p. 177.

62   A. Moravcsik, 'Why the European Community Strengthens the State: Domestic Politics and International Cooperation', paper presented at the Annual Meeting of the American Political Science Association, New York, 1–4 September 1994, p. 3; quoted in G. Marks et al., 'European Integration from the 1980s: State-centric v. Multi-level Governance', *Journal of Common Market Studies*, 34, no. 3, 1996, pp. 345–6.

63   H. Abromeit, 'How to Democratise a Multi-level, Multi-dimensional Polity', in A. Weale and M. Nentwich (eds), *Political Theory and the European Union:*

Legitimacy, Constitutional choice, and Citizenship, London and New York: Routledge, 1998, p. 116.

64 B. Barry, *Political Argument*, London: Routledge, 1965, p. 317; quoted in A. Weale, 'Between Representation and Constitutionalism in the European Union', in A. Weale and M. Nentwich (eds), *Political Theory and the European Union: Legitimacy, Constitutional Choice and Citizenship*, London and New York: Routledge, 1998, p. 56.

65 S. Bulmer, 'The European Council and the Council of the European Union: Shapers of a European Confederation', *Publius*, 23, no. 3, p. 32.

66 P. Taylor, 'The Politics of the European Communities: The Confederal Phase', *World Politics*, 27, no. 3, 1975, p. 346.

67 A. M. Sbragia, 'Thinking about the European Future: The Uses of Comparison', in A. M. Sbragia (ed.), *Euro-politics: Institutions and Policy-making in the 'New' European Community*, Washington, DC: The Brookings Institution, 1992, p. 289.

68 S. Hix, *The Political System of the European Union*, Basingstoke: Macmillan, 1999, p. 203.

69 B. Laffan et al., *Europe's Experimental Union: Rethinking Integration*, London and New York: Routledge, 1999, p. 190.

70 Taylor, *European Union in the 1990s*, p. 181.

71 *The European*, 3 November 1994, p. 13; quoted in B. Laffan, 'The Politics of Order and Identity in the European Union', *Journal of Common Market Studies*, 34, no. 1, 1996, p. 95.

72 R. L. Watts, *Comparing Federal Systems*, 2nd edn, Montreal and Kingston: McGill-Queen's University Press, 1999, p. 36.

73 Ibid., pp. 36–7.

74 J. Shaw, *European Community Law*, London: Macmillan, 1993, p. 333.

75 K. Lenaerts, 'Subsidiarity and Community Competence in the Field of Education', *The Columbia Journal of European Law*, 1, no. 1, 1994/95, p. 23.

76 For more on this see, D. N. Chryssochoou, *Democracy in the European Union*, London and New York: I. B. Tauris, 1998, pp. 233–5.

77 Taylor, *International Organization*', p. 87.

78 Lenaerts, 'Subsidiarity and Community Competence', p. 4.

79 G. de Búrca, 'Reappraising Subsidiarity's Significance after Amsterdam', Harvard Jean Monnet Working Paper, no. 7/99, 1999, p. 19.

80 See D. Z. Cass, 'The Word that Saves Maastricht? The Principle of Subsidiarity and the Division of Powers in the European Community', *Common Market Law Review*, 29, 1992, pp. 1112–28.

81 A. G. Toth, 'The Principle of Subsidiarity in the Treaty of Maastricht', *Common Market Law Review*, 29, 1992, pp. 1090–1.

82 J. H. H. Weiler, 'Journey to an Unknown Destination: A Retrospective and Prospective on the European Court of Justice in the Arena of Political Integration', in S. Bulmer and A. Scott (eds), *Economic and Political Integration in Europe: Internal Dynamics and Global Context*, Oxford: Blackwell, 1994, p. 152.

83 *The Times*, 11 December 1992.

84 F. W. Scharpf, 'Negative and Positive Integration in the Political Economy of European Welfare States', in G. Marks et al. (eds), *Governance in the European Union*, London: Sage, 1996, pp. 33–4.

85 Centre for Economic Policy Research, *Making Sense of Subsidiarity: How Much Centralization for Europe?*, Annual Report no. 4, London, 1993, p. 22.

86   P. Demaret, 'The Treaty Framework', in D. O'Keefe and P. M. Twomey (eds), *Legal Issues of the Maastricht Treaty*, London: Wiley Chancery Law, 1994, p. 16.
87   Toth, 'Principle of Subsidiarity', p. 1081.
88   Ibid.
89   Ibid., p. 1092.
90   de Búrca, 'Reappraising Subsidiarity's Significance', p. 16.
91   W. Streeck, 'Neo-voluntarism: A New European Social Policy Regime?', in Marks et al. (eds), *Governance in the European Union*, p. 79.
92   Lenaerts, 'Subsidiarity and Community Competence', p. 25.
93   Ibid.
94   de Búrca, 'Reappraising Subsidiarity's Significance', p. 24.
95   Ibid., pp. 24–5.
96   Commission of the European Communities, 'The Principle of Subsidiarity', SECK(92) 1990, Brussels, 27 October 1992; quoted in Taylor, *European Union in the 1990s*, p. 66.
97   Taylor, *European Union in the 1990s*, p. 66.
98   Ibid., p. 188.
99   Cass, 'Word that Saves Maastricht', p. 1136.
100 A. Moravcsik and K. Nikolaïdis, 'Federal Ideas and Constitutional Realities in the Treaty of Amsterdam', *Journal of Common Market Studies*, 36 (1997 Annual Review of Activities), 1998, p. 14.
101 P. C. Schmitter, 'Federalism and the Euro-polity', *Journal of Democracy*, 11, no. 1, 2000, p. 44.
102 Y. Devuyst, 'Treaty Reform in the European Union: The Amsterdam Process', *Journal of European Public Policy*, 5, no. 4, 1998, p. 615.
103 *The Economist*, 21 June 1997, p. 37.
104 P. Manin, 'The Treaty of Amsterdam', *The Columbia Journal of European Law*, 4, no. 1, 1998, p. 26.
105 Ibid., p. 5.
106 For a comprehensive treatment of the Union's international politics, as well as the new CFSP provisions in relation to the model of confederal consociation, see D. N. Chryssochoou et al., *Theory and Reform in the European Union*, Manchester: Manchester University Press, 1999, esp. ch. 5.
107 F. Vibert, *A Core Agenda for the 1996 Inter-governmental Conference (IGC)*, London: European Policy Forum, 1995, p. 54.
108 K. Armstrong and J. Shaw, 'Integrating Law: An Introduction', *Journal of Common Market Studies*, 36, no. 2, 1998, p. 150.
109 A. Duff (ed.), *The Treaty of Amsterdam: Text and Commentary*, London: Sweet and Maxwell, 1997, pp. 152–3.
110 Ibid., p. 145.
111 Ibid., p. xxxvi–ii, 143.
112 Manin, 'Treaty of Amsterdam', p. 13.
113 de Búrca, 'Reappraising Subsidiarity's Significance', p. 45.
114 W. Wessels, 'Flexibility, Differentiation and Closer Integration: The Amsterdam Provisions in the Light of the Tindemans Report', in M. Westlake (ed.), *The European Union after Amsterdam: New Concepts of European Integration*, London and New York: Routledge, 1998, p. 95. Cf. J. Shaw, 'The Treaty of Amsterdam: Challenges of Flexibility and Legitimacy', *European Law Journal*, 4, no. 1, 1998, pp. 63–86.
115 G. Edwards and G. Wiessala, 'Editorial: Flexibility, Legitimacy and Identity

in Post-Amsterdam Europe', *Journal of Common Market Studies*, 36 (1997 Annual Review of Activities), 1998, p. 9.

116   J. Shaw and A. Wiener, 'The Paradox of the European "Polity"', in M. Green Cowles and M. Smith (eds), *State of the European Union, Volume 5: Risks, Reform, Resistance, and Revival*, Oxford: Oxford University Press, 2000, p. 85.

117   Devuyst, 'Treaty Reform', p. 623.

118   Ibid., p. 624. For a similar view, see W. Sauter, 'The Economic Constitution of the European Union', *The Columbia Journal of European Law*, 4, no. 1, 1998, pp. 35–6.

119   T. A. Spragens, Jr, *Civic Liberalism: Reflections on our Democratic Ideals*, Lanham: Rowman and Littlefield, 1999, p. 214.

120   See Devuyst, 'Treaty Reform'.

121   See also M. J. Tsinisizelis and D. N. Chryssochoou, 'The European Union: Trends in Theory and Reform', in Weale and Nentwitch, *Political Theory and the European Union*, pp. 83–97.

122   P. Taylor, 'The United Nations in the 1990s: Proactive Cosmopolitanism and the Issue of Sovereignty', *Political Studies*, 47, no. 3, 1999, p. 560.

123   Ibid.

124   J. de Areilza, 'Sovereignty or Management? The Dual Character of the EC's Suparanationalism Revisited', Harvard Jean Monnet Papers, no. 2/95, 1995, p. 9.

125   B. Laffan, 'The European Union: A Distinctive Model of International-ization', *Journal of European Public Policy*, 5, no. 2, p. 242.

126   Laffan et al., *Europe's Experimental Union*, p. 96.

127   T. Christiansen and K. E. Jørgensen, 'The Amsterdam Process: A Structurationist Perspective on EU Treaty Reform', European Integration Online Papers, 3, no. 1, 1999, p. 4.

128   Taylor, 'The United Nations in the 1990s', p. 538.

129   R. O. Keohane and S. Hoffmann, 'Conclusions', in W. Wallace (ed.), *The Dynamics of European Integration*, London: Pinter, 1990, p. 281.

130   See B. Kohler-Koch, 'Europe in Search of Legitimate Governance', ARENA Working Papers, no. WP 99/27, 1999.

131   Taylor, 'The United Nations in the 1990s', p. 564.

132   Lijphart, *Democracy in Plural Societies*, p. 2.

133   P. C. Schmitter, 'Some Alternative Futures for the European Polity and their Implications for European Public Policy', in Y. Mény et al. (eds), *Adjusting to Europe: The Impact of the European Union on National Institutions and Policies*, London and New York: Routledge, 1996, p. 31. Cf. W. Wallace, 'Government without Statehood: The Unstable Equilibrium', in H. Wallace and W. Wallace (eds), *Policy-making in the European Union*, Oxford: Oxford University Press, 1996, p. 450.

134   E. B. Haas, 'The Study of Regional Integration: Reflections on the Joy and Anguish of Pretheorising', *International Organization*, 24, no. 4, 1970, p. 635.

135   On the state of the European economy during the time of the Amsterdam negotiations, see A. Scott, 'Developments in the Economies of the European Union', *Journal of Common Market Studies*, 36 (1997 Annual Review of Activities), 1998, pp. 111–29.

136   Moravcsik and Nikolaïdis, 'Federal Ideas', p. 33.

PART FOUR

METATHEORY

6

Capturing the Normative Turn

CONTENTS

Introduction

The thesis advanced in this chapter is that the increasingly overwhelming literature on European integration still leaves much to be desired from a metatheoretical perspective. That is to say, from the standpoint of theorizing both about a fast-growing corpus of regional integration theory and about the study of the discipline using the language of normative discourse. Indeed, a considerable part of the theoretical *acquis* is largely informed by the explanations, as well as analytical and methodological insights, offered by various state-centric and euro-centric approaches to the structural arrangements, behavioural characteristics and operational dynamics of politics, policy and governance in the EU. This chapter puts forward the foundations of a metatheoretical research agenda and claims that the time has come for a certain type of meta-analysis to be applied to the theoretical study of the European polity.[1]

Today, EU scholarship is confronted with a fundamental theoretical challenge: to (re)conceptualize the emerging patterns of interaction between the collectivity and the segments through the intersection of different theoretical approaches. The aim is twofold: on the one hand, to enhance our understanding of the systemic properties and dynamics of European governance and, on the other, to improve the explanatory power of regional integration theory by examining how the political system of the Union actually works. In this context, the following questions warrant our attention. What is new about European polity-formation in the post-Amsterdam era? Is it possible to classify the emerging polity and its functionally structured subsystems under a comprehensive model of governance? If yes, then what conceptual lenses should be employed? What are the limits and possibilities of an 'ever closer union' among distinct politically organized states and demoi? Has a terminal state of integration become discernible? What is the dominant character of the relationship between large-scale democratization and polity-building?

In this chapter, such an ensemble of concepts and ideas is treated within a wider metatheoretical laboratory of European polity-formation, pointing to a profound locking together of democratically organized units within a larger, purposive whole. The idea is to theorize about regional integration theory so as to arrive at conceptual and ideational formulations that transcend theory itself. Or, in Ritzer's metatheoretical terms, the aim is to develop 'transcendent perspectives',[2] as well as a clearer, or perhaps less nebulous, epistemological awareness within the discipline, by engaging in a normativist 'meta-discourse' about the study of European integration *qua* polity-formation and its implications for further theory development and, where possible, new theory creation. The wider intellectual justification of a 'second-order discourse' becomes easily apparent when questioning the hermeneutic capacity of the more positivistic accounts of European governance – themselves trapped in the legacy of functionalist-driven, task-oriented and problem-solving modes of collective action. Hence, there is a corresponding need to call attention to questions of polity, democracy, identity and legitimate governance within the evolving 'EU order'. But for the European project to be subjected to effective normative scrutiny, the existing body of integration theory should become an object of study and/or a subject matter in its own right. After all, it is thanks to such normative undertakings that the polity's ontological conundrum forms part of an open intellectual challenge, rather than merely a studied case of empirical realities. As Bellamy and Castiglione put it:

> [Second-order discourse] does not simply use value-laden arguments or try to apply them, but also enquires into the strength of conviction that normative arguments carry with them, and their internal cohesion and external feasibility. This is what really distinguishes appeals to norms, as done in first-order literature, from the exploration of the reasons underlying norms, which is what the literature on the normative turn is supposed to contribute to European studies.[3]

A point of conceptual clarification is in order here: the term 'normative' is used neither as the opposite of 'realism', nor as synonymous with 'idealism',[4] but rather as a 'system of ideas' that attaches *a priori* importance to questions of bringing the Union closer to its citizens. To quote once more from Bellamy and Castiglione on the recent 'normative turn' in EU studies: 'The EU still awaits its Madison . . . capable of combining normative and practical considerations in equal measure. However, a Publius needs an audience and a context that only normative debate about the EU is likely to create.'[5]

From theory to metatheory

There is often a mistaken assumption that metatheory is about the development of an essentialist perspective capable of explaining the totality of relations in a given social phenomenon. This fallacy is compounded even further in contemporary EU studies by the fact that existing theories of integration, be they middle-range or designed to apply at the macro-level, fall short of capturing the interplay between normative and empirical trends in European governance. But metatheory has never aspired to any such claims. Instead, it is about the way in which research agendas are set so as to include substantive questions about the ontology and epistemology of the phenomenon under investigation or about the conduct of the discipline concerned. Put differently, metatheory does not treat 'theory' as distinct from the process of theorizing about theory itself. It is thus not to be confused with the development of a 'grand theory' whose aim is to explain all different aspects of a given social reality, or for that matter with the formulation of generalized assumptions about how things are and how they ought to be. Although metatheory may well entail elements of both, its primary task is to transcend conventional ways of theorizing and generate a foundational discourse on the subject matter. To underline a crucial distinction between the two concepts: whereas theory organizes and conditions the object of inquiry, metatheory treats theory as the *raison d'être* of the object of inquiry, with theory becoming more than an intellectual construct that gives meaning to that which is empirically observed. It now constitutes an object of study in itself.

What follows aims to capture the missing link between theorizing European integration as a dynamic macro-political phenomenon, whose explanation rests on an understanding of its structure, functions and actors, and 'second-order theorizing', instead focusing on *a priori* substantive issues by resorting to 'first principles' or 'foundational assumptions' about the nature of the European composite polity. What metatheory clearly contributes to the study of the Union's pluralistic process is a sense of theoretical direction as to what, precisely, we value as primary or secondary questions about the physiognomy of a union that defies any authoritative definition on the basis of both its structure and dynamics. More specifically, the crucial question does not so much concern the actual way in which the Union operates as a multi-logical political system, but rather its civic core: in whose name are publicly binding decisions taken in Brussels, or what really makes for the polity's 'constituting authority'? A single demos, several demoi, or simply their national governments? The fundamental normative unit in this line of inquiry is not the component nation-state systems, nor is it the governance institutions of the larger polity. Rather, it is the European civic body itself: an endogenous, multifaceted as well as self-constituting variable, whose infusion into the theoretical trajectory of EU studies transcends the conventional wisdom of formal integration theories. Indeed, if 'theories help to construct the world they describe',[6] metatheory helps to reach a more penetrating understanding of what clearly counts as legitimate lines of inquiry upon which one or the other type of theorizing can apply. Moreover, a metatheoretical approach offers a sense of self-reflection, thus creating additional intellectual spaces to be explored. Finally, metatheory bestows on integration scholarship 'a broader theoretical consciousness' in relation to an evolving and, arguably, ever perplexing EU reality – i.e. 'one of the most extraordinary manifestations of human governance undertaken in the twentieth century'[7] – that has successfully managed to escape any concrete measure of scholarly authoritativeness over its ontology. To borrow from Rosamond: 'Thinking thoroughly about what we do should be a routine act of reflection for social scientists and the most effective way to contextualise in this way is to keep the [meta]theoretical flag flying.'[8]

A second area of concern challenging our conventional ways of theorizing European integration is the question of a 'democratic deficit' in its structures. In a period when much scholarly debate on the subject focuses on procedural mechanisms and inter-institutional relations, if not indeed inter-institutional politics, its equally important socio-psychological aspects remain largely unexplored: the absence of a fully fledged European demos and its implications for the Union's social legitimacy, as '[t]he most important . . . quality of a particular configuration of political authority'.[9] This metatheoretical shift in emphasis rests on the assumption that European democracy presupposes the existence of a 'European civic, value-driven demos' (an identifiable citizen body whose unity is constituted by a shared civic identity) as the necessary popular infrastructure upon which majority rule is to apply.[10] Arguably, the application of majority rule in a system of democratic polities presupposes the existence of certain levels of social unity among the constituent publics which, in turn, presupposes that the 'opponents' who constitute the larger number are also an integral part of a self-conscious 'whole', within which 'minorities can be distinguished and the majority may legitimately claim to rule'.[11] Or, as Weiler categorically puts it: 'People accept the majoritarian principle of democracy within a polity to which they see themselves as belonging.'[12]

Accordingly, 'democracy' and 'demos' are ultimately expressions of a sense of belonging to a 'political community'. Otherwise, the Union will remain *in limbo* between a system of democratic governments and a democratic system of governance, or between a collection of separate national demoi and the breaking of a new, transnational demos. As for the latter term, Zürn makes the point that it contains at least five substantive but analytically separable components. They include: rights (acknowledgement of each other as autonomous individuals with a right to personal self-fulfillment); trust (acceptance that transnational obligations must be complied with); public spirit (a sense of collective identity translated into a concern for the well-being of the collectivity); public discourse (capacity for public communication across borders); and solidarity (willingness to self-sacrifice for the general good and acceptance of redistributive policies and processes).[13] Today, however, Europe's constituent demoi, despite their common citizenship status, are characterized by high levels of political fragmentation, amounting to a 'semi-sovereign' collection of individuals who still lack the means to mark their impact on the actual governance of the Union. For we have not yet witnessed the creation of concrete avenues for the expression of the sovereign power of European citizens in relation to the larger polity. What we have instead is a fragmented citizenry in the sense of a 'polycracy': 'a separable multiplicity made up of the unit "each one"'.[14] It is on this premise that the democratic transformation of the Union should result from the spread of new ideas and ways of relating European citizens to an 'inclusive', albeit composite, regional polity. The aim here is to transform a politically amorphous aggregate of national demoi into a transnational demos, whose members are capable of directing their democratic claims to, and via, the central institutions. This constitutes a fundamental democratic prerequisite for the development of a common civic identity at the grassroots. But where does the present Union fit in the above metatheoretical discussion?

A first point to make is that the transformation of the Union from democracies to democracy, and, hence, from a 'policy-generating enterprise' to a 'polity-creating' one, requires that the positive feelings of the subunits must be stronger and deeper than any divisive issues that may arise as integration proceeds. As Cohen puts it, 'there can be no larger part unless the larger part and the smaller parts are indeed parts of one whole.'[15] Thus, the more the larger polity relies on democratic procedures, the more it depends on whether elements of 'belonging to' a larger polity are embodied in the constituent demoi. It also follows that the emergence of a common civic identity patterned on a substantive corpus of shared democratic values among the member publics is imperative, leading to a self-constituting process that respects cultural pluriformity and multiple identity-holding. Above all, however, for a European demos to exist, its members should recognize their collective existence as such, rather than merely being granted common citizenship rights. Closa explains: 'The idea of democracy as a procedural arrangement linking individuals is only possible if a hypostatisation of real individuals into the idea of citizen is made.'[16] As will be shown below, citizenship becomes more than just a legal status, that is, a set of rights and obligations in the meaning codified by the traditional constitutional doctrine. Accordingly, transnational demos-formation is best conceptualized as a dynamic process of self-transformation in so far as the Union aspires to meet the requirements of what Dahl calls '*a fully democratic process in relation to a demos*',[17] and develop effective European 'civic competence'. By the latter term is meant the institutional capacity of citizens to be actively engaged in the governance of the larger polity. For this is what essentially gives substance to a corpus of citizenship rights and, more generally, civic entitlements, transforming a 'governing people' into a decisive 'civic body'.

Turning to the metatheoretical implications of this line of inquiry, the following analytical question is in order: is the existing laboratory of concepts and ideas drawn from the domain of EU studies firmly enough established to capture the 'normative turn' in the relationship between the Union (as a compound polity) and 'the civic' (as a composite citizen body) and, hence, to allow for such metatheoretical interrogations? In other words, to investigate the fundamental norms, principles and values under-pinning the development of a democratic process of union and formulate a set of presuppositions about the conditions of European polity-formation. The crucial question is whether an analysis of this type will help to investigate issues that are somewhat subsumed by the more descriptive accounts of European governance and how the internal dynamics of the latter relate to or influence the development of national polities. The view taken here is that metatheory is capable of redirecting our analytical *foci* to issues relating to the kind of questions we ask and the type of answers we offer. As Wendt points out, it focuses on 'the ontological and episte-mological issues of what constitute important or legitimate questions and answers for . . . scholarship, rather than on the structure and dynamics of the . . . system *per se*'.[18] In the context of normative discourse, metatheory navigates and at the same time challenges our basic assumptions about what it is that we try to establish when examining complex social and political phenomena like the democratic legitimation of the European polity and with it the possible means of systematizing an emerging body of common citizenship rights. Again, the crucial question to ask is not 'who governs?', but rather 'who is governed?' Wiener and Della Sala raise a similar concern:

> There has been, in the literature on constitutionalism, less regard for the debate as to who will be governed by this new structure, on what basis will they be defined as members of the political community, what role they will play in defining the basis of political authority, the rights they will have entrenched, and why they would accept the legitimate authority of the polity even if it passed the liberal democratic procedural test. The example of the EU illustrates that the challenge is not simply a procedural one of finding the right mix of liberal democratic institutions, procedures and principles. Rather,

there is a tension that . . . may be understood as a product of emerging forms of . . . 'citizenship practice'; that is, the process that contributes to the institutionalization of citizenship.[19]

Interestingly, although the Union appears as a living manifestation of a 'part-formed' body politic whose nascent demos still lacks the vantage point from which to see the general system as a coherent political whole inclusive of a deliberative public sphere, it displays a psychological need to cultivate its civic consciousness and create a new democratic environment by transcending 'the boundaries of the political'. In other words, the struggle for a more democratic process of union will be won when the emerging European demos consolidates its collective civic identity and sees the purpose of its own activities in the larger political association. But as long as the European public acts only as a passive receiver of elite-centred integrative initiatives, it will be this distinctive form of consensus elite government that will continue unchallenged to steer the Union and command the major hierarchies of power in its political architecture. The aim, then, is to find appropriate ways of reforming the European polity so as to create what Tassin called a 'politically constituted public sphere'.[20] And since no single body of theory is capable of ascribing the final word to what democracy is and is not, it is analytically more profitable to understand first what popular democratic assumptions are all about, and then distinguish between democratic and non-democratic approaches to European integration.

So far, the case has been made for a metatheoretical discourse to question the fundamental assumptions or 'first principles' underlying existing research agendas, and to challenge the primacy of 'first-order theorizing' about EU polity-building: metatheory may itself 'open up (or close down) avenues for substantive theory and thereby exercise an important regulatory influence on the latter'.[21] Or, as Christiansen et al. assert, taken as a research strategy, metatheory opens avenues for social science inquiry where several theories '*reduce* features that can be investigated'.[22] Especially in those studies concerned with the building of a democratically viable Union constituted not by a set of interstate contractual arrangements but by a profound popular basis, this requires the transcendence of purely statist and predominantly institutional considerations, and the forging of a new methodological commitment to addressing *a priori* substantive issues about grassroots European political developments, the growing chasm between democratic theory and EU practice, and the sociopsychological conditions of transnational democracy-building.

In this light, metatheory helps to articulate an explicit alternative to existing institutional approaches to the Union's democratic pathology, by formulating a demos-oriented conceptual and analytical apparatus which, to borrow from Schattschneider, perceives democracy first as 'a state of mind'.[23] This approach is firmly rooted in the assumption that the ever-increasing array of policy competences acquired by European governing institutions through government delegation (and legal interpretation) needs to be counterbalanced by the affirmation of substantive 'civic competence' at the grassroots. For it is not the various institutional arrangements *per se* that ultimately bear a major political impact on the governance of the European polity, but rather the meaning of democracy to its respective citizens. A new notion of citizenship thus emanates not as 'a bundle of rights', but rather as 'a state of mind' which, following Soltan's analysis, 'is also a form of membership in a collectivity . . . [defined] by the knowledge, motives, ideals, abilities, and skills associated with it'.[24] This constitutive process of civic self-determination will eventually prove capable of bridging what Habermas calls the 'ever greater gap between being affected by something and participating in changing it'.[25] The proposed metatheoretical agenda, therefore, not only aims to discover a 'reflexivist' avenue to the study of the European polity and, by extension, to redefine the ontological and epistemological foundations of the discipline, but also aspires to transcend our ordinary ways of thinking about the democratization of the collectivity, allowing us to focus on the constitutive elements of transnational demos-formation.[26] Although this type of meta-analysis does not claim to possess all the answers, it offers alternative procedures for answering (as well as for setting) important questions, which take us beyond our path-dependent conceptions of large-scale democracy-building through institutional design.[27]

The strand in EU theorizing that has come closer to a 'second-order discourse' is represented by constructivist approaches to the study of European integration. A special issue of an academic journal, which was devoted to the 'Social Construction of Europe', acknowledged the importance of a normatively informed, metatheoretical research context to EU polity-building, by systematically investigating the impact of constitutive norms and rules; the role of ideas and communicative action; the uses of language and deliberative processes; the interplay of routinized practices, socialization, symbolism and institutional interaction; and the relationship between agent identity and interests. The whole exercise was meant to herald a 'constructivist turn' in EU studies: 'to go beyond explaining variation [in politics and policy] within a fixed setting' and to stress 'the impact of "intersubjectivity" and "social context" on the continuing process of European integration . . . [in brief, to call attention to] the constructive force of the process itself'.[28]

The starting-point of this research trend is an aspect of change since integration has 'a *transformative* impact on the European state system and its constituent units', as well as a firm belief in taking the logic and methods of social science inquiry seriously and incorporate into the process of understanding social reality 'human consciousness' and 'ideational factors' with a normative as well as instrumental dimension.[29] The gist of the argument is that there exists 'a socially constructed reality' as an expression of what Ruggie calls 'collective intentionality'.[30] Keeping in mind that there is both a realist and an idealist component in constructivist thought, constructivism is a social theory with a strong interdisciplinary reach, straddling the lines between the various subfields of social science research. This interdisciplinary trend is exemplified, *inter alia*, in the writings of Shaw and Wiener, whose underlying purpose is 'to track norms from "the social" to "the legal" . . . [and] trace the empirically observable process of norm construction and change . . . with a view to examining aspects of "European" constitutionalism [and citizenship practice]'.[31] The core set of conclusions to be drawn from their research findings is that EU constitutional politics as 'day-to-day practices in the legal and political realm as well as the high dramas of IGCs and new Treaties' is about 'fundamental ordering principles which have a validity outwith the formal setting of the nation state', that 'norms may achieve strong structuring power . . . [and] are created through interaction', and that '[t]he processes of norm construction and rule-following are mutually constitutive'.[32]

In general, the question posed by constructivist theorists in the field of European integration is 'to what extent, and in which ways, a new polity is being constructed in Europe'.[33] The aim is to problematize the changing social ontologies of European polity-formation. It is on this premise that middle-range constructivist theorizing becomes well suited to contemporary EU studies, directing our research *foci* to 'the juridification and institutionalization of politics through rules and norms; the formation of identities and the construction of political communities; the role of language and discourse'.[34] Although it would be rather difficult, as it would be unfair, to reach an authoritative conclusion on the overall contribution of constructivism to the field, for it is both a recent and a continuing attempt 'to enlarge the theoretical toolbox of EU studies',[35] a multitude of useful epistemological and analytical insights can be drawn from an interdisciplinary constructivist research programme that places metatheoretical thinking at the centre of understanding the social ontology of the European polity, thus creating 'an arena in which ontological shifts and metatheoretical moves can be debated'.[36]

So far, an attempt has been made to project an alternative methodological approach to European integration *qua* polity-formation by distinguishing between integration theory as conventionally understood and metatheory as a means of attaining a more profound understanding of the normative implications underlying the study of the European polity. This represents a critical normative turn in EU studies since the means and ends of the democratic legitimation of the Union are increasingly becoming the objects of analysis. In this context, the emphasis has not been on the question of which body of theory can best explain the constitutive norms of European governance, but rather which type of theorizing offers a deeper understanding of the Union's political physiognomy in relation to the sociopsychological conditions of transnational democracy-building. Whether this metatheoretical approach will contribute to the emergence of a conceptual consensus about the construction of a democratic theory of European integration – a task requiring the refinement of integration theory and the development of 'transcendent perspectives' on a range of conventional dispositions – is difficult to foresee. Yet, the point is made that familiarity with metatheory is a two-way process: it helps to develop 'overarching theoretical perspectives' and appreciate their relevance to 'first-order theorizing'.

Applied to the current configuration of authority in the EU, this form of meta-analysis reveals that the component states, although now parts of a compound polity, have lost nothing of their anxiety to preserve the integrity of their polities against the more substantive issues confronting the making of a new democratic *civitas* in Europe. Indeed, 'top-down' attempts at a substantive re-ordering of national political spaces and public spheres – i.e. their qualitative structural adjustment and functional incorporation into a novel regional order – have failed to produce a sense of civic attachment to a supranational polity, let alone a 'postnational' regime in which sovereignty is embedded in the central institutions as an expression of an overarching European social legitimacy. Thus, the relationship between sovereignty and the scope and level of integration is still relevant when trying to explain the evolving European polity. Finally, the point is clearly made about the need to institutionalize European 'civic competence' so as to achieve greater and better democracy in the general system. In conclusion, for a polity that is constantly under the scrutiny of international scholarship, but where no substantive consensus exists (as yet) on its very ontology, the search for clear answers (and questions) is no easy task. But this will be even more so should we fail to investigate the normative implications that a second-order discourse generates for EU polity-building.

The case for European civic competence

It has been suggested that 'to this date the [integration] process has not generated a new political consciousness that would demand and sustain further institutional and democratic transformations.'[37] Likewise, Schmitter admits that public opinion data 'do not show any monotonic tendency towards an increasing sense of "feeling European" or of "being a citizen of Europe" – indeed, this personal identification has decreased rather than increased in the aftermath of the Single European Act and the Treaty on European Union'.[38] Integration has not in other words fostered the normative qualities needed for the nurturing of a common European civicness, itself a prerequisite for the configuration of a shared civic identity at the grassroots. Notwithstanding the contrary rhetoric, the Amsterdam reforms fell short of rectifying this gross democratic deficiency, leaving instead the relationship between the Union and 'the civic' as problematic as ever. In fact, the integrative project can be said to have become even more technical, reflecting the prevalence of a new regulatory aetiology of 'post-parliamentary governance' based on the politics of 'expertology', 'managerialism' and 'technocratic elitism'.[39] Underlying this empirical pragmatism is the functionalist-inspired idea of 'management committee government', particularly evident in the highly technocratic operations of existing 'comitology' structures. Loyal to the segments' traditions of civic statehood, the Amsterdam product failed to provide a sense of civic attachment to the European polity sustained by an independent source of 'input-oriented legitimacy' and, in Bellamy's terms, 'to forge a common identity able to sustain a shared sense of the public good . . . '.[40] Instead, as Shaw categorically asserts, 'the vision of legitimacy driving the political masters of the Treaty is rather a managerial, top-down view of legitimacy as changes to the Treaty framework tend to deliver a rather passive form of citizen consent.'[41]

Before examining the extent to which the AMT affected the democratic quality of European governance, let us sketch a normative perspective on Union citizenship. According to Article B TEU, its general objectives are 'to strengthen the protection of the rights and interests of the nationals of its Member States . . . ', while Articles 8a–e EC [now Articles 17–22 EC] set out the content of such rights. They include: the right to move and reside freely anywhere within the territory of the member states; the right to vote or stand for election in local and European elections for citizens residing in a member state other than their own; the right to diplomatic protection by the consular authority of any member state in third countries; the right to petition the EP; and the right to direct complaints to the European Ombudsman. The first point to make is that the era of the national state as the only legitimate actor in determining the politics of citizenship belongs to the past. For the once nationally determined fix between norms of citizenship and the territorial state is increasingly being eroded by the effects of global communications as well as by the processes of institution-building and polity-formation that take place alongside, and some would argue beyond, the nation-state. As d'Oliveira puts it with reference to Union citizenship, 'It represents a loosening of the metaphysical ties between persons and a State, and forms a symptom of the cosmo-politization of citizenship.'[42] Meehan makes a similar point when she argues that 'a reconceptualization is taking place in which . . . the citizen's legal status and the content of his or her rights are not determined by nationality alone'.[43] This view does not classify Union citizenship as being either 'neo-national' or 'neo-imperial', but as a form of regulating a common order out of distinct publicly organized national settings: 'both statuses will co-exist, representing two different principles of political organization'.[44] As Meehan concludes:

> While the complexity of this framework is intimidating in the demands it makes in finding our way around the European public space, it can provide many openings for challenging authority, for expressing our various loyalties associated with our various identities, and for exercising our rights and duties in more than one arena.[45]

But citizenship also symbolizes an internally oriented relationship that the demos shares with the institutions of the polity to which its members belong.[46] In spite, therefore, of its explicit treaty-based character and corollary constitutional shortcomings, Union citizenship carries an undisputed political symbolism, which may entail far-reaching implications for the development of a common European civicness and the embodiment of a stronger *Gemeinschaft* element among the constituent publics. Union citizenship, as a novel form of collective civic identity, may thus gradually develop into a meaningful object of citizen identification capable of shaping pre-existing individual identities. But perhaps the most celebrated property of citizenship is the range and depth of participatory opportunities it offers to fulfil the democratic potential (deliberative or other) of the demos in the exercise of political authority. This view, which does not presuppose an organic form of social unity, accords with an active notion of citizenship *qua* 'substantive public engagement' – i.e. citizenship not just as a legal status or a means of protecting rights, but as an attitude towards public life – whereby civic participation constitutes a highly valued feature, if not a virtue in itself. In this embracing civic space, a feature central to the democratic process becomes crucial, that of 'civic competence': the institutional capacity of citizens *qua* social equals to enter the realm of political influence, shape the political agenda and affect the making of publicly binding decisions.

The pairing of 'civic' and 'competence' does not embody a category mistake, but rather acts in the interests of empowering citizens to engage themselves actively in the management of public affairs. It thus issues an invitation to institutionalize, through the granting of substantive civic entitlements, a normative commitment to core democratic principles in the actual governance of the polity. In doing so, civic competence offers a meaningful conceptual framework and gives a concrete institutional face to a central task of legitimate rule, that of encouraging deliberative civic engagement and responsible governance. At the same time, it creates a multitude of opportunities for meaningful democratic choice by individual and organized citizens, enabling them to direct their claims through a publicly organized political space which promotes open dialogue and enhances their ability to have a real impact on the political process. On the basis of this essentially civic, if not neo-republican (see Chapter 1), conception of structuring citizen involvement in the emerging European political order, joint decision-making becomes more transparent, political issues more visible and transnational power-holders more accountable in the public realm for their actions or inaction. Strengthening European civic competence would, therefore, make a profound contribution to the building of a democratic polity in Europe based on an active and participative community of citizens.

The preceding discussion makes it plausible to argue that the democratic potential of Union citizenship appears to be threefold: it sets up a transnational system of rights that are not nested in the component nation-states but rather are designed to give access and voice to the constituent demoi; it induces further integrative popular sentiment by motivating greater civic participation in the affairs of the larger system; and it strengthens the bonds of belonging to an 'active polity' by facilitating the process of positive European awareness-formation at the grassroots, thus performing a crucial identity function. The question to ask here is whether Union citizenship should simply entail a re-arrangement of existing civic entitlements, thus acting as a functionalist project at the disposal of national authorities, or whether it should attribute effective civic competence based on a new 'civic contract' between peoples, states and central authorities. Whether, in other words, it should generate the social capital and assorted sense of common civicness needed for the making of a larger, composite demos. The answer becomes clear by employing a meta-institutional approach to Union citizenship – the prefix 'meta' denotes the transcendence of purely institutional variables – whereby the distribution of European civic competence passes through the capacity of citizens to determine the political functions of the larger polity. Such an approach alludes to the view that what is vital both to the moral ontology of democratic governance and to the prevailing value spheres of collective civicness is the existence of a civic contract between 'decision-makers' and 'decision-receivers'. Arguably, should a demos-oriented 'arrangement' of this type fail to materialize, then the social legitimacy of the polity is challenged *ab intra* and a corresponding state of 'illegitimacy' prevails. From this meta-institutional account of the political orientation and deliberative potential of Union citizenship, the European demos acquires a higher normative authority, its status being elevated into a truly sovereign entity in the public realm of a transnational polity.

Union citizenship offers the opportunity to incorporate but not amalgamate the separate civic contracts of the component polities into a European civic space, where the consent of citizens to the larger scale of decisions is organized 'from below' within a horizontally structured union of peoples. It thus respects the principle of 'value pluralism', according to which 'diversity is *valuable* in itself, and not, as often happens, just an inconvenient fact that must be regulated in order to ensure better "coexistence"'.[47] Indeed, as the nation-state has been 'the necessary vehicle for the establishment of a modern social contract',[48] so the Union could create *ex novo* a plurinational civic contract that is responsive to the concerns of a diversified citizen body, and whose value lies in the idea of symbiotic legitimation structures among different democratic publics. Union citizenship does not and should not thus employ a universalist approach aimed at the regulation of collective national differences of identity, but rather their incorporation into a polycentric public sphere by means of constitutionalizing what, in Requejo's words, amounts to 'a plurality of ways of belonging to and participating in the *polity*'.[49] This conception of citizenship not only is fully in line with a defence of democratic pluralism, but also aspires to the co-constitution of different civic components of national identities. In this context also, the idea of 'demos before ethnos' becomes a practical political reality leading to the forging of cross-national public allegiances and multiple group affiliations.

The preceding reflections suggest that the making of a European demos should be distinguished from any assimilationst processes of enforced homogeneity, evident in the nation-building experiences of the component polities. Moreover, without any solid pre-political ties among the constituent publics, the substance of Union citizenship becomes closer, in Mouffe's words, to 'the construction of a "we" in a context of diversity which reflects the core values of the "uniting" parts'.[50] The point here is that the idea of a European demos overrides any territorial and ethno-cultural conceptions of political organization, especially those associated with propagandistic means of consciousness-raising and artificial collective identifications. Its constituent parts are instead based on what Etzioni calls a 'core curriculum':[51] a body of shared values which keep its members together not as a homogeneous citizenry, but rather as an identifiable civic unit that has a say in the making of collective binding decisions at the larger level. Whereas nation-building implies the formal merging of pre-existing nations or members of a single nation within an amalgamated state appara-tus (whose legitimacy rests on specific ethno-cultural characteristics), demos-formation implies a different kind of group consciousness that is based on adherence to the democratic process, as opposed to feelings of belonging to or wishing to form one state, in the form of a territorially defined entity which possesses ultimate legal authority and maintains (often by coercive means) a general hierarchy of power upon which public life is organized. Unlike, then, formal amalgamation, whereby different peoples legally come to form the core population of a larger territory, which in turn becomes the privileged site of domestic social discipline and control, transnational demos-formation aims to make the European peoples feel, look and act more as a composite demos than as several and fragmented citizen bodies.

What is more, although both nation-building and demos-formation can facilitate political integration, the former aims to achieve a natural 'community of fate' whose constituted unity lies in the conception of one 'nationality' (also aimed at achieving a cultural match between statehood and peoplehood), while the latter purports to lay down the foundations for a self-conscious and civic-minded citizen body capable of identifying with the institutions of governance operating above or alongside the traditional state. This is a critical distinction for it clears away any notion that the idea of the component demoi forming a collective civic identity may itself invoke a kind of European nationalism, or that the larger polity 'will be able to reproduce on an enlarged scale the same intensity of collective sentiment that was once characteristic of its member nation-states . . . '.[52] In short, transnational demos-formation is concerned with the transfor-mation of exclusive loyalties and affiliations into a dynamic 'network' of concentric identities, according to which less encompassing units, such as the participating state polities or their respective substate communities, are situated within more encompassing ones such as the Union.

Thus envisaged, a European civic demos is neither the creature of law based on the granting of political rights to a community composed of different nationalities, nor is it a by-product of a process akin to national integration that purports to create a sense of 'national identity' and pride through national symbols or by employing tactics of political socialization so as to eradicate constitutive loyalties and identities.[53] Weiler concurs:

> The substance of membership (and thus of the demos) is in a commitment to the shared values of the Union as expressed in its constituent documents, a commitment, *inter alia*, to the duties and rights of a civic society covering discrete areas of public life, a commitment to membership in a polity which privileges exactly the opposites of nationalism – those human features which transcend the differences of ethno-culturalism. In this reading, the conceptualisation of a European demos should not be based on real or imaginary trans-European cultural affinities or shared histories nor on the construction of a European 'national' myth of the type which constitutes the identity of the organic nation. The decoupling of nationality and citizenship opens the possibility, instead, of thinking of co-existing multiple demoi.[54]

In the same vein, Connolly's plea for supporting 'a more cosmopolitan democratic imagination' exemplifies the ethos of transnational demos-formation well: 'to cultivate respect for a politics of democratic governance', by pluralizing 'democratic energies, alliances and spaces of action that exceed the closures of territorial democracy'.[55]

But for Union citizenship to elevate the constituent demoi into the symbol and source of 'strong democracy',[56] it requires the evolution of the 'member-state citizen' from a 'functionalist' or 'fragmented citizen' to an 'indirect' or 'derived' one, and then to an 'interactive citizen'.[57] The transition from one stage to the other should come about as a conscious act of civic self-development: an exercise in 'political self-identification'.[58] As Herzog puts it, 'European citizenship must proceed from the desire and the capacity of the persons concerned to found an active community seeking to serve common goals.'[59] Among such measures to build on the occurrence of a transnational civic identity are: the detachment of Union citizenship from the 'nationality requirement' and its placing on an independent sphere of civic entitlements; the institutionalization of citizens' right to information on all EU issues; the creation of protective legal mechanisms against any infringement of fundamental liberties, collective or individual; the enrichment of the citizens' social and economic rights relating to the four freedoms of movement, social welfare, working conditions and labour-management relations; and the recognition of political rights to legally resident third-country nationals, which in turn requires the transcendence of liberal statist norms of inclusion and the rejection of a 'dissociational-type democracy'.[60] As for now, Habermas's lament continues to hold true: 'The European passport [and let us add the elements of a European capital city, flag, anthem, and driving licence] is not as yet associated with rights constitutive for democratic citizenship.'[61]

Central to the above discussion is the principle of additionality, in that Union citizenship rights should be established in addition to those already embedded in the status of national citizenship. Put differently, they should be attached to a novel *status civitatis* or, conversely, divorced from 'the classical [organic] democratic model of nationally derived belonging and identity'.[62] Instead, they should be linked to the capacity of citizens to improve the participatory quality of European governance by engaging themselves 'in the construction of the norms, institutions and visions that will define . . . [their] rights, access and a sense of belonging to the new Europe',[63] as well as by contributing to the process of overcoming collective-action problems through public deliberation. It is only then that the Union could foster the bonds between itself and an emergent European civic body, and give rise to a new concept of plurinational citizenship. As Bellamy notes, the only significant change to citizenship provisions brought about by the AMT amounted, in large measure, to a point of clarification: 'Citizenship of the Union shall complement and not replace national citizenship.'[64] This provision, he continues, 'neatly captures the continued dual character of the Union, as both inter-national and supranational'.[65] It is still the case, however, courtesy of Article 8(1) EC, that the status of Union citizenship is contingent upon the granting of nationality in one of the member states, a process which remains firmly under the control of their respective authorities. Moreover, like Maastricht, Amsterdam failed to incorporate any substantive civic rights in a formal 'constitutional' document addressed to the citizen directly. Such a decision clearly reflected the political rationale of sovereignty-conscious states to insist on a fairly acceptable but modest citizenship package, representing, in the words of Anderson et al., 'a codification of existing trends in jurisprudence and legislation which added little to what was already in the pipeline or being practiced'.[66] Schmitter makes this point well:

> Most of the TEU provisions concerning Euro-citizenship were not novel. They had already been 'acquired' without much fanfare through the internal regulations of the EP or the ECJ, or included in various treaties sponsored by the Council of Europe. Many of them are not even exclusive to EU membership, but apply to legally resident aliens and firms as well. Even if one were to assemble a list of all the rights that Euro-citizens have acquired since the EEC's founding in 1958 – regardless of their source or substance – it might be difficult to convince most individuals that they had gained much that their respective national governments were not already providing.[67]

Although the language used in both treaties implies that there was no intention on the part of national governments to give birth to a 'new political subject' – i.e. a genuine *civis europeus* – from a developmental macro-political perspective, the mere inclusion of Union citizenship into the treaty framework 'could be seen as an interesting example of Member States feeding (relatively) new ideas into the policy-making and, in this case, the constitution-forming, process'.[68] Notwithstanding Herzog's point that Union citizenship has established 'an important federal precedent', or Duff's view that it 'postulates the existence of a common popular sovereignty to complement – or rival – the common sovereignty of the states', O'Keeffe is right to comment that the importance of common citizenship provisions 'lies not in their content but rather in the promise they hold for the future'.[69] And so is Shaw's dynamic account of Union citizenship as 'a form of "post-national" political membership which represents a vital building-block in the ongoing process of polity-formation within Europe'.[70] Nevertheless, the prospects for European civic competence rest as much on legal requirements, judicial mechanisms and procedural guarantees, as they do on public responses themselves. From this normative angle, it must be concluded that the development of Union citizenship within a multi-level civic order composed of national and transnational forms of fellowship as well as a multitude of non-territorial associative relations among diverse socio-political forces aims at harnessing the democratic ethos of a nascent European civic body. Hence, the relationship between the extension and deepening of the conditions and terms of Union citizenship and the democratic legitimation of the emerging regional polity becomes immediately synergetic, assigning meaning to the civic orientation of European political society, while espousing a new participatory ethos and a profound reconceptualization of citizen-polity relations.

At the macro-level, the trinity *symbiosis – synergy – osmosis* corresponds to the three stages in the making of a European civic demos: the first describes the current state of the relationship between the collectivity (as a compound polity) and the segments (as distinct but constitutive polities); the second points to the development of horizontal links among the component demoi and a strengthening of existing ties among their respective elites; the third represents a culmination of the previous two in a democratic 'sympolity' emphasizing the importance of civic competence for the composite demos to act in an extended political space. To borrow from Sołtan: 'Strengthening civic competence can be seen, first, as an instrument of democratization . . . More broadly (and ambitiously), strengthening civic competence is also an instrument of reform that improves the quality of government and of social life more generally.'[71] The significance of tying the self-image of the elites to the dialectic between Union citizenship and transnational demos-formation is that no sense of common civic identity may come into being unless all major actors in European governance see themselves as part of a multi-level political space that has to evolve from reciprocal interactions at the lower level 'upwards'; that is to say, from the everyday networks of civic engagement. Equally important here is for the constitutive civic values and democratic claims of European citizens to be identified, debated, challenged and ultimately accommodated through the institutions of the general system.

If by democracy is meant the highest form of civic association for embracing the participation of the demos in the shaping of its political environment, then the above conception does not refer to a theoretical transformation derived from a 'pure' political sociological approach to legitimate forms of governance, thus being deprived of any empirical implications. Rather, it points to a highly interactionist activity carried on through processes of public deliberation so as to generate and sustain a belief in the members of the composite demos that they are the decisive actors in the transnational political process by assuming shared civic responsibilities for shaping and steering the Union as 'a polity belonging to its citizens rather than nationals . . . '.[72] As the next section will clearly illustrate, however, the Amsterdam treaty reforms leave much to be desired regarding the transition of the Union's democratic orientation 'from paternalism to citizenship', or from 'top-down elitism' to what Bellamy and Warleigh term 'a participatory ethics of governance'.[73] This said, it seems fair to conclude that, without an inclusive normative framework for the development of a common European civicness, the possibilities for institutionalizing a fully working transnational civic order, which will allow the Union to acquire its distinctive model of democratic citizenship, remain particularly grim, at least for the foreseeable future.

But let us now offer a typology of civic governance (see Figure 6.1). The Union presently occupies the upper left box in the figure since there are clear signs of the development of a large-scale civil society composed of transnational policy communities, partnership arrangements, structures of functional representation, patterns of interest intermediation, umbrella organizations, networking activities and a plethora of organized pressure groups pursuing their interests at the larger level of aggregation. Although these factors arguably play a growing role in the initiation and formulation of common policies, the development of a shared civic identity on the part of its constituent demoi has not yet met the institutionalization of civic competence at the larger level. As the typology in Figure 6.1 illustrates, this mix of variables is necessary for the emergence of a European civic space composed of an interactive transnational demos. But the Union has not equally met the conditions for the institutionalization of a political public sphere, within which citizens deliberate through public argument and reasoning over possible ways of improving the democratic quality of European governance. After all, this is exactly what the process of civic governance based on the discursive qualities of free public deliberation is all about.

The normative content of the envisaged regional order refers to discourse-centred processes of civic engagement in the transnational political process. Whether or not formally instituted, such processes serve the goal of a polycentric civic space, for they direct the democratic claims of the citizen body towards those centres of authoritative decision-making that are entitled to commit the polity as a whole. Otherwise, a novel yet easily discernible form of political domination will determine the

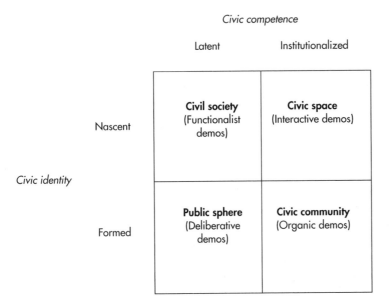

FIGURE 6.1 *Typology of civic governance*

relationship between executive-centred elites and the affected public. The point here is that, without a principled public discourse to steer the civic orientation of the European polity, it would be naïve to expect the structural transformation of a shadowy political space into a purposeful *res publica*: a pluralist polity within which citizens operate at different levels and sites of power and are entitled 'to negotiate fair compromises amongst the plurality of interests and ideals involved'.[74] Such normative commitment to instituting a transnational public sphere *ab integro* may act as an antidote to the growing impoverishment of national civic space, where a decline of public discourse is met by a shrinking democratic legitimacy of the political space. But it also performs a crucial formative function, by shaping the behaviour of citizens, encouraging public participation and creating an inclusive political process within which the notion of citizenship amounts to something much more than the aggregate of its parts: it becomes a normative quality to guarantee certain values. The next section examines the extent to which the Amsterdam reforms missed the opportunity to bring about a more demos-orientated process of union.

The false promise of Amsterdam

Regardless of one's pro/contra integrationist convictions, the phasing-in of questions of polity and democracy into the EU's political agenda has not yet transcended the anxiety of states to safeguard their own prerogatives, even when these questions became crucial to the political viability of the general system. Instead of focusing on issues that constitute the essence of any well thought out process of democratic reform, the unimaginative quality of proposals submitted to the 1996/97 IGC highlighted the absence of a clear democratic vision to take the Union dynamically into the new millennium. Shaw concurs: 'there is no strong evidence that the Treaty of Amsterdam has dealt with the fundamental legitimacy issues which emerged most clearly in the early 1990s.'[75] And so does Weiler, arguing that, '[w]hereas in its founding period Europe was positioned as a *response* to a crisis of confidence, fifty years later it has shifted to become one of the causes of that crisis.'[76] Amsterdam failed in these accounts, for it lacked a kind of 'innovative reflection' on the construction of an enlarged civic space out of the segments' varied traditions. Rather, it focused on 'distributive compromises'[77] so as to accommodate the particularistic attitudes of self-interested actors, inviting a sacrifice in democratic input for greater efficiency in output. As Shaw points out, the AMT 'is more about "managing" reactions to the EC/EU than it is about seeking to engage in citizen participation'.[78]

In addition to the above, the AMT lacked a 'departure of substance' for the creation of 'norms of polity' centred on the specific constructions of legitimate forms of governance. As a result, it failed to rediscover 'a sense of process' (and of purpose too) *vis-à-vis* such normative orientations as the structural transformation of a plurality of demoi into a pluralistic demos and, hence, the emergence of a new European *pouvoir constituant* as 'the ultimate legitimising referent of the [Euro-]polity'.[79] This is linked to yet another crucial transformation the Union ought to undertake: 'from an ethics of integration to an ethics of participation'; 'a deliberative process whereby citizens reach mutually acceptable agreements that balance their various communitarian commitments in ways that reflect a cosmopolitan regard for fairness'.[80] In the words of Mény: 'There is a need for a new civic culture . . . which allows for multiple allegiances, which combines the "right to roots" with the "right to options" . . . '.[81] From a metatheoretical perspective, what these assertions seek to identify is a new normative basis for EU polity-building, ensuring that such a process 'is founded on civic and deliberative debate'.[82]

But the areas upon which the review conference focused concerned primarily the rationalization and simplification of joint decision-making procedures (parliamentary co-decision) and decision-taking adjustments (reweighting of votes), the Council's voting mechanisms (extension of QMV) and, in general, measures concerning the effectiveness of joint decision-making as a precondition for guaranteeing the future functioning, but not social legitimation, of the larger system. Ironically enough, this elaborate exercise in rationalized institutionalism originally aimed at rectifying a long-standing criticism of the Community as a 'joint decision-system' producing sub-optimal policy outputs,[83] and at the level of negotiated package-deals an inequitable *status quo*. Dehousse has amply described one of the major reasons for the Union's 'unstable equilibrium': 'although the parliamentary system remains by far the dominant paradigm in the discourse on the reform of European institutions, the last decade has witnessed a gradual emergence of issues and instruments which do not correspond to the parliamentary tradition.'[84] As Kohler-Koch puts it: 'the EU is not just institutionally retired, but lives in a social environment that does not fulfil the prerequisites for representative democracy.'[85] Arguably, the AMT placed the EP closer to the *locus decidendi* of the general system by extending the scope of parliamentary co-decision (largely by replacing 'cooperation') and by simplifying the procedures therein (changing the 'default condition' in the conciliation process). In doing so, it sought to address the Union's 'parliamentary deficit' and facilitate the emergence of a bicameral system. Although co-decision 'applies to only 8 out of 36 new competences attributed to the [Community] by the Amsterdam Treaty . . . there are 22 new *issues under codecision* which come in addition to the 15 set out in the Maastricht Treaty.'[86] But it failed to link increased parliamentary co-decision with greater QMV in the Council, to extend the EP's right of assent in third-pillar issues affecting the citizen and, crucially, to grant the EP constitutional competence over treaty reform.

Let us now turn to the issue of transparency for it has overlapping consequences for the relationship between the Union and its citizens. This principle, inspired by notions of 'open government', is vital for the Union to eliminate the gap between the functioning of its institutions and citizen identification with its governance structures. The term is linked to the granting to Union citizens of a right of information and the need for a more simplified and comprehensible treaty. Although Amsterdam succeeded in meeting the first requirement through a (conditional) right of public access to official EU documents, and, in Dehousse's words, by covering 'the practical modalities of access',[87] it did not achieve much on the latter: the simplification of the co-decision procedure was coupled with the institutionalization (or even instrumentalization) of other practices such as flexibility, exceptions, reservations, safeguards, protocols, declarations and the rest, which arguably represent an exercise in 'cognitive difficulty'.[88] On balance, though, a formalization of transparency procedures has taken place: their *de jure* incorporation into the treaty framework. Whereas these were previously determined by inter-institutional arrangements and rules of procedure, the ECJ can now monitor the implementation of a norm of legislative openness as an operational principle of European governance. For all their shortcomings, since they still conform to the regulatory model of technocratic or network governance, the new transparency rules are now part of the Union's 'primary law'.[89] Yet as a member of the EP has observed, contrary to the stated aims of the Amsterdam negotiators, the end-product deserved 'a first prize for complexity, lack of clarity and transparency'.[90] Or, as Cram et al. categorically put it, 'the post-Amsterdam EU is even more arcane and complex than its already impenetrable predecessor.'[91]

Before turning to our conclusions, it is worth recalling that Amsterdam's largest deficiency was its emphasis on policy rather than polity, efficiency rather than democracy, distributive compromise rather than integrative accommodation, functionalist structures rather than shared normative commitments and the rationalist exercise of competences rather than symbiotic legitimation. It thus emerges as a managerial type of reform where affective/identitive politics still remains out of reach. Its core rests not on the need for cementing the constitutive (even dialectical) norms of a polycentric civic sphere as a precondition for deliberative equity and substantive civic engagement, but rather on an exclusionary politics of consensus elite government determined by sub-optimal exchanges in complex negotiations. The general assessment is that a European civic order patterned on the mutual constitution of normative structures is yet to emerge. The final section that follows summarizes the limits of EU polity-building by revisiting Amsterdam's failure to institutionalize democratic norm-orientation through formal treaty reform.

Drawing insights

Theorizing European integration has so far impelled many promising theoretical departures but has managed to achieve only a few concrete theoretical arrivals. At a time when the Union remains much of an unspeci-fied entity with an open-ended political *telos*, its dynamism is caught between federalist aspirations to become a more congruent polity and a modified type of intergovernmentalism which confirms the centrality of states in managing the regional arrangements. The overall conclusion to be drawn is that, despite its continued political and constitutional evolution, and gradual accretion of substantive policy competences, the Union has not developed the attributes of a sovereign entity. It has, however, evolved into a fully fledged political system whose proper conceptualization is to be found outside pre-existing statist categories, despite the rather paradoxical fact, at least from a realist state-centric perspective, that it does share a multitude of state-like characteristics. It is precisely this dialectical union of integrative and autonomy forces operating at the same time across distinct but interdependent policy domains and levels of governmental and societal action that constitutes the fundamental stability of the Union.

All the above contribute to an understanding of the Union as a compound polity best captured by the term 'confederal consociation': a consensual form of polity that has achieved a level of integration that is comparable to many plurinational federal polities, without however threatening in any fundamental way the sovereignty of its component states. Instead, the common management and joint exercise of separate sovereignties have acquired a new qualitative dynamic, assisted by an accommodationist process of political co-determination. Above all, the validity of our claim to present the Union as an image of a confederal con-sociation lies in the varied possibilities the model offers for encompassing what seems to be the cornerstone of a constitutionally viable, politically stable and socially acceptable European non-state form of polity: 'unity in diversity'. But, as also mentioned in Chapter 1, a relatively accurate understanding of this novel form of transnational polity is to be found within the confines of a largely asymmetrical and often analytically incongruent synthesis of insights drawn from the intersection of various theoretical strands. It thus appears that the most reliable trajectory for developing a more profound understanding of the European polity process is towards an interdisciplinary research programme that combines both theoretical and metatheoretical perspectives.

In the midst of a near-chaotic state of theorizing integration, the norma-tive agents of legitimate governance and 'postnational constitutionalism',[92] along with the gradual Europeanization of civil society, have clearly raised the expectations of the Amsterdam process to bestow upon the Union a clearer political and constitutional identity. Yet, by consolidating national autonomy in terms of acknowledging the need of states to retain ultimate political control over both European constitutional choice and change, the limits of these reforms clearly illustrated the limits of EU polity-building in the late 1990s. Even the new qualitative dialectic between sovereignty and integration carried the implication of an explicit right to political co-determination, without however committing the member state polities to the framing of a comprehensive strategy for democratizing the Union with the view to strengthening transnational civic competence, 'deepening' European citizenship rights and dissociating its fragile political legitimacy from collective policy performance. Far from being a *cause célèbre* for a substantive re-ordering of civic spaces and public spheres, the Amsterdam reforms amount to a series of 'partial offsets' to key democratic problems confronting the Union. Thus, the new dynamic tension between democracy and integration became manifest not only after Amsterdam, but also because of Amsterdam. For, what the latter failed to produce was not a common democratic vision *per se*, but rather a belief that such a vision remains out of reach, at least for the foreseeable future.

This criticism is justified further by perceiving the AMT as the product of a predominantly utilitarian, cost–benefit calculus between divergent national interests and competing 'polity-ideas', along the lines of an overall rationalist settlement. As Moravcsik and Nikolaïdis summarized the primary lesson of Amsterdam: 'no amount of institutional facilitation or political enterpreneurship, supranational or otherwise, can overcome underlying divergence or ambivalence of national interests.'[93] To that, one could safely add that it is hardly possible to democratize the Union without civic participation, now that the once unquestionable 'permissive consen-sus' can no longer generate the necessary public commitment to an EU politics where public needs are met through a process of consensus elite government. If anything, the exclusion of citizens from the governance of the Union, compounded by the lack of effective European civic competence, is at the expense of popular fragmentation itself. And so is the failure to arrive at a European citizenship model to broaden civic participation in the determination of collective policy outcomes and the resolution of collective-action problems. But it is also against the interests of better equipping citizens to become agents of civic change: to elevate their status into a system-steering agency within a nascent pluralist order.

The absence of this normative trend from the logic of the Amsterdam process was exactly the opposite of what neofunctionalists had hoped to achieve: instead of politicization becoming an additional weapon in the strategic arsenal of pro-integrationist forces, it is effectively employed by the more sceptical actors, making it difficult for a new democratic equilibrium to emerge between the Union and 'the civic' and act as an invitation to civic inclusiveness, decisional transparency and principled public discourse. True, for a polity that was founded and is still based on a system of international treaty rules, and whose incipient but fragmented citizen body lacks effective civic competence, the transition from democracies to democracy and, hence, from an aggregative to a deliberative model of governance is neither easy nor linear, let alone automatic. Yet, as Spragens tellingly warns us, 'Forgetfulness about important things can be dangerous.'[94] It is on this premise that the making of a democratic polity in Europe should counsel an end to that neglect. The challenge is thus set: to discover a sense of civic process within which politics is not treated as the art of the possible, but rather as the art of *creating* the possible. This represents more than just a democratic wish for the shape of things to come and, admittedly, less than a concrete strategy for large-scale democratization. But it is a virtuous cause and, above all, one that could assign meaning to a new concept of politics, civility and hope.

Notes and references

1 See also D. N. Chryssochoou, 'Meta-theory and the Study of the European Union: Capturing the Normative Turn', *Journal of European Integration*, 22, no. 2, 2000, pp. 123–44.
2 G. Ritzer, *Metatheorizing in Sociology*, Lexington: Lexington Books, 1991, p. 4.
3 This distinction draws on R. Bellamy and D. Castiglione, 'The Normative Turn in European Union Studies: Legitimacy, Identity and Democracy', mimeo, 1999, p. 3. By kind permission of the authors.
4 Ibid., p. 1.
5 Ibid., p. 11.

6 B. Rosamond, 'Theorising the European Union Past, Present and Future: On Knowledge, Disciplines and "Thinking Thoroughly" about Integration Theory', *Current Politics and Economics of Europe*, 9, no. 2, 1999, p. 155.

7 Ibid., p. 158.

8 Ibid.

9 N. Walker, 'Sovereignty and Differentiated Integration in the European Union', *European Law Journal*, 4, no. 4, 1998, p. 381.

10 On different conceptions of a European demos, see J. H. H. Weiler et al., 'European Democracy and its Critique', in J. Hayward (ed.), *The Crisis of Representation in Europe*, London: Frank Cass, 1995; and D. N. Chryssochoou, 'Europe's Could-be Demos: Recasting the Debate', *West European Politics*, 19, no. 4, 1996, pp. 787–801.

11 C. Cohen, *Democracy*, Athens: The University of Georgia Press, 1971, p. 47.

12 J. H. H. Weiler, 'After Maastricht: Community Legitimacy in Post-1992 Europe', in W. J. Adams (ed.), *Singular Europe: Economy and Polity of the European Community after 1992*, Ann Arbor: University of Michigan Press, 1992, p. 22.

13 M. Zürn, 'The Social Pre-requisites of European Democracy', in *Governance and Citizenship in Europe: Some Research Directions*, Luxembourg: Office for the Official Publications of the European Communities, Conference Proceedings, 1999, pp. 39–40.

14 G. Sartori, *The Theory of Democracy Revisited*, Chatham NJ: Chatham House, 1987, p. 22.

15 Cohen, *Democracy*, p. 46.

16 C. Closa, 'Supranational Citizenship and Democracy: Normative and Empirical Dimensions', in M. La Torre (ed.), *European Citizenship: An Institutional Challenge*, Dordrecht: Kluwer, 1999, p. 419.

17 R. A. Dahl, *Democracy and its Critics*, New Haven, CT: Yale University Press, 1989, p. 114.

18 A. Wendt, 'Bridging the Theory/Meta-Theory Gap in International Relations', *Review of International Studies*, 17, no. 4, 1991, p. 383.

19 A. Wiener and V. Della Sala, 'Constitution-making and Citizenship Practice: Building the Democracy Gap in the EU?', *Journal of Common Market Studies*, 35, no. 4, 1997, pp. 597–8.

20 E. Tassin, 'Europe: A Political Community?', in C. Mouffe, (ed.), *Dimensions of Radical Democracy*, London and New York: Verso, 1992, p. 171.

21 Wendt, 'Bridging the Theory/Meta-theory Gap', p. 383.

22 T. Christiansen et al., 'The Social Construction of Europe', *Journal of European Public Policy*, 6, no. 4, 1999, p. 538.

23 E. E. Schattschneider, *Two Hundred Million Americans in Search of a Government*, New York: Holt, Rinehart and Winston, 1969, p. 42.

24 K. E. Soĺtan, 'Introduction: Civic Competence, Democracy, and the Good Society', in S. L. Elkin and K. E. Soĺtan (eds), *Citizen Competence and Democratic Institutions*, University Park, PA: Pennsylvania State University Press, 1999, p. 2.

25 J. Habermas, 'Citizenship and National Identity', in B. van Steenbergen (ed.), *The Condition of Citizenship*, London: Sage, 1994, p. 30.

26 D. N. Chryssochoou, *Democracy in the European Union*, London and New York: I. B. Tauris, 1998, esp. pp. 89–96.

27 This is not to negate the importance of institutional arrangements and

constitutional engineering, either through the ECJ's rulings or through treaty reform itself, in the making of a viable European democracy.

28 Christiansen et al., 'The Social Construction of Europe', pp. 528–9.
29 Ibid., p. 529.
30 Quoted in ibid., p. 529. For the original argument, see J. G. Ruggie, *Constructing the World Polity: Essays on International Institutionalization*, New York: Routledge, 1998, p. 33.
31 J. Shaw and A. Wiener, 'The Paradox of the "European Polity"', in M. Green Cowles and M. Smith (eds), *State of the European Union, Volume 5: Risks, Reform, Resistance, and Revival*, Oxford: Oxford University Press, 2000, pp. 67–8.
32 Ibid., pp. 75, 87.
33 Christiansen et al., 'The Social Construction of Europe', p. 537.
34 Ibid., p. 538.
35 Ibid., p. 543.
36 Shaw and Wiener, 'Paradox of the "European Polity"', p. 68.
37 J. de Areilza, 'Sovereignty or Management? The Dual Character of the EC's Supranationalism Revisited', Harvard Jean Monnet Papers, no. 2/95, 1995, p. 9.
38 P. C. Schmitter, 'Citizenship in an Eventual Euro-democracy', European University Institute, July 1996, mimeo, p. 9. By kind permission of the author.
39 S. S. Andersen and T. Burns, 'The European Union and the Erosion of Parliamentary Democracy: A Study of Post-parliamentary Governance', in S. S. Andersen and K. A. Eliassen (eds), *The European Union: How Democratic Is It?*, London: Sage, 1996, pp. 227–51. For an empirical analysis of post-parliamentary processes of European governance and citizenship practice, see A. Warleigh, 'The Hustle: Citizenship Practice, NGOs and "Policy Coalitions" in the European Union – The Cases of Auto Oil, Drinking Water and Unit Pricing', *Journal of European Public Policy*, 7, no. 2, 2000, pp. 229–43.
40 R. Bellamy, *Liberalism and Pluralism: Towards a Politics of Compromise*, London and New York: Routledge, 1999, p. 190.
41 J. Shaw, 'The Treaty of Amsterdam: Challenges of Flexibility and Legitimacy', *European Law Journal*, 4, no. 1, 1998, p. 85.
42 H. J. d'Oliveira, 'European Citizenship: Its Meaning, its Potential', in R. Dehousse (ed.), *Europe after Maastricht: An Ever Closer Union?*, Munich: Law Books in Europe, 1994, p. 147; quoted in J. Shaw, 'The Interpretation of European Union Citizenship', *The Modern Law Review*, 61, no. 3, 1998, p. 308.
43 E. Meehan, *Citizenship in the European Community*, London: Sage, 1993, pp. 8–9.
44 Ibid., pp. 7, 14. The quotation is from U. Preuss, 'Two Challenges to European Citizenship', *Political Studies*, 44, 1996, p. 551.
45 Meehan, *Citizenship in the European Community*, pp. 159–60.
46 P. Close, *Citizenship, Europe and Change*, London: Macmillan, 1995, pp. 2–3.
47 F. Requejo, 'Cultural Pluralism, Nationalism and Federalism: A Revision of Democratic Citizenship in Plurinational States', *European Journal of Political Research*, 35, 1999, p. 261.
48 S. García, 'Identity and Citizenship in the European Union: Some Points for Future Research', in *Governance and Citizenship in Europe*, p. 44.
49 Requejo, 'Cultural Pluralism', p. 265.
50 C. Mouffe, *The Return of the Political*, London: Verso, 1993, p. 69.
51 A. Etzioni, *The Spirit of Community: The Reinvention of American Society*, New York: Simon and Schuster, 1993, pp. 147–51.

52 Schmitter, 'Citizenship', p. 10.

53 See A. H. Birch, *Nationalism and National Integration*, London: Urwin Hyman, 1989, p. 37.

54 J. H. H. Weiler, 'Does Europe Need a Constitution? Demos, Telos and the German Maastricht Decision, *European Law Journal*, 1, no. 3, 1995, p. 252.

55 W. E. Connolly, 'Democracy and Territoriality', in M. Ringrose and A. J. Lehrner (eds), *Reimagining the Nation*, Buckingham: Open University Press, 1993, pp. 66, 70.

56 This term has been used by Etzioni as the antithesis of 'faulty democracy', namely as a means of making government 'more representative, more participatory, and more responsive to all members of the community'; see Etzioni, *The Spirit of Community*, p. 155. See also B. Barber, *Strong Democracy: Participatory Politics for a New Age*, Berkeley, CA: University of California Press, 1984, p. 132.

57 K. Neunreither, 'Citizens and the Exercise of Power in the European Union: Towards a New Social Contract?', in A. Rosas and E. Antola (eds), *A Citizens' Europe: In Search of a New Order*, London: Sage, 1995, p. 10.

58 Ibid., p. 13.

59 European Parliament, 'Report on the Functioning of the Treaty on European Union with a View to the 1996 Intergovernmental Conference', 1995, p. 67.

60 C. Taylor, 'The Dynamics of Democratic Exclusion', *Journal of Democracy*, 9, no. 4, 1998, pp. 143–56. Cf. A. Geddes, 'Immigrant and Ethnic Minorities and the EU's "Democratic Deficit"', *Journal of Common Market Studies*, 33, no. 2, 1995, pp. 197–217.

61 J. Habermas, 'Remarks on Dieter Grimm's "Does Europe Need a Constitution?"', *European Law Journal*, 1, no. 3, 1995, p. 303.

62 Wiener and Della Sala, 'Constitution-making and Citizenship Practice', p. 609.

63 Ibid., p. 604.

64 As stated in Article 17.1 of the new Treaty.

65 Bellamy, *Liberalism and Pluralism*, p. 204.

66 M. Anderson et al., 'European Citizenship and Cooperation in Justice and Home Affairs', in A. Duff et al. (eds), *Maastricht and Beyond: Building the European Union*, London: Routledge, 1994, p. 338. Although this may change with the adoption of a European Charter of Fundamental Rights, it is still important to note that national governments, rather than those forming the basis of a European civil society, remain the decisive actors in negotiating and finalizing the content of such a charter.

67 Schmitter, 'Citizenship', p. 17.

68 Shaw, 'Interpretation of European Union Citizenship', 'Report', p. 308.

69 See respectively, European Parliament, 'Report', p. 67; A. Duff, 'The Main Reforms', in Duff (ed.), *Maastricht and Beyond*, p. 29; and D. O'Keefe, 'Union Citizenship', in D. O'Keefe and P. M. Twomey (eds), *Legal Issues of the Maastricht Treaty*, London: Wiley Chancery Law, 1994, p. 106.

70 Shaw, 'Interpretation of European Union Citizenship', p. 294.

71 Soʃtan, 'Introduction', p. 12.

72 J. H. H. Weiler, *The Constitution of Europe: 'Do the New Clothes Have an Emperor?' and Other Essays on European Integration*, Cambridge: Cambridge University Press, 1999, p. 262.

73 R. Bellamy and A. Warleigh, 'From an Ethics of Integration to an Ethics of

Participation: Citizenship and the Future of the European Union', *Millennium*, 27, no. 3, 1998, p. 456.

74 R. Bellamy, 'Citizenship Beyond the Nation State: The Case of Europe', in N. O'Sullivan (ed.), *Political Theory in Transition*, London and New York: Routledge, 2000, p. 109.

75 J. Shaw, 'The Emergence of Postnational Constitutionalism in the European Union', Exeter Political Theory Workshop, November 1998, pp. 3–4.

76 J. H. H. Weiler, 'Bread and Circus: The State of European Union', *The Columbia Journal of European Law*, 4, 1998, p. 230.

77 R. Bellamy and M. Hollis, 'Consensus, Neutrality and Compromise', *Critical Review of International Social and Political Philosophy*, 1, no. 3, 1998, p. 63.

78 Shaw, 'Treaty of Amsterdam', p. 85.

79 J. H. H. Weiler, 'Legitimacy and Democracy of Union Governance', in G. Edwards and A. Pijpers (eds), *The Politics of European Treaty Reform: The 1996 Intergovernmental Conference and Beyond*, London: Pinter, 1997, p. 250.

80 Bellamy and Warleigh, 'From an Ethics of Integration', p. 448.

81 Y. Mény, 'The People, the Elites and the Populist Challenge', Jean Monnet Chair Paper RSC, no. 98/47, European University Institute, 1998, p. 9.

82 Z. Bañkowski et al., 'Guest Editorial', *European Law Journal*, 4, no. 4, 1998, p. 339.

83 F. W. Scharpf, 'The Joint-decision Trap: Lessons from German Federalism and European Integration', *Public Administration*, 66, no. 3, 1988, pp. 239–78.

84 R. Dehousse, 'European Institutional Architecture after Amsterdam: Parliamentary System or Regulatory Structure?', EUI Working Paper RSC, no. 98/11, 1998, p. 13.

85 B. Kohler-Koch, 'Europe in Search of Legitimate Governance', ARENA Working Papers, no. WP 99/27, 1999, p. 9.

86 M. Nentwich and G. Falkner, 'The Treaty of Amsterdam: Towards a New Institutional Balance', European Integration Online Papers, 1, no. 15, 1997, p. 45.

87 Dehousse, 'European Institutional Architecture', p. 10.

88 R. A. Dahl, 'The Future of Democratic Theory', Estudios Working Papers, no. 90, 1996, pp. 13–14.

89 Nentwich and Falkner, 'The Treaty of Amsterdam', p. 11.

90 L. J. Brinkhorst (1997) 'Pillar III', in European Policy Centre, *Challenge Europe: Making Sense of the Amsterdam Treaty*, Brussels, 1997, p. 49; quoted in G. Edwards and G. Wiessala, 'Editorial: Flexibility, Legitimacy and Identity in Post-Amsterdam Europe', *Journal of Common Market Studies*, 36 (1997 Annual Review of Activities), 1998, p. 7.

91 L. Cram et al., 'The Evolving European Union', in L. Cram et al. (eds), *Developments in the European Union*, London: Macmillan, 1999, p. 363.

92 J. Shaw, 'Postnational Constitutionalism in the European Union', *Journal of European Public Policy*, 6, no. 4, 1999, pp. 579–97.

93 A. Moravcsik and K. Nikolaïdis, K. 'Explaining the Treaty of Amsterdam: Interests, Influence, Institutions', *Journal of Common Market Studies*, 37, no. 1, 1999, p. 83.

94 T. A. Spragens, Jr, *Civic Liberalism: Reflections on our Democratic Ideals*, Lanham: Rowman and Littlefield, 1999, p. 208.

Bibliography

Abromeit, H. (1998) 'How to Democratise a Multi-level, Multi-dimensional Polity', in A. Weale and M. Nentwich (eds), *Political Theory and the European Union: Legitimacy, Constitutional Choice, and Citizenship*, London and New York: Routledge.

Adler, E. (1997) 'Seizing the Middle Ground: Constructivism in World Politics', *European Journal of International Relations*, 3 (3).

Adler, E. and Barnett, M. (1998) 'Security Communities in Theoretical Perspective', in E. Adler and M. Barnett (eds), *Security Communities*, Cambridge: Cambridge University Press.

Adonis, A. (1990) 'Subsidiarity: Myth, Reality and the Community's Future', House of Lords Select Committee on the European Communities, London, June.

Albertini, M. (1990) 'The Ventotene Manifesto: The Only Road to Follow', in L. Levi (ed.), *Altiero Spinelli and Federalism in Europe and in the World*, Milano: Franco Angeli.

Allison, G. (1971) *Essence of Decision: Explaining the Cuban Missile Crisis*, Boston: Little Brown.

Almond, G.A. (1956) 'Comparative Political Systems', *Journal of Politics*, 18 (3).

Althusius, J. (1995) [1603] *Politica*, ed. and trans. F.S. Carney, Indianapolis: Liberty Fund.

Andersen, S.S. and Burns, T. (1996) 'The European Union and the Erosion of Parliamentary Democracy: A Study of Post-parliamentary Governance', in S.S. Andersen and K.A. Eliassen (eds), *The European Union: How Democratic Is It?*, London: Sage.

Anderson, M. et al. (1994) 'European Citizenship and Cooperation in Justice and Home Affairs', in A. Duff et al. (eds), *Maastricht and Beyond: Building the European Union*, London: Routledge.

Apter, D. (1966) *The Political Kingdom in Uganda: A Study in Bureaucratic Nationalism*, Princeton, NJ: Princeton University Press.

Archer, C. (1992) *International Organizations*, 2nd edn, London: Routledge.

de Areilza, J. (1995) 'Sovereignty or Management? The Dual Character of the EC's Supranationalism Revisited', Harvard Jean Monnet Papers, no. 2/95.

Armstrong, K. and Bulmer, S. (1998) *The Governance of the Single European Market*, Manchester: Manchester University Press.

Armstrong, K. and Shaw, J. (1998) 'Integrating Law: An Introduction', *Journal of Common Market Studies*, 36 (2).

Bailey, S.D. (1948) *United Europe: A Short History of the Idea*, London: National News-Letter.

Bańkowski:, Z. et al. (1975) 'Guest Editorial', *European Law Journal*, 4 (4).

Barber, B. (1984) *Strong Democracy: Participatory Politics for a New Age*, Berkeley, CA: University of California Press.

Barry, B. (1965) *Political Argument*, London: Routledge.

Barry, B. (1975) 'Political Accommodation and Consociational Democracy', *British Journal of Political Science*, 5 (4).

Bellamy, R. (1999) *Liberalism and Pluralism: Towards a Politics of Compromise*, London and New York: Routledge.

Bellamy, R. (2000) 'Citizenship Beyond the Nation State: The Case of Europe', in N. O'Sullivan (ed), *Political Theory in Transition*, London and New York: Routledge.

Bellamy, R. and Castiglione, D. (1997) 'Building the Union: The Nature of Sovereignty in the Political Architecture of Europe', *Law and Philosophy*, 16 (4).

Bellamy, R. and Castiglione, D. (1999a) 'Democracy, Sovereignty and the Constitution of the European Union: The Republican Alternative to Liberalism', EurCit Working Papers, no. 99/1.

Bellamy, R. and Castiglione, D. (1999b) 'The Normative Turn in European Union Studies: Legitimacy, Identity and Democracy', mimeo.

Bellamy, R. and Hollis, M. (1998) 'Consensus, Neutrality and Compromise', *Critical Review of International Social and Political Philosophy*, 1 (3).

Bellamy, R. and Warleigh, A. (1998) 'From an Ethics of Integration to an Ethics of Participation: Citizenship and the Future of the European Union', *Millennium*, 27 (3).

Beloff, M. (1950) 'False Analogies from Federal Example of United States', *The Times*, 4 May.

Birch, A.H. (1989) *Nationalism and National Integration*, London: Unwin Hyman.

Blalock, H. (1984) *Basic Dilemmas in the Social Sciences*, Beverly Hills, CA: Sage.

Bluhm, W.T. (1968) 'Nation-building: The Case of Austria', *Polity*, 1.

Bodin, J. (1992) [1576] *On Sovereignty: Four Chapters from the Six Books of the Commonwealth*, ed. and trans. J.H. Franklin, Cambridge: Cambridge University Press.

Bolick, C. (1994) 'European Federalism: Lessons from America', Occasional Paper no. 93, London: The Institute of Economic Affairs.

Bosco, A. (1992) 'The Federalist Project and Resistance in Continental Europe', in A. Bosco (ed.), *The Federal Idea*, Vol. II: *The History of Federalism since 1945*, London and New York: Lothian Foundation Press.

Bosco, A. (1994) 'What is Federalism?', paper presented at the Second ECSA–World Conference, Brussels, 4–6 May.

Boulle, L.J. (1984) *Constitutional Reform and the Apartheid State: Legitimacy, Consociationalism and Control in South Africa*, New York: St Martin's Press.

Bowie, R.R. (1987) 'The Process of Federating Europe', in A.W. Macmahon (ed.), *Federalism: Mature and Emergent*, Garden City, NY: Doubleday.

te Brake, W. (1998) *Shaping History: Ordinary People in European Politics, 1500–1700*, Berkeley, CA: University of California Press.

Branch, A.P. and Øhgaard, J.C. (1999) 'Trapped in the Supranational–Intergovernmental Dichotomy: A Response to Stone Sweet and Sandholtz', *Journal of European Public Policy*, 6 (1).

Breckinridge, R.E. (1997) 'Reassessing Regimes: The International Regime Aspects of the European Union', *Journal of Common Market Studies*, 35 (2).

Brewin, C. (1987) 'The European Community: A Union of States without Unity of Government', *Journal of Common Market Studies*, 26 (1).

Brinkhorst, L.J. (1997) 'Pillar III', in European Policy Centre, *Challenge Europe: Making Sense of the Amsterdam Treaty*, Brussels.

Bulmer, S. (1983) 'Domestic Politics and European Community Policy-making', *Journal of Common Market Studies*, 21 (4).

Bulmer, S. (1993) 'The Governance of the European Union: A New Institutionalist Approach', *Journal of Public Policy*, 13 (4).

Bulmer, S. (1996) 'The European Council and the Council of the European Union: Shapers of a European Confederation', *Publius*, 23 (4).

Bulmer, S. (1997) 'New Institutionalism, the Single Market and EU Governance', ARENA Working Papers, no. WP 97/25.

Bulmer S. and Scott, A. (1994) 'Introduction', in S. Bulmer and A. Scott (eds), *Economic and Political Integration in Europe: Internal Dynamics and Global Context*, Oxford: Blackwell.

Bulmer, S. and Wessels, W. (1988) *The European Council: Decision-making in European Politics*, London: Macmillan.

Búrca, G. de (1999) 'Reappraising Subsidiarity's Significance after Amsterdam', Harvard Jean Monnet Working Paper, no. 7/99.

Burgess, M. (1984) 'Federal Ideas in the European Community: Altiero Spinelli and European Union', *Government and Opposition*, 19 (3).

Burgess, M. (1993) 'Federalism as Political Ideology: Interests, Benefits and Beneficiaries in Federalism and Federation', in M. Burgess and A-G. Gagnon (eds), *Comparative Federalism and Federation*, New York: Harvester Wheatsheaf.

Calhoun, J.A. (1943) [1853] *A Disquisition on Government*, New York: Peter Smith.

Caporaso, J. (1996) 'The European Union and Forms of State: Westphalian, Regulatory or Post-modern?', *Journal of Common Market Studies*, 34 (1).

Caporaso, J. (1998) 'Regional Integration Theory: Understanding our Past and Anticipating our Future', *Journal of European Public Policy*, 5 (1).

Carney, F.S. (1995) 'Translator's Introduction', in J. Althusius, *Politica*, ed. and trans. F.S. Carney, Indianapolis: Liberty Fund.

Cass, D.Z. (1992) 'The Word that Saves Maastricht? The Principle of Subsidiarity and the Division of Powers in the European Community', *Common Market Law Review*, 29.

Centre for Economic Policy Research (1993) *Making Sense of Subsidiarity: How Much Centralization for Europe?*, Annual Report no. 4, London.

Checkel, J.T. (1998a) 'The Constructivist Turn in International Relations Theory', *World Politics*, 50 (1).

Checkel, J.T. (1998b) 'International Institutions and Socialization', ARENA Working Papers, no. WP 99/5.

Christiansen, T. (1994) 'European Integration between Political Science and International Relations Theory: The End of Sovereignty?', EUI Working Paper no. 94/4.

Christiansen, T. (1997) 'Reconstructing European Space: From Territorial Politics to Multilevel Governance', in K-E. Jørgensen (ed.), *Reflective Approaches to European Governance*, Basingstoke: Macmillan.

Christiansen, T. et al. (1999) 'The Social Construction of Europe', *Journal of European Public Policy*, 6 (4).

Chryssochoou, D.N. (1994) 'Democracy and Symbiosis in the European Union: Towards a Confederal Consociation?, *West European Politics*, 17 (4).

Chryssochoou, D.N. (1996) 'Europe's Could-be Demos: Recasting the Debate', *West European Politics*, 19 (4).

Chryssochoou, D.N. (1997) 'New Challenges to the Study of European Integration: Implications for Theory-building', *Journal of Common Market Studies*, 35 (4).

Chryssochoou, D.N. (1998a) *Democracy in the European Union*, London and New York: I.B. Tauris.

Chryssochoou, D.N. (1998b) 'Federalism and Democracy Reconsidered', *Regional and Federal Studies*, 8 (2).

Chryssochoou, D.N. (2000) 'Meta-theory and the Study of the European Union: Capturing the Normative Turn', *Journal of European Integration*, 22 (2).

Chryssochoou, D.N. et al. (1999) *Theory and Reform in the European Union*, Manchester and New York: Manchester University Press.

Church, C.H. (1993) *The Not So Model Republic? The Relevance of Swiss Federalism to the European Community*, Discussion Papers in Federal Studies, no. FS93/4, University of Leicester, November.

Church, C.H. (1996) *European Integration Theory in the 1990s*, European Dossier Series, no. 33, University of North London.

Claes, D.H. (1999) 'What do Theories of International Regimes Contribute to the Explanation of Cooperation (and Failure of Cooperation) among Oil-producing Countries?', ARENA Working Papers, no. WP 99/12, University of Oslo.

Claude, I.L., Jr (1964) *Swords into Plowshares*, 3rd edn, New York: Random House.

Closa, C. (1999) 'Supranational Citizenship and Democracy: Normative and Empirical Dimensions', in M. La Torre (ed.), *European Citizenship: An Institutional Challenge*, Dordrecht: Kluwer.

Close, P. (1995) *Citizenship, Europe and Change*, London: Macmillan.

Cohen, C. (1971) *Democracy*, Athens: The University of Georgia Press.

Collier, D. (1993) 'The Comparative Method', in A. Finifter (ed.), *Political Science: The State of the Discipline*, Washington, DC: American Political Science Association.

Commission of the European Communities (1992) 'The Principle of Subsidiarity', SECK(92) 1990, Brussels, 27 October.

Conlan, T. (1988) *New Federalism*, Washington, DC: The Brookings Institution.

Connolly, W.E. (1993) 'Democracy and Territoriality', in M. Ringrose and A.J. Lehrner (eds), *Reimagining the Nation*, Buckingham: Open University Press.

Cox, R. (1981) 'Social Forces, States and World Orders: Beyond International Relations Theory', *Millennium*, 10 (2).

Cox, R (1986) 'Social Forces, States and World Orders', in R.O. Keohane (ed.), *Neorealism and its Critics*, New York: Columbia University Press.

Cram, L. (1997) *Policy-making in the European Union: Conceptual Lenses and the Integration Process*, London and New York: Routledge.

Cram, L. et al. (1999) 'The Evolving European Union', in L. Cram et al. (eds), *Developments in the European Union*, London: Macmillan.

Daalder, H. (1971) 'On Building Consociational Nations: The Cases of The Netherlands and Switzerland', *International Social Science Journal*, 23 (3).

Daalder, H. (1974) 'The Consociational Democracy Theme', *World Politics*, 26 (4).

Dahl, R.A. (1956) *A Preface to Democratic Theory*, Chicago: University of Chicago Press.

Dahl, R.A. (1989) *Democracy and its Critics*, New Haven, CT: Yale University Press.

Dahl, R.A. (1996) 'The Future of Democratic Theory', Estudios Working Papers, No. 90.

Dahrendorf, R. (1967) *Society and Democracy in Germany*, London: Weidenfeld and Nicolson.

Dehousse, R. (1995) 'Constitutional Reform in the European Community: Are

There Alternatives to the Majority Rules?, in J. Hayward (ed.), *The Crisis of Representation in Europe*, London: Frank Cass.

Dehousse, R. (1998) 'European Institutional Architecture after Amsterdam: Parliamentary System or Regulatory Structure?', EUI Working Paper RSC, no. 98/11.

Demaret, P. (1994) 'The Treaty Framework', in D. O'Keefe and P.M. Twomey (eds), *Legal Issues of the Maastricht Treaty*, London: Wiley Chancery Law.

Deudney, D. (1996) 'Binding Sovereigns: Authorities, Structures, and Geopolitics in Philadelphian Systems', in T. Biersteker and C. Weber (eds), *State Sovereignty as Social Construct*, Cambridge: Cambridge University Press.

Deutsch, K.W. (1967) *Nationalism and Social Communication: An Inquiry into the Foundations of Nationality*, 2nd edn, Cambridge, MA: MIT Press.

Deutsch, K.W. (1971) *The Analysis of International Relations*, Englewood Cliffs, NJ: Prentice-Hall.

Deutsch, K.W. et al. (1957) *Political Community and the North Atlantic Area*, Princeton, NJ: Princeton University Press.

Devuyst, Y. (1998) 'Treaty Reform in the European Union: The Amsterdam Process', *Journal of European Public Policy*, 5 (4).

Dogan, M. and Pelassy, D. (1984) *How to Compare Nations: Strategies in Comparative Politics*, Chatham: Chatham House.

Duchacek, I.D. (1970) *Comparative Federalism: The Territorial Dimension of Politics*, London: Holt, Rinehart and Winston.

Duff, A., (1994) 'The Main Reforms', in A. Duff et al. (eds), *Maastricht and Beyond: Building the European Union*, London: Routledge.

Duff, A. (ed.) (1997) *The Treaty of Amsterdam: Text and Commentary*, London: Sweet and Maxwell.

Eastby, J. (1985) *Functionalism and Interdependence*, Lanham: University Press of America.

Edwards, G. and Wiessala, G. (1998) 'Editorial: Flexibility, Legitimacy and Identity in Post-Amsterdam Europe', *Journal of Common Market Studies*, 36 (1997 Annual Review of Activities).

Elazar, D.J. (1987) *Exploring Federalism*, Tuscaloosa: University of Alabama Press.

Elazar, D.J. (1995a) 'Althusius' Grand Design for a Federal Commonwealth', in J. Althusius, *Politica*, ed. and trans. F.S. Carney, Indianapolis, Liberty Fund.

Elazar, D.J. (1995b) 'Federalism', in S.M. Lipset (ed.), *The Encyclopedia of Democracy*, Vol. II, London: Routledge.

Elazar, D.J. (1998) *Constitutionalizing Globalization: The Postmodern Revival of Confederal Arrangements*, Lanham: Rowman and Littlefield.

Elazar D.J. et al. (1994) *Federal Systems of the World: A Handbook of Federal, Confederal and Autonomy Arrangements*, 2nd edn, London: Longman.

Eleftheriadis, P. (1998) 'Begging the Constitutional Question', *Journal of Common Market Studies*, 36 (2).

Etzioni, A. (1993) *The Spirit of Community: The Reinvention of American Society*, New York: Simon and Schuster.

European Community (1995) 'Report of the Council of Ministers on the Functioning of the Treaty on European Union', April, Annex IV.

European Parliament (1995) 'Report on the Functioning of the Treaty on European Union with a View to the 1996 Intergovernmental Conference'.

Everling, U. (1994) 'The Maastricht Judgement of the German Federal

Constitutional Court and its Significance for the Development of the European Union', *Yearbook of European Law*, 14: 1–19.

Finnemore, M. (1996) 'Norms, Culture and World Politics: Insights from Sociology's Institutionalism', *International Organization*, 50 (2).

Forsyth, M. (1981) *Unions of States: The Theory and Practice of Confederation*, Leicester: Leicester University Press.

Forsyth, M. (1994) 'Federalism and Confederalism', in C. Brown (ed.), *Political Restructuring in Europe: Ethical Perspectives*, London and New York: Routledge.

Forsyth, M. (1995a) 'Political Science, Federalism and Europe', Discussion Papers in Federal Studies, no. FS95/2, University of Leicester.

Forsyth, M. (1995b) 'Towards a New Concept of Confederation', in *The Modern Concept of Confederation*, European Commission for Democracy through Law, Council of Europe, Conference Proceedings.

Forsyth, M. (1996) 'The Political Theory of Federalism: The Relevance of Classical Approaches', in J.J. Hesse and V. Wright (eds), *Federalizing Europe? The Costs, Benefits, and Preconditions of Federal Political Systems*, Oxford: Oxford University Press.

Friedrich, C.J. (1955) 'Federal Constitutional Theory and Emergent Proposals, in A.W. Macmahon (ed.), *Federalism: Mature and Emergent*, Garden City, NY: Doubleday.

Friedrich, C.J. (1968) *Trends of Federalism in Theory and Practice*, London: Pall Mall Press.

Furnivall, J.S. (1948) *Colonial Policy and Practice: A Comparative Study of Burma and Netherlands India*, Cambridge: Cambridge University Press.

García, S. (1999) 'Identity and Citizenship in the European Union: Some Points for Future Research', in *Governance and Citizenship in Europe: Some Research Directions*, Luxembourg: Office for the Official Publications of the European Communities, Conference Proceedings.

Garrett, G. and Tsembelis, G. (1996) 'An Institutionalist Critique of Intergovernmentalism', *International Organization*, 46 (2).

Geddes, A. (1995) 'Immigrant and Ethnic Minorities and the EU's "Democratic Deficit"', *Journal of Common Market Studies*, 33 (2).

George, A.L. (1979) 'Case Studies and Theory Development: The Method of Structured, Focused Comparison', in P.G. Lauren (ed.), *Diplomacy: New Approaches in History, Theory and Policy*, New York: The Free Press.

Goetz, K.H. (1995) 'National Governance and European Integration: Inter-governmental Relations in Germany', *Journal of Common Market Studies*, 33 (1).

Gourevitch, P. (1978) 'The Second Image Reversed: The International Sources of Domestic Politics', *International Organization*, 32 (4).

Greider, W. (1997) *One World, Ready or Not: The Manic Logic of Global Capitalism*, New York: Simon and Schuster.

Grodzins, M. (1967) 'American Political Parties and the American System', in A. Wildavsky (ed.), *American Federalism in Perspective*, Boston: Little Brown.

Groom, A.J.R. (1990) 'The Setting in World Society', in A.J.R. Groom and P. Taylor (eds), *Frameworks for International Co-operation*, London: Pinter.

Groom, A.J.R. (1993) 'The European Community: Building Up, Building Down, and Building Across', in Conference Proceedings, *People's Rights and European Structures*, Manresa: Centre Unesco de Catalunya, September.

Haas, E.B. (1958) *The Uniting of Europe: Political, Social and Economic Forces 1950–1957*, London: Stevens.

Haas, E.B. (1964) *Beyond the Nation-state: Functionalism and International Organization*, Stanford: Stanford University Press.

Haas, E.B. (1970) 'The Study of Regional Integration: Reflections on the Joy and Anguish of Pretheorising', *International Organization*, 24 (4).

Haas, E.B. (1975) *The Obsolescence of Regional Integration Theory*, Berkeley, CA: Institute of International Studies.

Habermas, J. (1994) 'Citizenship and National Identity', in B. van Steenbergen (ed.), *The Condition of Citizenship*, London: Sage.

Habermas, J. (1995) 'Remarks on Dieter Grimm's "Does Europe Need a Constitution?"', *European Law Journal*, 1 (3).

Hague, R., Harrop, M. and Breslin, S. (1992) *Comparative Government and Politics: An Introduction*, Basingstoke: Macmillan.

Hall, P. and Taylor, R. (1996) 'Political Science and the Three Institutionalisms', *Political Studies*, 44 (5).

Hallowell, J.H. (1954) *The Moral Foundation of Democracy*, Chicago: University of Chicago Press.

Halpern, S.M. (1986) 'The Disorderly Universe of Consociational Democracy', *West European Politics*, 9 (2).

Hamlyn, D.W. (1995) *Metaphysics*, Cambridge: Cambridge University Press.

Harris, P. (1976) *Foundations of Political Science*, 2nd edn, London: Hutchinson.

Harrison, R.J (1990) 'Neo-functionalism', in A.J.R. Groom and P. Taylor (eds), *Frameworks for International Co-operation*, London: Pinter.

Harrison, R.J. (1974) *Europe in Question: Theories of Regional International Integration*, London: Allen and Unwin.

Hasenclever, A. et al. (1997) *Theories of International Regimes*, Cambridge: Cambridge University Press.

Held, D. et al. (1999) *Global Transformations*, Cambridge: Polity Press.

Helman D.H. (ed.) (1988) *Analogical Reasoning*, Dortrecht: Reidel.

Herdegen, M. (1994) 'Maastricht and the German Constitutional Court: Constitutional Restraints for an "Ever Closer Union"', *Common Market Law Review*, 31 (2).

Hirst, P. (1994) *Associative Democracy: New Forms of Economic and Social Governance*, Cambridge: Polity Press.

Hix, S. (1994) 'The Study of the European Community: The Challenge to Comparative Politics', *West European Politics*, 17 (4).

Hix, S. (1998) 'The Study of the European Union II: The "New Governance" Agenda and its Rival', *Journal of European Public Policy*, 5 (1).

Hix, S. (1999) *The Political System of the European Union*, Basingstoke: Macmillan.

Hoffmann, S. (1966) 'Obstinate or Obsolete? The Fate of the Nation State and the Case of Western Europe', *Daedalus*, 85 (3).

Holden, B. (1993) *Understanding Liberal Democracy*, 2nd edn, London: Harvester Wheatsheaf.

Hooghe, L. (1995) 'Subnational Mobilisation in the European Union', in J. Hayward (ed.), *The Crisis of Representation in Europe*, London: Frank Cass.

Hopf, T. (1998) 'The Promise of Constructivism in International Relations Theory', *International Security*, 23 (1).

Hughes, C. (1963) *Confederacies*, Leicester: Leicester University Press.

Ionescu, G. (ed.) (1972) *The New Politics of European Integration*, London: Macmillan.

Jachtenfuchs, M. (1994) 'Theoretical Perspectives on European Governance', *European Law Journal*, 1 (2).

Jachtenfuchs, M. et al. (1998) 'Which Europe? Conflicting Models of a Legitimate European Political Order', *European Journal of International Relations*, 4 (4).

Jervis, R. (1983) 'Security Regimes', in S.D. Krasner (ed.), *International Regimes*, Ithaca, NY: Cornell University Press.

Joffe, J. (1999) 'Rethinking the Nation-state: The Many Meanings of Sovereignty', *Foreign Affairs*, 78 (6).

Jørgensen, K.E. and Christiansen, T. (1999) 'The Amsterdam Process: A Structurationist Perspective on EU Treaty Reform', European Integration Online Papers, 3 (1).

Jørgensen, K.E. (1997) 'Studying European Integration in the 1990s', *Journal of European Public Policy*, 3 (3).

Kamenka, E. (1989) *Bureaucracy*, Oxford: Blackwell.

Kamrava, M. (1996) *Understanding Comparative Politics: A Framework for Analysis*, London and New York: Routledge.

Katzenstein, P.J. (ed.) (1996a) *The Culture of National Security: Norms and Identity in World Politics*, New York: Columbia University Press.

Katzenstein, P.J. (1996b) 'Regionalism in Comparative Perspective', ARENA Working Papers, no. 1.

Kegley, W. and Wittkopf, E. (eds) (1984) *The Global Agenda: Issues and Perspectives*, New York: Random House.

Keohane, R.O. (1984) *After Hegemony: Cooperation and Discord in the World Political Economy*, Princeton, NJ: Princeton University Press.

Keohane, R.O. (1989) 'Neoliberal Institutionalism: A Perspective on World Politics', in R.O. Keohane (ed.), *International Institutions and State Power: Essays in International Relations Theory*, Boulder, CO: Westview Press.

Keohane, R.O. and Hoffmann, S. (1990) 'Conclusions', in W. Wallace (ed.), *The Dynamics of European Integration*, London: Pinter.

Keohane, R.O. and Hoffmann, S. (1991) 'Institutional Change in Europe in the 1980s', in R.O. Keohane and S. Hoffmann (eds), *The New European Community: Decisionmaking and Institutional Change*, Boulder, CO: Westview Press.

Keohane, R.O. and Nye, J.S. (1977) *Power and Interdependence: World Politics in Transition*, Boston: Little Brown.

Keohane, R.O. and Nye, J.S. (1993) 'Introduction: The End of the Cold War in Europe', in R.O. Keohane et al. (eds) *After the Cold War: International Institutions and State Strategies in Europe, 1989–1991*, Harvard, MA: Harvard University Press.

Kincaid, J. (1999) 'Confederal Federalism and Compounded Representation in the European Union', *West European Politics*, 22 (2).

King, G. et al. (1994) *Designing Social Inquiry: Scientific Inference in Qualitative Research*, Princeton, NJ: Princeton University Press.

King, P. (1982) *Federalism and Federation*, London: Croom Helm.

King, P. (1993) 'Federation and Representation', in M. Burgess and A-G. Gagnon (eds), *Comparative Federalism and Federation*, New York: Harvester Wheatsheaf.

Kirchner, E.J. (1992) *Decision Making in the European Community: The Council Presidency and European Integration*, Manchester: Manchester University Press.

Kitzinger, U. (1967) *The European Common Market and Community*, London: Routledge.

Kitzinger, U. (1973) 'Time-lags in Political Psychology', in J. Barber and B. Reeds (eds), *European Community: Vision and Reality*, London: Croom Helm.

Knudsen, O.F. (1991) 'The Parochial Scholar: Barriers to Communication in European International Studies', *NUPI Notat*, no. 140.

Kohler-Koch, B. (1996) 'Catching Up with Change: The Transformation of Governance in the European Union', *Journal of European Public Policy*, 3 (3).

Kohler-Koch, B. (1999a) 'Europe in Search of Legitimate Governance', ARENA Working Papers, no. WP 99/27.

Kohler-Koch, B. (1999b) 'The Evolution and Transformation of European Governance', paper presented at the Sixth Biennial ECSA–USA Conference, Pittsburgh, Pennsylvania, 2–5 June.

Kohli, A., Evans, P., Katzenstein, P.J., Przeworski, A., Hoeber, S., Scott, J.C. and Skocpol, T. (1996) 'The Role of Theory in Comparative Politics: A Symposium', *World Politics*, 48 (1).

Krasner, S.D. (ed.) (1983) *International Regimes*, Ithaca, NY: Cornell University Press.

Krasner, S.D. (1983) 'Structural Causes and Regime Consequences: Regimes as Interviewing Variables', in S.D. Krasner (ed.), *International Regimes*, Ithaca: NY: Cornell University Press.

Kuhn, T.S. (1962) *The Structure of Scientific Revolutions*, Chicago: University of Chicago Press.

Laffan, B. (1996) 'The Politics of Order and Identity in the European Union', *Journal of Common Market Studies*, 34 (1).

Laffan, B. (1998) 'The European Union: A Distinctive Model of Internation-alization', *Journal of European Public Policy*, 5 (2).

Laffan, B. et al. (1999) *Europe's Experimental Union: Rethinking Integration*, London and New York: Routledge.

Landau, M. (1961) 'On the Uses of Metaphors in Political Analysis', *Social Research*, 28.

Lane, J-E. and Ersson, S. (2000) *The New Institutional Politics: Performance and Outcomes*, London and New York: Routledge.

Laski, H.J. (1938) *A Grammar of Politics*, London: Allen and Unwin.

Lehmbruch, G. (1975) 'Consociational Democracy in the International System', *European Journal of Political Research*, 3.

Lejeune, Y. (1995) 'Contemporary Concept of Confederation in Europe – Lessons Drawn from the Experience of the European Union', in Conference Proceedings, *The Modern Concept of Confederation*, European Commission for Democracy through Law, Council of Europe.

Lenaerts, K. (1994/95) 'Subsidiarity and Community Competence in the Field of Education', *The Columbia Journal of European Law*, 1 (1).

Leslie, P.M. (1996) 'The Cultural Dimension', in J.J. Hesse and V. Wright (eds), *Federalizing Europe? The Costs, Benefits, and Preconditions of Federal Political Systems*, Oxford: Oxford University Press.

Levi, L. (1990) 'Recent Developments in Federalist Theory', in L. Levi (ed.), *Altiero Spinelli and Federalism in Europe and in the World*, Milano: Franco Angeli.

Levi, L. (1992) 'Altiero Spinelli, Mario Albertini and the Italian Federalist School: Federalism as Ideology', in A. Bosco (ed.), *The Federal Idea: The History of Federalism since 1945*, Vol. II, London and New York: Lothian Foundation Press.

Lieber, R.J. (1973) *Theory and World Politics*, London: Allen and Unwin.

Lijphart, A. (1968a) *The Politics of Accommodation: Pluralism and Democracy in The Netherlands*, Berkeley, CA: University of California Press.

Lijphart, A. (1968b) 'Typologies of Democratic Systems', *Comparative Political Studies*, 1 (1).

Lijphart, A. (1969) 'Consociational Democracy', *World Politics*, 21 (2).

Lijphart, A. (1974) 'Cultural Diversity and Theories of Political Integration', *Canadian Journal of Political Science*, 4 (1).

Lijphart, A. (1977) *Democracy in Plural Societies: A Comparative Exploration*, New Haven, CT: Yale University Press.

Lijphart, A. (1979) 'Consociation and Federation: Conceptual and Empirical Links', *Canadian Journal of Political Science*, 12 (3).

Lijphart, A. (1981) 'Karl W. Deutsch and the New Paradigm in International Relations', in R.L. Meritt and B.M. Russett (eds), *From National Development to Global Community: Essays in Honor of Karl W. Deutsch*, London: Allen and Unwin.

Lindberg, L.N. (1963) *The Political Dynamics of European Economic Integration*, Stanford: Stanford University Press.

Lindberg, L.N. (1967) 'The European Community as a Political System', *Journal of Common Market Studies*, 5 (4).

Lindberg L.N. and Scheingold, S.A. (1970) *Europe's Would-be Polity: Patterns of Change in the European Community*, Englewood Cliffs, NJ: Prentice-Hall.

Lister, F.K. (1996) *The European Union, the United Nations and the Revival of Confederal Governance*, Westport, CT: Greenwood Press.

Lister, F.K. (1999) *The Early Security Confederations: From the Ancient Greeks to the United Colonies of New England*, Westport, CT: Greenwood Press.

Lodge, J. (1978) 'Loyalty and the EEC: The Limits of the Functionalist Approach', *Political Studies*, 26 (2).

Lorwin, V.R. (1971) 'Segmented Pluralism: Ideological Cleavages and Political Cohesion in Small European Democracies', *Comparative Politics*, 3 (2).

Lowndes, V. (1996) 'Varieties of New Institutionalism: A Critical Appraisal', *Public Administration*, 74 (2).

Lustick, I. (1979) 'Stability in Deeply Divided Societies: Consociationalism versus Control', *World Politics*, 30 (3).

MacCormick, N. (1997) 'Democracy, Subsidiarity, and Citizenship in the "European Commonwealth"', *Law and Philosophy*, 16.

MacFarquhar, R. (1978) 'The Community, the Nation-state and the Regions', in B. Burrows et al. (eds), *Federal Solutions to European Issues*, London: Macmillan.

MacIver, R.M. (1936) *Community: A Sociological Study*, London: Macmillan.

McKay, D. (1994) 'On the Origins of Political Unions', paper presented at the Second ECSA–World Conference, Brussels, 4–6 May.

McKenzie, W.J. (1967) *Politics and Social Science*, Harmondsworth: Penguin.

Mackie, T. and Marsh, D. (1995) 'The Comparative Method', in D. Marsh and G. Stoker (eds), *Theory and Methods in Political Science*, London: Macmillan.

Majone, G. (1994) 'The Rise of the Regulatory State in Europe', *West European Politics*, 17 (3).

Majone, G. (ed.) (1996) *Regulating Europe*, London and New York: Routledge.

Majone, G. (1999) 'The Regulatory State and its Legitimacy Problems', *West European Politics*, 22 (1).

Manin, P. (1998) 'The Treaty of Amsterdam', *The Columbia Journal of European Law*, 4 (1).

March, J. and Olsen, J. (1984) 'Institutional Perspectives on Political Institutions', *Governance*, 9 (3).

March, J. and Olsen, J. (1989) *Rediscovering Institutions: The Organizational Basis of Politics*, New York: Free Press.

Marks, G. et al. (1996a) 'Competencies, Cracks and Conflicts: Regional Mobilization in the European Union', in G. Marks et al. (eds), *Governance in the European Union*, London: Sage.

Marks, G. et al. (1996b) 'European Integration from the 1980s: State-centric *v.* Multi-level Governance', *Journal of Common Market Studies*, 34 (3).

Mattli, W. (1999) 'Explaining Regional Integration Outcomes', *Journal of European Public Policy*, 6 (1).

Meehan, E. (1993) *Citizenship in the European Community*, London: Sage.

Mény, Y. (1998) 'People, the Elites and the Populist Challenge', Jean Monnet Chair Paper RSC, no. 98/47, European University Institute.

Merton, R.K. (1957) *Social Theory and Social Structure*, New York: Free Press.

Milward, A.S. (1992) *The European Rescue of the Nation State*, London: Routledge.

Milward, A.S. and Sørensen, V. (1993) 'Interdependence or Integration? A National Choice', in A.S. Milward et al. (eds), *The Frontier of National Sovereignty: History and Theory 1945–1992*, London and New York: Routledge.

Mitrany, D. (1932) *The Progress of International Government*, New Haven, CT: Yale University Press.

Mitrany, D. (1966) [1943] *A Working Peace System*, Chicago: Quadrangle.

Mitrany, D. (1975) *The Functional Theory of Politics*, London: Martin Robertson.

Mjøset, L. (1999) 'Understanding of Theory in the Social Sciences', ARENA Working Papers, no. WP 99/33.

Moravcsik, A. (1991) 'Negotiating the Single Act', in R.O. Keohane and S. Hoffmann (eds), *The New European Community: Decisionmaking and Institutional Change*, Boulder, CO: Westview Press.

Moravcsik, A. (1993) 'Preferences and Power in the European Community: A Liberal Intergovernmentalist Approach', *Journal of Common Market Studies*, 31 (4).

Moravcsik, A. (1994) 'Why the European Community Strengthens the State: Domestic Politics and International Cooperation', paper presented at the Annual Meeting of the American Political Science Association, New York, 1–4 September.

Moravcsik, A. (1998) *The Choice for Europe: Social Purposes and State Power from Messina to Maastricht*, Ithaca, NY: Cornell University Press.

Moravcsik, A. and Nikolaïdis, K. (1998) 'Federal Ideas and Constitutional Realities in the Treaty of Amsterdam', *Journal of Common Market Studies*, 36 (1997 Annual Review of Activities).

Moravcsik, A. and Nikolaïdis, K. (1999) 'Explaining the Treaty of Amsterdam: Interests, Influence, Institutions', *Journal of Common Market Studies*, 37 (1).

Mouffe, C. (1993) *The Return of the Political*, London: Verso.

Murphy, A. (1995) 'Belgium's Regional Divergence: Along the Road to Federation' in G. Smith (ed.), *Federalism: The Multiethnic Challenge*, London and New York: Longman.

Mutimer, D. (1989) '1992 and the Political Integration of Europe: Neofunctionalism Reconsidered', *Journal of European Integration*, 13 (1).

Mutimer, D. (1994) 'Theories of Political Integration', in H.J. Michelmann and P. Soldatos (eds), *European Integration: Theories and Approaches*, Lanham: University Press of America.

Nentwich, M. and Falkner, G. (1997) 'The Treaty of Amsterdam: Towards a New Institutional Balance', European Integration Online Papers, 1 (15).

Neunreither, K. (1994) 'The Syndrome of Democratic Deficit in the European Community', in G. Parry (ed.), *Politics in an Interdependent World: Essays Presented to Ghita Ionescu*, London: Edward Elgar.

Neunreither, K. (1995) 'Citizens and the Exercise of Power in the European Union: Towards a New Social Contract?', in A. Rosas and E. Antola (eds), *A Citizens' Europe: In Search of a New Order*, London: Sage.

Newman, M. (1996) *Democracy, Sovereignty and the European Union*, New York: St Martin's Press.

Novick, L.R. (1988) 'Analogic Transfer: Processes and Individual Differences', in D.H. Helman (ed.), *Analogical Reasoning*, Dortrecht: Reidel.

O'Keefe, D. (1994) 'Union Citizenship', in D. O'Keefe and P.M. Twomey (eds), *Legal Issues of the Maastricht Treaty*, London: Wiley Chancery Law.

d'Oliveira, H.J. (1994) 'European Citizenship: Its Meaning, its Potential', in R. Denousse (ed.), *Europe after Maastricht: An Ever Closer Union?*, Munich: Law Books in Europe.

Olsen, J.P. (2000) 'Organising European Institutions of Governance: A Prelude to an Institutional Account of Political Integration', ARENA Working Papers, no. WP 00/2.

Olsen J.P. and Peters, B.G. (1996) 'Learning from Experience', ARENA Reprints, no. 96/5.

O'Neill, M. (1999) 'Theorising the European Union: Towards a Post-foundational Discourse', *Current Politics and Economics of Europe*, 9 (2).

Pentland, C. (1973) *International Theory and European Integration*, London: Faber and Faber.

Peters, B.G. (1998) *Comparative Politics: Theory and Methods*, London: Macmillan.

Peters, B.G. (1999) *Institutional Theory in Political Science: The 'New Institutionalism'*, London and New York: Pinter.

Peterson, J. (1995a) 'Decision-making in the European Union: Towards a Framework of Analysis', *Journal of European Public Policy*, 2 (1).

Peterson, J. (1995b) 'Policy Networks and European Union Policy Making: A Reply to Kassim', *West European Politics*, 18 (2).

Pierson, P. (1996) 'The Path to European Integration: A Historical Institutionalist Analysis', *Comparative Political Studies*, 29 (2).

Pinder, J. (1993) 'The New European Federalism', in M. Burgess and A-G. Gagnon (eds), *Comparative Federalism and Federation*, New York: Harvester Wheatsheaf.

Pistone, S. (1991) 'Altiero Spinelli and a Strategy for the United States of Europe', in A. Bosco (ed.), *The Federal Idea*, Vol. I: *The History of Federalism from the Enlightenment to 1945*, London and New York: Lothian Foundation Press.

Pollack, M.A. (1996) 'The New Institutionalism and EC Governance: The Promise and Limits of Institutional Analysis', *Governance*, 9 (4).

Powell, B.G., Jr (1982) *Contemporary Democracies: Participation, Stability, and Violence*, Cambridge, MA: Harvard University Press.

Prokhovnik, R. (1999) 'The State of Liberal Sovereignty', *British Journal of Politics and International Relations*, 1 (1).

Pryce, R. (1994) 'The Maastricht Treaty and the New Europe', in A. Duff et al. (eds), *Maastricht and Beyond: Building the European Union*, London: Routledge.

Przeworski A. and Tenue, H. (1970) *The Logic of Comparative Social Inquiry*, New York: Wiley-Interscience.

Puchala, D.J. (1972) 'Of Blind Men, Elephants and International Integration', *Journal of Common Market Studies*, 10 (3).

Puchala, D.J. (1984) 'The Integration Theorists and the Study of International Relations', in C.W. Kegley and E. Wittkopf (eds), *The Global Agenda: Issues and Perspectives*, New York: Random House.

Puchala, D. J. (1999) 'Institutionalism, Intergovernmentalism and European Integration', *Journal of Common Market Studies*, 37 (2).

Putnam, R.D. (1988) 'Diplomacy and Domestic Politics: The Logic of Two-levels Games', *International Organization*, 42 (3).

Rapopport, A. (1958) 'Various Meanings of "Theory"', *American Political Science Review*, 52.

Requejo, F. (1999) 'Cultural Pluralism, Nationalism and Federalism: A Revision of Democratic Citizenship in Plurinational States', *European Journal of Political Research*, 35.

Ress, G. (1994) 'Democratic Decision-making in the European Union and the Role of the European Parliament', in D. Curtin and T. Heukels (eds), *Institutional Dynamics of European Integration: Essays in Honour of Henry G. Schermers*, Vol. II, Dortrecht: Martinus Nijhoff.

Rhodes, R.A.W. (1995) 'The Institutional Approach', in D. Marsh and G. Stoker (eds), *Theory and Methods in Political Science*, London: Macmillan.

Rhodes, R.A.W. (1996) 'The New Governance: Governing without Government', *Political Studies*, 44 (5).

Richardson, J. (1996) 'Policy-making in the EU: Interests, Ideas and Garbage Cans of Primeval Soup', in J. Richarson (ed.), *European Union: Power and Policy-making*, London and New York: Routledge.

Ridley, F.F. (1975) *The Study of Politics: Political Science and Public Administration*, Oxford: Martin Robertson.

Riker, W.H. (1996) 'European Federalism: The Lessons of Past Experience', in J.J. Hesse and V. Wright (eds), *Federalizing Europe? The Costs, Benefits, and Preconditions of Federal Political Systems*, Oxford: Oxford University Press.

Risse-Kappen, T. (1996) 'Exploring the Nature of the Beast: International Relations Theory and Comparative Policy Analysis Meet the European Union', *Journal of Common Market Studies*, 34 (1).

Ritzer, G. (1991) *Metatheorizing in Sociology*, Lexington: Lexington Books.

Robinson, K. (1961) 'Sixty Years of Federation in Australia', *Geographical Review*, 51 (1).

Rosamond, B. (1995) 'Mapping the European Condition: The Theory of Integration and the Integration of Theory', *European Journal of International Relations*, 1 (3).

Rosamond, B. (1999) 'Theorising the European Union Past, Present and Future: On Knowledge, Disciplines and "Thinking Thoroughly" about Integration Theory', *Current Politics and Economics of Europe*, 9 (2).

Rosamond, B. (2000) *Theories of European Integration*, Basingstoke: Macmillan.

Rose, R. (1991) 'Comparing Forms of Comparative Analysis', *Political Studies*, 39 (3).

Rosenau, J.N. (1966) 'Pre-theories and Theories of Foreign Policy', in R.B. Farrell (ed.), *Approaches to Comparative and International Politics*, Evaston, IL: Northwestern University Press.

Rosenau, J. (1992) 'Governance, Order and Change in World Order', in J. Rosenau (ed.), *Governance without Government: Order and Change in World Politics*, Cambridge: Cambridge University Press.

de Rougemont, D. (1972) 'The Campaign of European Congresses', in G. Ionescu (ed.), *The New Politics of European Integration*, London: Macmillan.

Ruggie, J.G. (1975) 'International Responses to Technology: Concepts and Trends', *International Organization*, 29 (3).

Ruggie, J.G. (1993) 'Territoriality and Beyond: Problematizing Modernity in International Relations', *International Organization*, 47 (1).

Ruggie, J.G. (1998) *Constructing the World Polity: Essays on International Internationalization*, New York: Routledge.

Sandholtz, W. (1996) 'Membership Matters: Limits of the Functional Approach to European Institutions', *Journal of Common Market Studies*, 34 (3).

Sandholtz, W. and Zysman, J. (1989) '1992: Recasting the European Bargain', *World Politics*, 42 (1).

Sartori, G. (1987) *Theory of Democracy Revisited*, Chatham, NJ: Chatham House.

Sartori, G. (1991) 'Comparing and Miscomparing', *Journal of Theoretical Politics*, 3.

Sauter, W. (1998) 'The Economic Constitution of the European Union', *The Columbia Journal of European Law*, 4 (1).

Sbragia, A.M. (1992) 'Thinking about the European Future: The Uses of Comparison', in A.M. Sbragia (ed.), *Euro-politics: Institutions and Policymaking in the 'New' European Community*, Washington, DC: The Brookings Institution.

Sbragia, A.M. (1993) 'The European Community: A Balancing Act', *Publius*, 23 (3).

Scharpf, F.W. (1988) 'The Joint-decision Trap: Lessons from German Federalism and European Integration', *Public Administration*, 66 (3).

Scharpf, F.W. (1996) 'Negative and Positive Integration in the Political Economy of European Welfare States', in G. Marks et al. (eds), *Governance in the European Union*, London: Sage.

Scharpf, F.W. (1999) *Governing in Europe: Effective and Democratic?*, Oxford: Oxford University Press.

Schattschneider, E.E. (1969) *Two Hundred Million Americans in Search of a Government*, New York: Holt, Rinehart and Winston.

Schmitter, P.C. (1971) 'A Revised Theory of Regional Integration', in L.N. Lindberg and S.A Scheingold (eds), *Regional Integration: Theory and Research*, Cambridge, MA: Harvard University Press.

Schmitter, P.C. (1996a) 'Citizenship in an Eventual Euro-democracy', European University Institute, July, mimeo.

Schmitter, P.C. (1996b) 'Examining the Present Euro-polity with the Help of Past Theories', in G. Marks et al. (eds), *Governance in the European Union*, London: Sage.

Schmitter, P.C. (1996c) 'Imagining the Future of the Euro-polity with the Help of New Concepts', in G. Marks et al. (eds), *Governance in the European Union*, London: Sage.

Schmitter, P.C. (1996d) 'Some Alternative Futures for the European Polity and their Implications for European Public Policy', in Y. Mény et al. (eds), *Adjusting to Europe: The Impact of the European Union on National Institutions and Policies*, London and New York: Routledge.

Schmitter, P.C. (2000) 'Federalism and the Euro-polity', *Journal of Democracy*, 11 (1).

Scott, A. (1998) 'Developments in the Economies of the European Union', *Journal of Common Market Studies*, 36 (1997 Annual Review of Activities).

Sharma, B.M. and Choudhry, L.P. (1967) *Federal Polity*, London: Asia Publishing House.

Shaw, J. (1993) *European Community Law*, London: Macmillan.

Shaw, J. (1998a) 'The Emergence of Postnational Constitutionalism in the European Union', Exeter Political Theory Workshop, November.

Shaw, J. (1998b) 'The Interpretation of European Union Citizenship', *The Modern Law Review*, 61 (3).

Shaw, J. (1998c) 'The Treaty of Amsterdam: Challenges of Flexibility and Legitimacy', *European Law Journal*, 4 (1).

Shaw, J. (1999) 'Postnational Constitutionalism in the European Union', *Journal of European Public Policy*, 6 (4).

Shaw, J. and Wiener, A. (2000) 'The Paradox of the European "Polity"', in M. Green Cowles and M. Smith (eds), *State of the European Union, Volume 5: Risks, Reform, Resistance, and Revival*, Oxford: Oxford University Press.

Smith, A.D. (1991) *National Identity*, Harmondsworth: Penguin.

Smith, M. (1996) 'The European Union and a Changing Europe: Establishing the Boundaries of Order', *Journal of Common Market Studies*, 34 (1).

Snyder, F. (1998) *General Course on Constitutional Law in the European Union*, Collected Courses on the Academy of European Law, VI, I.

Sołtan, K.E. (1999) 'Introduction: Civic Competence, Democracy, and the Good Society', in S.L. Elkin and K.E. Sołtan (eds), *Citizen Competence and Democratic Institutions*, University Park, PA: Pennsylvania State University Press.

Spinelli, A. (1967) 'European Union and the Resistance', *Government and Opposition*, April–July.

Spinelli, A. and Rossi, E. (1944) *Il Manifesto di Ventotene*, Pavia.

Spragens, T.A., Jr (1999) *Civic Liberalism: Reflections on our Democratic Ideals*, Lanham: Rowman and Littlefield.

Stavridis, S. (1993) 'Democracy in Europe: West and East', in *People's Rights and European Structures*, Manresa: Centre Unesco de Catalunya, Conference Proceedings, September.

Stein, A.A. (1983) 'Coordination and Collaboration: Regimes in an Anarchic World', in S. Krasner (ed.), *International Regimes*, Ithaca, NY: Cornell University Press.

Steiner, J. (1971) 'The Principles of Majority and Proportionality', *British Journal of Political Science*, 1 (1).

Stevenson, G. (1982) *Unfulfilled Union: Canadian Federalism and National Unity*, rev. edn, Toronto: Gage.

Stoker, G. (1995) 'Introduction', in D. Marsh and G. Stoker (eds), *Theory and Method in Political Science*, Basingstoke: Macmillan.

Strange, S. (1983) '*Cave! Hic Dragones*: A Critique of Regime Analysis', in S.D. Krasner (ed.), *International Regimes*, Ithaca, NY: Cornell University Press.

Strange, S. (1996) *The Retreat of the State: The Diffusion of Power in the World Economy*, Cambridge: Cambridge University Press.

Streeck, W. (1996) 'Neo-voluntarism: A New European Social Policy Regime?', in G. Marks et al. (eds), *Governance in the European Union*, London: Sage.

Tarrow, S. (1998) 'Building a Composite Polity: Popular Contention in the European Union', Institute for European Studies Working Paper, no. 98/3, Cornell University.

Tassin, E. (1992) 'Europe: A Political Community?', in C. Mouffe (ed.), *Dimensions of Radical Democracy*, London and New York: Verso.

Taylor, C. (1998) 'The Dynamics of Democratic Exclusion', *Journal of Democracy*, 9 (4).

Taylor, P. (1968) 'The Concept of Community and the European Integration Process', *Journal of Common Market Studies*, 12 (2).

Taylor, P. (1971) *International Co-operation Today: The European and the Universal Patterns*, London: Elek.

Taylor, P. (1975) 'The Politics of the European Communities: The Confederal Phase', *World Politics*, 27 (3).

Taylor, P. (1978) 'Confederalism: The Case of the European Communities', in P. Taylor and A.J.R. Groom (eds), *International Organization: A Conceptual Approach*, London: Pinter.

Taylor, P. (1980) 'Interdependence and Autonomy in the European Communities: The Case of the European Monetary System', *Journal of Common Market Studies*, 18 (4).

Taylor, P. (1983) *The Limits of European Integration*, New York: Columbia University Press.

Taylor, P. (1990a) 'A Conceptual Typology of International Organization', in P. Taylor and A.J.R. Groom (eds), *Frameworks for International Co-operation*, London: Pinter.

Taylor, P. (1990b) 'Federation and Consociation as Approaches to International Integration', in A.J.R. Groom and P. Taylor (eds), *Frameworks for International Co-operation*, London: Pinter.

Taylor, P. (1990c) 'Functionalism: The Approach of David Mitrany', in Groom A.J.R. and Taylor P. (eds), *Frameworks for International Co-operation*, London: Pinter.

Taylor, P. (1991) 'The European Community and the State: Assumptions, Theories and propositions', *Review of International Studies*, 17 (2).

Taylor, P. (1993) *International Organization in the Modern World: The Regional and the Global Process*, London: Pinter.

Taylor, P. (1996) *The European Union in the 1990s*, Oxford: Oxford University Press.

Taylor, P. (1999) 'The United Nations in the 1990s: Proactive Cosmopolitanism and the Issue of Sovereignty', *Political Studies*, 47 (3).

Teasdale, A. (1993) 'The Life and Death of the Luxembourg Compromise', *Journal of Common Market Studies*, 31 (4).

Teune, H. (1990) 'Comparing Countries: Lessons Learned', in E. Oyen (ed.), *Comparative Methodology: Theory and Practice in International Social Research*, London: Sage.

Tilly, C. (2000) 'Relational Origins of Inequality', Columbia University, mimeo.

Tindemans, Leo (1976) Report to the European Council, *Bulletin of the European Communities*, supplement 1–1976.

Tocqueville, A. de (1969) [1839, 1840] *Democracy in America*, New York: Harper and Row.

Tönnies, F. (1974) [1887] *Community and Association*, trans. and supplemented by C.P. Loomis, London: Routledge and Kegan Paul.

Toth, A.G. (1992) 'The Principle of Subsidiarity in the Treaty of Maastricht', *Common Market Law Review*, 29.

Tranholm-Mikkelsen, J. (1991) 'Neo-functionalism: Obstinate or Obsolete? A Reappraisal in the Light of the New Dynamism of the EC', *Millennium*, 20 (1).

von Treitschke, H. (1970) 'State Confederations and Federated States', Book III, in M. Forsyth et al. (eds), *The Theory of International Relations*, London: Allen and Unwin.

Tsinisizelis, M.J. and Chryssochoou, D.N. (1998) 'The European Union: Trends in Theory and Reform', in A. Weale and M. Nentwich (eds), *Political Theory and the European Union: Legitimacy, Constitutional Choice, and Citizenship*, London and New York: Routledge.

Unger, R.M. (1975) *Knowledge and Politics*, New York: Free Press.

Vasovic, V. (1992) 'Polyarchical or Consociational Democracy?', in T. Vanhanen (ed.), *Strategies of Democratization*, Washington: Crane Russak.

Vibert, F. (1995) *A Core Agenda for the 1996 Inter-governmental Conference (IGC)*, London: European Policy Forum.

Walker, N. (1988) 'Sovereignty and Differentiated Integration in the European Union', *European Law Journal*, 4 (4).

Wallace, H. (1993) 'European Governance in Turbulent Times', *Journal of Common Market Studies*, 31 (3).

Wallace, W. (1982) 'Europe as a Confederation: The Community and the Nation-state', *Journal of Common Market Studies*, 21 (1–2).

Wallace, W. (1983) 'Less than a Federation, More than a Regime: The Community as a Political System', in H. Wallace et al. (eds), *Policy-making in the European Community*, Chichester: John Wiley.

Wallace, W. (1994) 'Theory and Practice in European Integration', in S. Bulmer and A. Scott (eds), *Economic and Political Integration in Europe: Internal Dynamics and Global Context*, Oxford: Blackwell.

Wallace, W. (1996) 'Government without Statehood: The Unstable Equilibrium', in H. Wallace and W. Wallace (eds), *Policy-making in the European Union*, Oxford: Oxford University Press.

Wallace, W. (2000) 'Collective Governance', in H. Wallace and W. Wallace (eds), *Policy-making in the European Union*, 4th edn, Oxford: Oxford University Press.

Warleigh, A. (2000a) 'History Repeating? Framework Theory and Europe's Multi-level Confederation', *Journal of European Integration*, 22 (2).

Warleigh, A. (2000b) 'The Hustle: Citizenship Practice, NGOs and "Policy Coalitions" in the European Union – The Cases of Auto Oil, Drinking Water and Unit Pricing', *Journal of European Public Policy*, 7 (2).

Watts, R.L. (1981) 'Federalism, Regionalism, and Political Integration', in D.M. Cameron (ed.), *Regionalism and Supranationalism: Challenges and Alternatives to the Nation-state in Canada and Europe*, London: The Institute on Research of Public Policy.

Watts, R.L. (1999) *Comparing Federal Systems*, 2nd edn, Montreal and Kingston: McGill-Queens University Press.

Weale, A. (1998) 'Between Representation and Constitutionalism in the European Union', in A. Weale and M. Nentwich (eds), *Political Theory and the European Union: Legitimacy, Constitutional Choice and Citizenship*, London and New York: Routledge.

Webb, C. (1983) 'Theoretical Perspectives and Problems', in H. Wallace et al. (eds), *Policy-making in the European Community*, Chichester: John Wiley.

Weiler, J.H.H. (1992) 'After Maastricht: Community Legitimacy in Post-1992 Europe', in W.J. Adams (ed.), *Singular Europe: Economy and Polity of the European Community after 1992*, Ann Arbor: University of Michigan Press.

Weiler, J.H.H. (1995) 'Does Europe Need a Constitution? Demos, Telos and the German Maastricht Decision', *European Law Journal*, 1 (3).

Weiler, J.H.H. (1994) 'Journey to an Unknown Destination: A Retrospective and Prospective on the European Court of Justice in the Arena of Political Integration', in S. Bulmer and A. Scott (eds), *Economic and Political Integration in Europe: Internal Dynamics and Global Context*, Oxford: Blackwell.

Weiler, J.H.H. (1997) 'Legitimacy and Democracy of Union Governance', in G. Edwards and A. Pijpers (eds), *The Politics of European Treaty Reform: The 1996 Intergovernmental Conference and Beyond*, London: Pinter.

Weiler, J.H.H. (1998) 'Bread and Circus: The State of European Union', *The Columbia Journal of European Law*, 4.

Weiler, J.H.H. (1999) *The Constitution of Europe: 'Do the New Clothes Have an Emperor?' and Other Essays on European Integration*, Cambridge: Cambridge University Press.

Weiler, J.H.H. et al. (1995) 'European Democracy and its Critique', in J. Hayward (ed.), *The Crisis of Representation in Europe*, London: Frank Cass.

Wendt, A. (1991) 'Bridging the Theory/Meta-theory Gap in International Relations', *Review of International Studies*, 17 (4).

Wendt, A. (1999) *Social Theory of International Politics*, Cambridge: Cambridge University Press.

Wessels, W. (1991) 'The EC Council: The Community's Decisionmaking Centre', in R.O. Keohane and S. Hoffmann (eds), *The New European Community: Decisionmaking and Institutional Change*, Boulder, CO: Westview Press.

Wessels, W. (1997a) 'The Amsterdam Treaty in View of the Fusion Theory', paper presented to the British International Studies Association, University of Leeds, 15–17 December.

Wessels, W. (1997b) 'An Ever Closer Fusion? A Dynamic Macropolitical View on Integration Processes', *Journal of Common Market Studies*, 35 (2).

Wessel, R.A. (1997c) 'The International Legal Status of the European Union', *European Foreign Affairs*, 2.

Wessels, W. (1998) 'Flexibility, Differentiation and Closer Integration: The Amsterdam Provisions in the Light of the Tindemans Report', in M. Westlake (ed.), *The European Union after Amsterdam: New Concepts of European Integration*, London and New York: Routledge.

Wheare, K.C. (1964) *Federal Government*, 4th edn, Oxford: Oxford University Press.

Wiener, A. and Della Sala, V. (1997) 'Constitution-making and Citizenship Practice: Bridging the Democracy Gap in the EU?', *Journal of Common Market Studies*, 35 (4).

Willets, P. (1990) 'Transactions, Networks and Systems', in A.J.R. Groom and P. Taylor (eds), *Frameworks for International Co-operation*, London: Pinter.

Wilson, W. (1899) *The State: Elements of Historical and Practical Politics*, London: Isbister.

Wincott, D. (1995a) 'Institutional Interaction and European Integration: Towards an Everyday Critique of Liberal Intergovernmentalism', *Journal of Common Market Studies*, 33 (4).

Wincott, W. (1995b) 'The Role of the Law or the Rule of the Court of Justice? An "Institutional" Account of Judicial Politics in the European Community', *Journal of European Public Policy*, 2 (4).

Young, O.R. (1980) 'International Regimes: Problems of Concept Formation', *World Politics*, 32 (3).

Young, O.R. (1986) 'International Regimes: Toward a New Theory of Institutions', *World Politics*, 39 (1).

Young, O.R. (1989) *International Cooperation: Building Regimes for Natural Resources and the Environment*, Ithaca, NY: Cornell University Press.

Zürn, M. (1999) 'The Social Pre-requisites of European Democracy', in Conference Proceedings, *Governance and Citizenship in Europe: Some Research Directions*, Luxembourg: Office for the Official Publications of the European Communities.

Index

additionality, 186
Adonis, A., 17
Albertini, M., 48
Allison, G., 10
Althusius, J., 134
Amsterdam, Treaty of 25, 154–9, 162, 193–4
  and citizenship, 164, 181, 186, 188
  and demos-oriented union, 189–92, 193
analogical reasoning, 22
Anderson, M., 186
Apter, D., 134
Aristotle, 118
asymmetrical authority overlap, 163
asymmetrical federalism, 94
authority, dispersed, 21
autonomy 78, 105, 110, 161, 193
  and federalism, 43, 44, 46
  and interdependence, 80–1
  loss of, 19
  segmental, 14, 48, 136, 140–1
  through control, 64–6

balanced constitution, 21–2
Barry, B., 143
Belgium, 94
Bellamy, R., 21, 172–3, 181, 186
Beloff, M., 48
Blalock, H., 118
Bosco, A., 45
Bowie, R.R., 45
Brake, W. te, 22
Brewin, C., 70
Bulmer, S., 30, 100, 113, 116–17
Búrca, G. de, 149, 152–3

Caporaso, J., 19–20, 98
Carney, F.S., 134

case studies, in comparative research, 119–20
Castiglione, D., 21, 172–3
Checkel, J.T., 72
Choudhry, L.P., 67
Christiansen, T., 177
Church, C.H., 10, 19, 25, 58, 70
citizenship, see EU citizenship
civic body, 174–5
  elites and, 138, 143, 187
civic competence, 144, 160, 176, 178, 182–9, 194
civic contract, 183–4
civic governance, typology of, 188–9
civic identity, 175, 177, 180, 182, 185, 187
Claes, D.H., 72
Claude, I.L., 66
Closa, C., 175–6
co-decision procedure, 156, 191
  see also, joint decision-making
co-determination, see political co-determination
Cohen, C., 175
collective action, 20, 38, 110
collective governance, 97, 98
comitology, 100, 157
Committee of the Regions, 98
Common Foreign and Security Policy, 99, 155
common interest, 40, 78–9
community, 55
  federalism and, 43–4
  functionalism and, 38–9
Community Acts, hierarchy of, 156
community-formation, 49, 50–1, 52
Community Method, 54, 66, 100
comparative analysis, 22–3, 118–24
competence allocation, 146–54, 157
competences 24, 47, 94, 153